Leon Gouré
Foy D. Kohler
Mose L. Harvey

THE ROLE OF
NUCLEAR FORCES
IN CURRENT
SOVIET STRATEGY

MONOGRAPHS IN INTERNATIONAL AFFAIRS

CENTER FOR ADVANCED INTERNATIONAL STUDIES
UNIVERSITY OF MIAMI

LEON GOURÉ is a Professor of International Studies and Director of Soviet Studies at the Center for Advanced International Studies at the University of Miami. A graduate of New York University, Columbia University School of International Affairs and Russian Institute, and Georgetown University, he is the author of *Civil Defense in the Soviet Union, The Siege of Leningrad,* and *Soviet Civil Defense 1969-70.* He also co-authored *Two Studies in Soviet Controls,* and co-edited Marshal V. D. Sokolovskii, *Soviet Military Strategy* . . . **FOY D. KOHLER,** career Ambassador of the United States and long associated with Soviet affairs, is Professor of International Studies at the Center for Advanced International Studies at the University of Miami. He is the author of *Understanding the Russians, A Citizen's Primer* and has contributed numerous articles to journals and magazines . . . **MOSE L. HARVEY** is a Professor of History and Director of the Center for Advanced International Studies at the University of Miami. He received his AB and MA from Emory University and his PhD from the University of California at Berkeley. A former U.S. Foreign Service Officer, he has served as Director of the Department of State's Office of Intelligence Research for the USSR and Eastern Europe and as a Senior Member of the Policy Planning Council. He is author of *East-West Trade and U.S. Policy,* and numerous articles on various aspects of the Soviet economy and Soviet-U.S. relations.

Library of Congress Catalog Number 74-81602
© University of Miami
Center for Advanced International Studies, 1974

Contents

PREFACE

This book is one of several which the Center for Advanced International Studies of the University of Miami has undertaken in reference to Soviet positions on specific aspects of the detente relationship between the US and the USSR. Our purpose in these studies is not confined to examining and analyzing current situations and prospects, but extends to the larger questions of long-time trends in Soviet policies and behavior that appear especially pertinent for US foreign policy interests and objectives.

The genesis of this particular effort was the selection, in consultation with specialists at other universities, research institutes, and in government agencies, of a series of questions which, while limited in compass, appeared both of critical importance in themselves and as offering together a key to an understanding of the basic elements that enter into Moscow's calculations regarding Soviet nuclear forces. We recognized, of course, that the product of our efforts would be far from comprehensive, that there would remain many other questions in need of examination and analysis before a full-scale picture could be drawn. We subsequently distributed a draft report on our research to a wide range of specialists for comment and criticism and received many helpful suggestions in response. To the extent possible within our frame of reference, these have been taken fully into account in the very extensive revisions of our draft preparatory to publication.

We naturally owe a great debt to those who so generously helped us in this manner and regret that the list is far too large for inclusion here. Beyond this group, we have received valuable assistance from colleagues in our Center at the University of Miami, including especially Vladimir Prokofieff, Richard Soll, Susan Kulchar, Margarita Pelleya, Florence Coey, and Mark Miller.

FOREWORD
by
Foy D. Kohler

The aim of this study is to provide insights that may be useful in current appraisals and debates relative to the new "detente" relationship between the United States and the Soviet Union, with particular emphasis on security implications for the US.

The study is limited to the examination and analysis, in the light of open Soviet sources, of certain critical aspects of current Soviet thinking and planning for the nuclear forces of the USSR. The specific problem areas addressed relate to Moscow's views on the purposes its nuclear forces serve and the relative weight it attaches to these purposes; how much in the way of nuclear forces Moscow considers necessary under present and prospective international conditions; how Moscow envisages the possible military use of its nuclear forces; and Moscow's perception of the relationship between the use of strategic nuclear forces and theater forces.

I

While the focus of the study is thus quite narrow, and deliberately so, we feel the issues involved are basic to the range of important questions that need to be weighed at this stage of detente. According to both US and Soviet authorities, the greatest of the fruits to be expected from detente is a reduction in the chances of a nuclear war between the two countries and, to this end, an amelioration of the conditions that might lead to nuclear war, including particularly a slowing of the arms race and a change in military doctrines and postures which might, if left intact, generate dynamics for the continuation of hostile attitudes and policies with their accompanying dangers. The Soviets, for their part, are paying close attention to developments in US positions in the area of weapons and military roles doctrines and treat any indication of a persistence of past patterns as a serious threat to detente. As a case in point, Georgii Arbatov, Director of the USSR Academy of Sciences Institute for the Study of the USA and one of the most heavily utilized Soviet spokesmen on the new US-Soviet relationship, wrote for *Problems of Peace and Socialism* in February 1974:

> Many representatives of the U.S. ruling circles [have not] yet renounced the hope that some future achievements of a military-technical nature will even now make it possible to increase the "viability" of employing military force and in some way to turn back the course of events . . . this explains, at least partially, one of the paradoxes of the contemporary strategic situation. On the one hand, the fact that military force is, in a way, powerless is becoming increasingly obvious, and the impossibility of employing it for politi-

cal purposes is becoming increasingly clear. On the other hand, in contrast to this, the arms race is continuing and, in some areas, even intensifying. From this ensues, too, another contradiction—that existing between the developing processes of political detente in the world and the major lagging behind in terms of military detente. Speaking at the recent World Peace Congress in Moscow, Comrade L. I. Brezhnev stressed that this situation cannot continue indefinitely. "If we want detente and peace to last," he pointed out, "we must halt the arms race."

It would seem only prudent that the US in its turn examine with care evidence as to what the Soviets may or may not be doing to adjust their own military doctrines and postures to the requirements of detente, and particularly in the nuclear sphere which is obviously central to the common objective of reducing the chances of general war. Is there a change in the pattern of Soviet thinking in response to the requirements of detente, as the Soviets demand of the US? Or is Moscow seeking the application of a double standard? The Soviets have discussed the issues freely and with apparent frankness. What do these discussions show?

A second consideration that appears to make desirable an in-depth look at a specific area of the detente spectrum is that the trend so far has been to concentrate on general aspects of the new situation. The atmospherics of an improvement in relations between the US and the USSR are important; it would seem in fact that given the course of events and attitudes of the past twenty-five years a change in atmospherics was an essential prelude to any sort of genuine progress between the two countries. But the real test must lie in the concrete results that follow the change in atmospherics. Several fields have been earmarked by the two sides for special efforts in direct state-to-state relations: closer trade and economic relations; more effective cultural and scientific-technical exchanges; cooperation in space; and of course movement toward arms limitation, beginning with nuclear arms. What has actually happened in these different fields and how has it affected pre-existing modes of thought and behavior, not only in the sense of performance against specific commitments but in the broader sense of implications for policy?

II

In this study we have sought to determine whether the changing relationship between the US and the USSR has led, or appears likely to lead, to significant modifications in Moscow's position regarding the nature and role of Soviet nuclear forces. To this end we have examined the mass of documentary materials bearing on the question that have appeared in the Soviet Union since the beginning of the nuclear era, but have concentrated primary attention on statements and publications immediately preceding and following the summit meetings of 1972 and 1973.

I might say at the outset that the results of this effort are not encouraging. Current Soviet positions, as revealed by public pronouncements, on the role of nuclear forces are very much now has they have been in the past, only more so. In simplest terms, Moscow continues to see nuclear weapons and forces, and particularly nuclear rocket forces, as central to all phases of Soviet military power. Today as much as at any time since the Kremlin finally effected in January 1960 its adjustment to the "revolutionary" implications of nuclear weapons for warfare, Soviet military theory, doctrine, strategy, war planning, force structure and organization, instruction and training programs, battle exercises, resource allocations, research and development programs and activities, civil defense efforts, indoctrination programs for the troops and for the population, war readiness measures, and so on are all keyed to and dominated by the nuclear weapons factor. We have found no evidence that agreements reached at the Moscow and Washington Summits of 1972 and 1973, or the general relaxation of tension between the US and the USSR, have brought any changes in Soviet positions. Neither SALT I nor on-going negotiations for SALT II have had any discernible impact on overall Soviet postures, activities, or plans relative to the further development and possible utilization of nuclear weapons. To the contrary, Moscow emphasizes that while the danger of a general war has been reduced, it continues to·exist and will as long as capitalism survives. Moreover, a general war is viewed as having become less likely only because the accelerating shift in the "world balance of forces" in favor of the Soviet Union, primarily in consequence of the steady growth of nuclear-based Soviet military might, has forced the US to recognize that under existing conditions it cannot hope to operate "from a position of strength" as against the USSR. However, it is said that this situation is tenuous and may be reversed in consequence of a number of possible developments during the further course of the inevitable "struggle between systems," and that the one guarantee that a war will not actually come is for the USSR to continue to strengthen its armed forces in all. possible ways and by all means. Especially important, according to Moscow, is for the USSR to avoid any possibility for the US securing any important technological advantage in weapons, or "illusion" of advantage, through constantly pressing forward with its own military research and development efforts.

Until quite recently, many analysts would have questioned the utility of Soviet public pronouncements in such an effort as we have made to determine actual Soviet attitudes, intentions and expectations. For a number of years after the war's end it was generally accepted among those concerned with Soviet affairs that the members of the ruling hierarchy of the USSR provide through their public utterances a substantially accurate account of what they are up to and why, both in a strategic sense and with respect to particular situations and moves, and that very often the ruling hierarchy have through such utterances signaled in advance their actual purposes and intended courses of action. Indeed, it appeared that we were severely handicapped in shaping US policies as against the USSR without readily available access and close attention to past and current authoritative Soviet statements as to Soviet positions. And it was only after shortcomings in these regards were overcome that the US, from both an intelligence and an operational standpoint, was able to break through the assumed enigma in which the Soviet Union was supposed to be wrapped.

However, fundamental documentary research of this nature came to be greatly curtailed and in many cases simply abandoned. In fact, there came to be considerable intellectual disdain for such documentary research which tended to be scornfully referred to as "Kremlinology." But this very skepticism has led to a superficial approach to understanding Soviet concepts and intentions and to a lot of wishful thinking. This tendency was pithily dealt with by Sir Hugh Seton-Watson in an article in *Interplay* of August-September 1969, in which he said: "What 200,000 Communist Party officials, from Brezhnev down to the secretaries of party branches in factories or collective farms, tell their subjects is all camouflage. The real views of the Soviet leaders are what some nice guy from the Soviet delegation at the UN said over a drink or what an itinerant midwestern scientist heard from some friendly academician in Novosibirsk." The tendency was for analysts to ascribe to Soviet leaders attitudes, values, and interests which in all important respects closely parallel our own, and to endow those leaders in their dealings with us with a growing "realism" or "pragmatism" in the Western sense of these words. The thought was that as a modern great state the Soviet Union faces situations, develops policies and determines courses of actions on the basis of essentially the same considerations and decision-making processes as does the United States. In other words, the tendency was to perceive the Soviet leaders as thinking and seeing things as we do and, in effect, to project into Soviet affairs a mirror-image of ourselves and our own concepts. The consequences of such an approach, as well as many closely related approaches based upon self-conceived assumptions about the Soviets and their conduct, is that it has led to serious misjudgments in understanding and forecasting Soviet behavior.

Fortunately, there has been a recent revival of respect for the value of the study of what the Soviets themselves say about their outlook and purposes, their policies and activities at home and abroad. Perhaps the most decisive factor responsible for this phenomenon was Soviet behavior with respect to the October 1973 Middle East war which ran so strongly counter to Western assumptions of Soviet positions regarding detente and Soviet purposes in the Middle East itself, as well as Western perceptions of the situation and possibilities in that region. In any event, it appears again to be widely accepted that in trying to understand and interpret Soviet affairs due attention and weight must be given to the "view from the Kremlin" as the Soviets themselves reveal that view.

III

Certainly for such a problem area as Moscow's purpose with respect to its nuclear forces, whether under conditions of detente or otherwise, a knowledgeable reading and analysis of what Soviet authorities have to say is essential for a realistic understanding and reliable judgment of actual Soviet positions. This is not to suggest that there is any set of fixed principles, or settled "doctrines," that govern for this or any similar area in the Soviet Union. There is, regrettably, no straight-line methodology to a solution of any · problem relative to Soviet policies and conduct. Any approach must allow for a mix of basic factors entering into and affecting Soviet decisions and actions, and must allow that this "mix is not constant but in continuous flux." Further, beyond the particular basic factors operating in a given situation, account must be taken of such variables as Soviet priorities, capabilities, risk calculations, and the costs and trade-offs which the Soviet leaders may see in the pursuit of competing objectives.

It cannot be assumed from the foregoing, however, that the Soviets in practice proceed essentially on the basis of the same considerations and in the same manner as we do in dealing with similar or even identical situations and problems. The actual record of Soviet behavior, as well as the explanations and justifications provided by the Soviets themselves, make clear that the considerations that determine Soviet policies and actions are not the product of conditions and practices similar to our own but are the product of an environment, a view of the world and a decision-making process entirely different from ours.

The Soviet environment and world outlook reflect elements that are peculiar to the Soviet Union, including the oligarchic system of rule with its unremitting urge to preserve itself; a set of unique historical experiences and geographic influences; Marxist-Leninist doctrine, especially its peculiar *Weltanschauung;* a long history of economic inferiority as against those it considers its adversaries; superpower status combined with a self-assumed role of leadership of a world-wide revolutionary movement; a sense of destiny with respect to rivalry with the US, the only other superpower and the leader of a competing world system; a special concern for China due to both national and ideological factors; and so on down a substantial list.

Similarly, the Soviet decision-making process is quite different from that of the US, being marked by the absolute authority of the party hierarchy with no mechanisms for public dissent and influence and with built-in imperatives to preserve established patterns of thought and rule. None of this is to say, however, that the Soviets make their decisions without regard to real world considerations and factors. Instead, they place great emphasis on being "realistic" in their courses of action. However, it should never be forgotten that what they operate on is their own perceptions of reality, not ours; and that their perceptions are derived from a set of circumstances quite different from our own. The Soviet view of the real world and its requirements and possibilities is a view from the Kremlin, not a view from Washington, London, Paris or Berlin.

Inherent in this view are what Moscow identifies as "immutable" considerations which it invariably takes into account in determining policies and actions, including particularly:

• The inevitability of a continuing East-West, or socialist-capitalist, struggle for predominance.
• The critical role of the East-West balance of forces, in which "forces" are understood to include not only Soviet perceptions of the military balance but also relative economic and scientific-technological capabilities and their utilization; the relative effectiveness of the socialist and capitalist systems to achieve desired ends; the relative degree of social-political and ideological cohesion of socialist as against capitalist countries; conflict within and among capitalist countries; the extent of popular acceptance of national objectives on the two sides; the question of relative national morale; and so on.
• A unique ability of the Soviet leadership to reach "scientifically" correct assessments of the "dominant" short and long-term trends in the competing groupings of states and in specific regions and countries based on the expectation of unavoidable interstate and class conflicts of interest and the effects of social-economic development.
• "Proletarian internationalism" as the essential base for the Soviet claim to leadership of the global "anti-imperialist struggle" and of global revolutionary and national liberation movements.

IV

Within the framework of such basic considerations the Soviets often change in their approaches and positions for even very fundamental questions and issues, and they quite evidently precede and accompany these changes with intensive and often heated debate and controversy, much of which is fully exposed—one can conjecture deliberately exposed—in the open media.

This is not a case of cynicism on the part of the leadership toward the Marxist-Leninist ideology to which they adhere. Despite the rigidity of the Soviet system of rule and decision-making and despite the constraints and compulsions inherent in the Soviet environment, both Soviet doctrine and practice allow for great flexibility in the area of strategy and tactics. The doctrinal line, first set by Lenin and continued by all leaders since, is that strategy as well as tactics must be constantly adjusted as changes take place in the "objective realities" at home and abroad. The "verities" of Marxist-Leninist ideology, while providing the framework in which the Soviet leadership appears intent on operating now and in the future, provide no barrier to even drastic shifts because the Central Committee of the CPSU (i.e., the Politburo or the dominant element in the Politburo) has the self-asserted authority not only to act as the sole interpreter of Marxism-Leninism but also to "creatively" develop it as conditions change. The standard position of the Soviet leaders, now and in the past, is to deplore "rigidity" and "doctrinairism" and to make a virtue of adjusting to concrete circumstances of any particular time or place through, as they put it, "compromises, zigzags, retreats, maneuvering, adopting new methods, combining and recombining and changing policies and approaches and forms of struggle," and so on.

In practice, the Soviet decision-making process for strategic and foreign policy matters, as revealed by Soviet sources, involves a succession of steps which are designed to bring into play a variety of interacting and possibly competing factors:

1. Determining the "doctrinal setting" in which the matter at issue must be viewed and handled (i.e., its relationship to basic goals as determined essentially by long-term environmental influences).
2. Development of policy options or alternatives in terms of "doctrinal" requirements.
3. Considering, weighing and adjusting policy alternatives in light of existing economic, military, diplomatic and other capabilities, taking into account competing requirements and various other "objective realities" that must be dealt with, such as the policies and activities and resources of adversaries and local opportunities and obstacles.
4. Subjecting any resultant proposals to a succession of Party-Government reviews at operational levels.
5. Review of all relevant proposals and considerations affecting them by the "Section" of the Central Committee Secretariat which has responsibility for the problem area involved and establishment of a "Party position" by the Section in question on controversial issues and questions and preparation of recommendations for the Politburo.
6. Examination (discussion and debate) within the Politburo of recommendations thus reached and submitted by the Section.
7. Arrival at a final decision by the Politburo (usually, according to Brezhnev, by "consensus" rather than vote), and communication of the decision to appropriate elements in the Party and Government where it has the force of unquestionable law. (Sooner or later, and often quite soon, the decision, unless it deals with a highly sensitive matter, together with its rationale, is also communicated in one way or another to Soviet society at large, e.g. through a *Pravda* editorial, a speech by a member of the top hierarchy, a published report on a Central Committee Plenum, guidelines for propaganda organizations, and so on and on—so as to insure the widespread understanding of and faithful adherence to the decision that the Soviet system requires.)

Until the last step in this process is reached, opportunities exist for the input of differing points of view and for debate by representatives of institutions and organizations which are directly concerned with the matters at issue or which may be affected by the decision reached. In actual practice, vested interest elements in the Soviet Party-Government structure, which are widely pervasive and deeply entrenched, almost always insure that through each of the steps debate will be intense, and often bitter, for any matter of significant import. On major matters, the debate passes from one level of the Soviet hierarchy to another up to and including members of the Politburo itself. Often, also, the debate is extended into party and government media, beginning usually with low-level commentaries in professional or ministerial organs and continuing, if the importance of the stakes appear to merit it, to higher and higher level statements and arguments utilizing ever more authoritative media or platforms. Once, however, the Politburo has arrived at a decision, which often comes only after extensive debate within that body, all further debate usually ceases and what has been decided is treated as binding on all elements of the hierarchy and on Soviet society generally. When exceptions occur, and of course they do occur, it can be assumed that something far-reaching is taking place within the Soviet leadership, that in fact something on the order of a power struggle is building up or underway for dominance in the party and country.

V

With respect to the particular question of the role of nuclear forces in Soviet strategy, Soviet sources themselves emphasize that a virtual revolution has been wrought in Soviet positions.

The revolution was not effected quickly or easily. It evolved over the years and only after the theory of strategy had undergone unusually great changes through extensive debate and controversy of the type just discussed. Almost on the morrow of the acquisition of a nuclear weapons capability by the USSR, questions evidently arose within the Soviet hierarchy as to the implications for basic Soviet tenets relative to the nature, requirements and role of future wars, questions which Stalin felt necessary to quell personally through public pronouncements before and in connection with the 19th Party Congress of October 1952. After Stalin's death, the questioning reemerged and at the top level. Council of Ministers Chairman Georgi Malenkov, ostensibly first among equals in the Stalin succession, implied in 1954 that with nuclear weapons a new general war had become unthinkable because it would result in the "destruction of civilization," and, further, advocated an easing of Soviet concentration on power building through shifting some of the resources from the military-heavy industry sector to the consumer sector (light industry, housing and agriculture), and he even went so far as to advocate the diversion of military grain reserves to meet immediate consumption needs. A great intra-leadership debate immediately ensued, with Khrushchev, then holding first place in the Party apparatus, leading the opposition to Malenkov's propositions. The debate quickly broke into the open for all the world to follow, with *Izvestiya,* the main organ of the Soviet government, serving as mouthpiece for Malenkov and his followers, and *Pravda,* the main organ of the Soviet party, serving the same role for Khrushchev's side. The outcome was the ouster of Malenkov as Premier in January 1955 amidst denunciations by Khrushchev and other leaders for his heresies and mistakes. A particularly prominent role went to Molotov who scornfully repudiated Malenkov's destruction-of-civilization contention on grounds that no change in weaponology, nuclear or otherwise, could alter the immutable laws of social development and that not civilization but only capitalism would be destroyed by a new world war.

Hardly had Khrushchev triumphed over Malenkov than he made his own break with Leninist-Stalinist orthodoxy. Avoiding Malenkov's line regarding the destruction of civilization, he asserted at the 20th Party Congress in February 1956 that because of the might of the USSR and the socialist camp another general war was no longer "fatalistically inevitable." While no voice was openly raised against Khrushchev's formulation, it soon became evident that this, along with other of his departures from the Stalinist past, was producing rumblings in the collective which was presumably sharing power in the party and government. Matters came to a head in July 1957 with a Politburo decision to oust Khrushchev. However, Khrushchev and his followers engineered a quick turnabout at the hands of the Party Central Committee which, reviving powers that had long since seemed dead, ousted Khrushchev's opponents in the Politburo as "Anti-Party" conspirators.

Thereafter Khrushchev further developed his thesis that war was no longer fatalistically inevitable, reaching the point of asserting that the danger of a new world war could actually be eliminated while capitalism still existed. Further, Khrushchev came to argue, and apparently with great effectiveness on those concerned with strategy in the Soviet Union, that given a strong Soviet nuclear capability the "imperialists" would not only be deterred from an attack on the USSR but would also be, if not provoked by "adventurist" threats and violence, increasingly deterred from activist policies and actions in furtherance of their world positions and interests. (Witness among other evidence his polemical exchanges with Peking that began in 1959.) In keeping with this line of thinking, Khrushchev, in January 1960, announced at a meeting of the Supreme Soviet the establishment of the Strategic Rocket Troops which would thenceforth serve as the main instrument of the Soviet armed forces. At the same time, he announced a substantial reduction in conventional forces.

The decision by Khrushchev to elevate nuclear forces to the prime position in the Soviet military structure represented the consummation of the "military-technical revolution" which had been in preparation for some time and which quite evidently had the full support of all principal elements in the Soviet hierarchy. It can be assumed, however, that given the supremacy long enjoyed by the ground forces this step was anything but popular among traditionalists within the Soviet military establishment, and all the more so since it was accompanied by reductions in ground and other conventional forces. Further, explanatory details provided by then Defense Minister Marshal Malinovsky could hardly have been very reassuring to the traditionalists. While "Rocket Troops of our Armed Forces," Malinovsky told the Supreme Soviet," undoubtedly are the main Service of the Armed Forces, . . . we realize that one Service alone cannot resolve all the tasks of war." In view of this, "we are keeping a definite number and corresponding sensible proportion of all the Services of the Armed Forces." However, "combat actions both in their organization and in methods . . . will bear little resemblance to those of the last war."

Apprehensive though they doubtless were, and in contrast to reactions to far less drastic changes in force relationships in the US, traditionalists in the armed forces made no discernible effort to contest the decisions reached by the leadership. Instead, the new setup, as announced by Khrushchev and explained by Malinovsky, was taken as doctrine which was dutifully echoed by military spokesmen and commentators up and down the line. Even the ouster of Khrushchev in October 1964, and the follow-up authoritative references (i.e., a *Pravda* editorial of October 17, 1964) to "harebrained scheming, hasty conclusions, rash decisions and actions based on wishful thinking, boasting, empty words, bureaucratism," and so on, did not produce any repercussions among the military or on behalf of the military. There was, in fact, no suggestion that Khrushchev's handling of military affairs was a factor in his dismissal, despite the fact that he had had to backtrack on his force reduction decision of January 1960 and authorize an emergency increase of approximately thirty percent in military expenditures in July 1961, as well as an increase in food prices in June 1962 because of urgent new "defense needs." Also, of course, there had been the Cuban missile fiasco. Khrushchev was later heavily criticized for his errors in a number of specific fields such as agriculture, but not in the military field.

Meanwhile, Marshal Malinovsky remained Defense Minister in the post-Khrushchev government and as such continued to talk of the new nuclear-centered military doctrine as he had in 1960, as indeed did all other military leaders and spokesmen. And what was true with Malinovsky has remained true with the new Defense Minister, Marshal Grechko, up to and including the present day. Thus, after some ten years of uncertainty and debate, the Soviet decision-making process was able in 1960 to settle upon a profound reorientation of concepts, organization, force assignments, and general direction of development for the Soviet armed forces, in response to what was considered the "objective" requirements of the nuclear age, and to secure unquestioned adherence to the new orientation among all affected elements of society, including particularly military elements, over the following years.

VI

Several important points relative to political-military relationships in the USSR are suggested by this course of events which are, in my view, particularly pertinent to the issues dealt with in this study.

At no time during either the period of uncertainty and debate regarding nuclear weapons or the period of decision or the long period of adherence that has followed, did the Soviet military as the military come out in opposition to the political authorities who rule the Soviet Union, or seek *as an organized entity* to induce acceptance of its point of view by the political authorities. In fact, never in Soviet history, even during the full militarization of the country in the Civil War period and World War II, has the military as such attempted to achieve any degree of *independent* political power or even independent political say so. The military obviously represents and has always represented a very powerful vested-interest group in the Soviet Union, and one that has been strongly supported by the ruling political authorities. But a price that has been successfully exacted from the military in return is that it play the game of politics according to the political authorities' rules. These rules permit the military a very strong voice in the decision-making process, but only up to the point of final resolution of a question or issue. They permit the military almost unlimited opportunities to protect and promote its interests, but only within the framework of the established Soviet way of doing things. And this way of doing things requires that the military, collectively and in its several parts, subordinate itself to the will and control of the rulers of the country, that it always act as a submissive instrument of the party, never as an active or potential rival.

The Soviet leadership, it might be noted, does not leave to chance the subordination of the military to its own will and control. It has effectively demonstrated over a period of many years that active membership in the CPSU or its preparatory organization, the Komsomol, is a virtual prerequisite for advancement in the military hierarchy. (Currently some ninety percent of all Soviet military officers are members of either the Communist Party or the Komsomol, with seventy-odd percent members of the former.) The leadership has also followed the practice of selecting key military figures to serve in Party organizations while continuing in their military posts. (Of the military officers who now occupy the 13 positions of Deputy Minister and above in the Ministry of Defense, ten are members of the Party Central Committee and one is a candidate member; the Chief of Staff of the Armed Forces is a member, as is the Director of the Main Political Administration of the Armed Forces.)

Most important of all, however, organized units of the Party, which are controlled by and responsible to the Party apparatus, are used throughout the armed forces (i.e., all administrative and functional branches and down to the company or battery level in combat units) to keep tabs on all phases of activity. It must be said that this particular aspect of Party control has from time to time been resisted by some military elements. This has not, however, been a case of resistance to political authority as such but to interference by non-specialists in highly professional affairs. The military during the early post-Stalin years conducted something of a running campaign against the practice. Defense Minister Marshal Zhukov, who rose to a position of seemingly great influence with Khrushchev during his struggle for ascendancy, brought the issue to a head. After a succession of steps reducing the power of the Political Department of the Soviet Army and Navy (now the Main Political Administration), which directs and controls party units in the armed forces, Zhukov managed to secure a Central Committee "Instruction" in May 1957, which ruled, among other things, that "criticism of the orders and decisions of commanders will not be permitted at Party meetings." But Zhukov's triumph was short-lived. In October 1957 he was summarily dismissed as Defense Minister and later expelled from his Party posts on grounds, as stated by the responsible Central Committee Plenum, that he had "violated the Leninist Party principles for the guidance of the armed forces, pursued a policy of curtailing the work of Party organizations, political organs and military councils, of abolishing the leadership and control of the Party . . . over the Army and Navy." The old rule as to direct party participation in military affairs was quickly reestablished. As explained by *Sovietskii Flot* on November 1, 1957, "Regardless of the rank or position of a Communist he not only can, but must, be subjected at Party meetings or conferences to criticism for shortcomings in his service." And this is the way it has remained in the armed forces ever since.

Basic to the Party-military relationship in the Soviet Union is, as I suggested above, the "unswerving solicitude of the Party and Government" for the armed forces. This solicitude, of course, reflects more than political expediency. Built into the Soviet system and the Soviet world outlook are factors which make, as the Soviets themselves say, the constant strengthening of the armed forces an "objective necessity." The military do not have to seek power to get what they feel they need; it ordinarily is given to them as a matter of settled policy. Where there has appeared to be any reluctance on the part of elements within the political leadership to go along with the "constant strengthening" formula, other elements have quickly and successfully sprung to the support of the military cause. In fact, a feature of struggles for power in the Soviet leadership has often been an effort of one faction to put into question the loyalty of a rival faction to the formula. Stalin used this tactic with great effectiveness. So too did Khrushchev in his contest with Malenkov. And the possibility that the same might be done to him by political rivals may well have served as a constraint on Khrushchev in his own policies toward the military.*

Beyond this use of the "military loyalty image" to undercut a rival in a power struggle, a political faction has sometimes successfully sought to use the military directly against an opponent. Evidently such a ploy played a decisive role in the elimination of Beria shortly after the death of Stalin. The same appears to have been true for Khrushchev in his 1957 contest with the "Anti-Party Group" in the Politburo. But in neither of these cases did the initiative come from the military; it came instead from the political side. And in neither did the military, or any element in the military, secure more than fleeting political advantages from its involvement, if that. After Beria was out, the Party leaders resumed full control and fought among themselves without any direct influence by the military. And within short months after Khrushchev's defeat of the Anti-Party Group in 1957, he unceremoniously dumped Marshal Zhukov, who had been used by Khrushchev to great benefit in effecting that defeat, from his high positions in the party and government.

VII

The fundamental question raised by the analysis presented in this study is whether the views on which the analysis is based reflect decisions, policies and purposes of the Soviet political leadership or merely doctrinal and strategic game-playing on the part of the military and military-minded civilians.

---

*While I was serving as American Ambassador in Moscow, Khrushchev told me that he would like to cut back on the military but could not do so. The best, he said, he could do was to hold them where they were. Actually at that time the regime had already embarked on a far-reaching program to close the strategic gap between the US and the USSR. (See my *Understanding the Russians: A Citizen's Primer* [New York, Harper and Row, 1970], pp. 247-48).

For my own part, I am convinced that, in light of such circumstances and factors as I have touched upon above, the views must be taken as reflective of positions of the political leadership.

The views are consonant with concepts relative to the role of nuclear forces in Soviet military strategy that have been repeatedly voiced by various members of the political leadership, over the past decade and more.

The views, it should be particularly stressed, rest solidly on pronouncements of General Secretary Brezhnev. There is, in other words, nothing reflected in the views to suggest any differences or conflicts between Brezhnev and his present policies and either military elements or political elements in the Soviet hierarchy.

The views flow directly from the body of Soviet military theory and doctrine that has developed since the mid-1950s under the direct aegis and with the explicit sanction of the political leadership.

The views accord with actual Soviet decisions and actions in the development and deployment of nuclear weapons and forces, and with currently indicated Soviet plans for the future development and deployment of nuclear weapons and forces.

The views as they apply to basic Soviet positions, intentions, and expectations cannot be meaningfully divided between military and non-military. When read without knowledge of origin an editorial article devoted to nuclear forces appearing in *Pravda* can hardly be distinguished from an editorial article appearing in *Red Star*. Suslov says much the same thing as Grechko and Grechko much the same as Brezhnev and Kosygin. A colonel writing in an obscure military journal makes essentially the same points as a professional party functionary writing in an obscure provincial newspaper.

Differences frequently do occur with regard to particular aspects of Soviet military matters, and not only as between military and non-military but also within the military itself. But these differences are invariably within the framework of the basic positions and principles established by the hierarchy. Also, military spokesmen talk much more about military affairs and in far greater detail than do non-military spokesmen. But this would seem natural in light of professional interests.

The views, in any event, could not conceivably have been voiced in such volume, with such a degree of general uniformity, and by way of such widespread and authoritative media without the sanction of the political leadership.

VIII

There is the further question of whether the Soviet leadership is not now in process of changing its positions regarding Soviet nuclear forces in consequence of the new detente relationship between the US and the USSR.

In attempts to answer this question, I feel it essential that account be taken of the fact that the Soviet leadership views the nature, requirements and implications of the new relationship with the US in an entirely different light than do most of us in the US.

In the US it is generally assumed that the Soviet situation as regards the relationship is very much the same as our own. Detente has given rise in the US to a whole range of expectations and interpretations concerning the future prospects of Soviet-US cooperation for international stability, reductions in the threat of nuclear war and the burdens of defense and even of progressive convergence between the systems. These expectations rest upon assumptions regarding the character of the Soviet leaders, their policies and priorities which go well beyond the specific commitments made by both governments in the agreements reached at summit meetings in Moscow in May 1972 and in Washington in June 1973. An important feature is the widespread belief that fundamental changes have taken place in the former opponent's motivations, priorities and intentions. Not only is the absence of war assumed but also the elimination of conditions which might lead to war, that is, a scaling down of mutually incompatible objectives, the absence of intense competition which infringes on important national interests, cessation of efforts by either side to gain a significant advantage over the other or to alter the existing or agreed-upon balance of power, especially military power. In brief, detente is taken to mean considerable cooperation in the preservation of international stability and the status quo, and as meaning that while competition between the countries may persist to a degree it will be conducted according to equal rules and within fixed bounds and that on all important issues cooperation will take precedence over competition.

The Soviets, for their part, seldom use the term detente in reference to the new relationship, and do so almost exclusively in pronouncements and commentaries aimed at Western targets. The Soviets use, instead, their own preferred term "peaceful coexistence." Moreover, they ordinarily add "between states with different social systems," thereby indicating not only the limits on their cooperation but also reflecting an underlying assumption of a dynamic international environment and of continuing and irreducible competition—the Soviet word is "struggle"—between the opposing systems. Unlike detente, "peaceful coexistence," as explained by the Soviets, does not assume or require the abandonment by either side of incompatible objectives. Its stated aim is not to maintain the *status quo* or to promote stability, but to facilitate changes favorable to the Soviet Union and its allies. Therefore, the Soviets see "peaceful coexistence" not only as a form of struggle with the West but also as a strategy of struggle aimed at achieving

Soviet global objectives. Since the Soviet leadership has gone to great lengths to spell out what it means by "peaceful coexistence" and the limits of that concept as well as its implications for Soviet foreign policies, there is no reason, as Soviet spokesmen themselves point out, why the West should harbor any "illusions" about it or persist in basing its expectations on different assumptions concerning Moscow's policies and actions.

According to Moscow's specifications the prime purpose of peaceful coexistence is to reduce the chances that the continuing struggle between systems will lead to war between the great powers, or, as Brezhnev has said, "will make possible a shift of the historically inevitable struggle [between systems] onto a path that will not threaten wars, dangerous conflicts and unrestricted arms race." Thus, according to *Pravda* of August 22, 1973, "Peaceful coexistence does not mean the end of the struggle of the two world social systems. The struggle between the proletariat and the bourgeoisie, between world socialism and imperialism will be waged right up to the complete and final victory of communism on a world scale." And according to the authoritative collective study *Leninism Today,* "Peaceful coexistence does not extinguish or cancel out class struggle . . . it is a new form of class struggle employed by the working class and the socialist countries in the world arena. It cancels only one type of struggle—war as a means of settling international issues." Further, according to an authoritative 1972 study of the USSR Academy of Sciences, *Problems of War and Peace,* "As for the policy of peaceful coexistence, it rests on a *system of principles* that make it possible to avoid a major international conflict in the course of development of revolutionary processes in individual countries."

Also, although peaceful coexistence appears at first glance to impose equal restraints on both sides to abstain from war or dangerous confrontations in settling disputes between them, in the Soviet view the primary purpose is to place the West and especially the United States under unilateral constraints. The Soviets take the position that it is only the West which threatens war, resorts to military "adventures" and violence against other nations, promotes the arms race, organizes political and military alliances and blocs against the Soviet Union and seeks to deal with Moscow "from a position of strength." In the Soviet view, therefore, the purpose of peaceful coexistence is to curb the West's aggressiveness, militarism and attempts to oppose by force the movement for the transformation of the world according to the Soviet model, or in Soviet terminology, to prevent the West from" exporting counterrevolution" and from trying to impinge upon the "rights of peoples" to utilize every available means, including "arms in hand," to liberate themselves from "reactionary" forces, whether of foreign or domestic origin, and with the aid and support of the Soviet Union.

As an overall matter and as I pointed out above, Moscow interprets US movement toward the new relationship with the USSR, that is US "acceptance of the principle of peaceful coexistence," as a result of, and a further step in, the decline of the power and influence of the US as against the USSR. Hardly had President Nixon left Moscow at the end of May 1972 before the vast propaganda apparatus of the USSR was proclaiming that,

> The strategic course of US policies is now changing before our very eyes from "pax Americana" . . . to a definite form of necessity for peaceful coexistence. We must clearly understand that this change is a *forced* one and that it is precisely the power—the social, economic, and ultimately, military power of the Soviet Union and the socialist countries—that is *compelling* American ruling circles to engage in an agonizing reappraisal of values.

Subsequently, Soviet spokesmen explained that US leaders had had no choice but "to concern themselves with ensuring that US foreign policy objectives, methods, and the doctrines for achieving them are proportionate to [its] dwindling resources," and that the new situation represented "a great victory for our Party and for all the Soviet people—an event of outstanding significance." That, however, much still remains to be done has been emphasized by Brezhnev himself.

> We soberly and realistically evaluate the current situation. Despite the successes in relaxing international tension, a hard struggle against the enemies of peace, national and social liberation faces us. Marxist-Leninists do not entertain any illusions in relation to the anti-peoples essence of imperialism and its aggressive aspirations.

It is against this background that I feel we must examine the question of whether the Soviet leadership may be changing its positions regarding Soviet nuclear forces in consequence of detente. It is also against this background that I feel we must weigh the significance of General Secretary Brezhnev's warning to President Nixon in Moscow that the USSR would continue to strengthen its strategic forces in all ways not specifically prohibited by the SALT I agreement. And it is against this background that I feel we must judge the implications of the post-SALT I testing and deployment of the first Soviet MIRV's; the testing and imminent deployment of four new families of Soviet ICBM's, each decidedly more advanced and effective than its predecessor; an accelerating program of production and deployment of Soviet SLBM's, and the prospective early testing of an entirely new family of SLBM's; and a solid Soviet push for a highly modernized strategic bomber capability.

I
AN OVERVIEW OF FINDINGS AND JUDGMENTS

THE POINT OF DEPARTURE

1. The basic theme which runs through current Soviet statements on East-West relations and matters relating to Soviet defense is that regardless of agreements between states the struggle for dominance between the communist bloc, led by the Soviet Union, and the capitalist bloc, led by the United States, is uncompromising and irreconcilable and will continue as long as capitalism survives.

2. A concomitant basic theme is that the danger of war will persist until the final demise of capitalism. With the recent improvement in US-Soviet relations, Soviet commentaries have emphasized that as a practical matter this danger has been greatly reduced. But this phenomenon is put not in terms of any change in heart or purposes of either the US or the Soviet Union, or any change in the fundamental antagonisms between the two systems which the US and the Soviet Union head. In these particulars class considerations are said to dominate as much now as in the past: there has not been and cannot be any change. The responsible factor, according to Soviet authorities, has been a forced adjustment in US policies and options to new "harsh realities" affecting its domestic and international situation. "We must clearly understand," Soviet spokesmen argued immediately after the Moscow Summit of May 1972, "that this change [in US policies] is a forced one and that it is precisely the power—the social, economic and ultimately, military power of the Soviet Union and the socialist countries—that is compelling American ruling circles to engage in an agonizing reappraisal of values." The standard Soviet line has been, and continues to be, that "the real alignment of forces in the world arena" has shifted against the US and has left US leaders with no choice but "to concern themselves with insuring that [US] foreign policy objectives, methods, and the doctrines for achieving them are proportionate to dwindling [US] resources . . . these factors . . . are pushing the US ruling circles toward a realization of the groundlessness of their former gamble on military strength as their main and almost only instrument of foreign policy." The US is said, however, not to have accepted its changed position as final: "The aggressive forces of imperialism," Brezhnev stated in July 1973, shortly after returning from the US, "will probably not lay down their arms for a long time yet; and there are still adventurists who . . . are capable of kindling a new military conflagration." For this reason, Brezhnev warned, the Soviets "consider it our sacred duty to pursue our policy in such a way that nothing catches us unawares."

3. In speaking of a shift in the balance, or "correlation," of world forces in

1

favor of the USSR and the socialist camp, the Soviet authorities make clear they have in mind a variety of factors beyond the military which they consider as operating to their advantage, including economic, political, social, ideological and psychological factors. They also make clear that they give emphasis to relative trends, as they see and interpret them, on the Soviet as against the US side. Thus they currently draw a sharp contrast between, on the one hand, the allegedly growing strength and viability of the Soviet economy and society, the cohesiveness of the socialist community of states, the momentum of the world liberation movement under Soviet leadership, and the like, and, on the other hand, the internal political, social, and economic problems of the US, the growing "contradictions" between the US and other industrialized nations of the West, failures and difficulties of the US with respect to Third World areas (Southeast Asia, the Middle East, Latin America), and the overall decline in US international economic and political influence. But the Soviet authorities leave no doubt that they consider as basic to all else that has happened, or may happen, in the way of a shift in the balance of world forces the growth of Soviet military power, and more particularly Soviet nuclear power.

4. The Soviet development of a large strategic missile-nuclear force has indeed propelled the USSR from the status of a self-proclaimed besieged fortress in a so-called "capitalist encirclement" to the rank of a world superpower which it shares only with the United States. It has, according to Brezhnev's assertions of 1973 and 1974, "insured more reliably than ever before . . . the security of the Soviet people," and at the same time has forced the capitalist world "to recognize the impossibility of solving militarily the historical differences between capitalism and socialism." Further, the nuclear-based might of the Soviet Union is said to have become a "mighty factor for preserving peace and security of the peoples, a factor which objectively promotes the development of world revolutionary forces." "Soviet nuclear and missile weapons," Politburo member Marshal Grechko argued in November 1973, "offer reliable protection to the peaceful life and security of the members of the socialist community and of all the freedom-loving people," and hence have provided both a shield and base for the varied other developments that have entered in the assumed shift in the balance of world forces.

5. Nevertheless, Soviet pronouncements show that the advent of the nuclear revolution in military affairs has produced complexities for the Kremlin leadership. Both party and military leaders have made clear that they are keenly aware that the new weapons technology has radically altered previous concepts of the balance of power, including new dangers for the USSR in consequence of the acquisition of nuclear capabilities by China and

to a lesser extent other present and potential Nth powers; of the character of war should it occur; and of Moscow's opportunities to achieve its immediate and long-term objectives; and that they are wrestling in many forums and in many ways with the ensuing problems.

6. Soviet views and debates on the implications of nuclear weapons and what is to be done about them demonstrate that the Soviet leaders approach this matter dialectically and perceive it in the context of a dynamic competition with the West for predominance. They demonstrate that it would be a profound error indeed to ascribe to these leaders attitudes, values, and interests which in all important respects closely parallel our own, or to endow them *a priori* with growing "realism," in our sense of the term, in consequence of either the danger inherent in new nuclear weapons or the increase in Soviet military power.

7. In more particular terms, Soviet public discussions indicate that the leadership has no thought of resting content with the present situation, but that it intends to press for further and ever more decisive shifts in the balance of world forces against the US and in favor of the USSR. Contrary to US views as to the meaning of the new peaceful coexistence, or detente, relationship, the Soviets do not consider the relationship as a formula for maintaining international stability or the status quo. Rather, they consider it as a formula for placing constraints on the US as an inherently "aggressive" and "reactionary" power, and allowing a freer hand to the USSR as an inherently "peace-loving" and "progressive" power. Far from inhibiting further advances of the socialist cause, it is said to create conditions more favorable to such advances. The Soviets avow, consequently, an intention to push forward within the framework of the peaceful coexistence relationship on all possible fronts of struggle short of the direct military.

8. Thus, it is specified that the Soviet Union, because of its "international class obligations," must and will intensify struggle in the ideological, political-diplomatic, economic and scientific-technical spheres, and in support of the world-wide "national liberation" movements, including military assistance for movements which "with arms in hand" are striving to eliminate "repressive" or "reactionary" forces. While on the one hand arguing that things have gone so far that the US will have little realistic recourse regardless of what happens, Soviet commentators on the other hand emphasize that new dangers and difficulties may be generated on the US side by new losses and threats of losses in the balance-of-forces equation and by pressures within the US to recapture its former "position of strength." In any event, it appears to be taken as axiomatic by the Soviets that given the "inevitability" of continued dynamic struggle between the US and the USSR and their respective systems, there will be an unavoidable need for continued

increases in Soviet military strength. This need is, in fact, called "a vital necessity, an objective law-governed pattern for the successful building of socialism and communism. It ensues from the nature of modern social development and the specific features of the class struggle between capitalism and socialism."

PURPOSES WHICH THE SOVIETS SEE
THEIR NUCLEAR FORCES AS SERVING

Deterrence of an Attack on the USSR and Its Allies

1. The utility of nuclear forces as a deterrent to a Western attack has been openly stressed by Moscow from the initial acquisition of a Soviet capability. As early as 1954 Soviet leaders were asserting that war against the Soviet Union would lead to the destruction of the West and the capitalist system. Since that time Soviet authorities have placed ever-increasing stress on, the importance of Soviet nuclear forces as a major factor restraining Western aggression against the USSR, including in the process the escalating premature claims of Krushchev concerning Soviet strategic capabilities. Today Moscow's ability to wreak massive nuclear destruction on any opponent or combination of opponents is fully accepted by all nations, a fact which Soviet spokesmen constantly emphasize and in connection with which they voice confidence that none but madmen would dare attack the Soviet Union.

2. Even so, the Soviet public position indicates continuing concern about the dependability of its deterrence posture. The oft-stated Soviet view is that "imperialism" is aggressive by nature and "rightly sees in socialism its deadly enemy." Consequently Western imperialism will continue to seek ways to destroy the Soviet system and cannot be relied upon to act "rationally"—in the Soviet view of rationality—at all times. In other words, as is frequently emphasized, the imperialists refuse, and will continue to refuse, "to voluntarily withdraw from the scene of history." Communist global successes, with the consequent foreshadowing of doom for the capitalist system, might well stimulate the US to even foolhardy adventures. Additionally, Soviet spokesmen frequently note the danger of an "unwanted" nuclear war through escalation of a local conflict. They also note the possibility that an ally of the US might embark on a course that could bring on a nuclear clash between the superpowers. The danger of an unprovoked attack is underscored, furthermore, by the Soviet belief, as expressed in its military doctrine, that major and possibly decisive advantages can be gained from a nuclear surprise attack. It is also underscored by Soviet charges of intensifying US efforts to effect a technological breakthrough in weapons development that might appear to the US to give it a momentary significant

4

advantage in a nuclear conflict. With respect to this latter possibility, one influential Soviet analyst was arguing in February 1974 that "given existing military-technical standards it is difficult to envisage any breakthrough in the foreseeable future which would radically alter the [existing] situation." Nevertheless, he warned: "A destabilizing effect can even be caused by the illusion that some advantage has been obtained. Such an illusion can engender among some circles the temptation, which is difficult to overcome, to make rapid use of the superiority supposedly obtained."

3. Even though Soviet leaders and spokesmen claim that the US has come to give increasing credence to Soviet nuclear deterrence capability and to be more inclined to shift the competition between the systems to non-violent methods, Soviet pronouncements especially since mid-1973 (as against 1972) increasingly warn of the adverse influence exercised in the US by "anti-detente" and militaristic forces and claim to see an intensification of efforts by the US for qualitative improvements in its strategic capability which Defense Minister Grechko and other military leaders describe as constituting a "preparation of world war" and as aimed against the Soviet Union.

4. There is, further, the problem of China which the Soviets treat as beyond any predictability as to the extremes to which Peking might go in furtherance of its anti-Soviet course, regardless of consequences.

5. The upshot is that the Soviets stress that fully reliable deterrence cannot be based solely on an assured second-strike capability but rather must depend on a "pre-war" fighting posture and ability which will face a threatening aggressor with "annihilation" and "defeat." The Soviets do not talk in terms of a "preventive war." Their position is that the Soviet Union never initiates war but only fights wars imposed by a foreign enemy. Nevertheless, Soviet comment consistently emphasizes the necessity of being able to face an enemy with an ability to "frustrate" or "disrupt" any attack, and makes clear that in Soviet thinking the only way in which this can be done is to have the capability to strike first, that is, a capability to launch a first counter-force nuclear strike which would seek not only to disarm an opponent but simultaneously to destroy his defense industry and major industrial complexes, as well as his administrative, military-political command and control, and vital communications and transportation centers.

Deterrence of US "Aggressions" and Initiatives
as Against Third Countries and Areas

1. Beyond the use of Soviet deterrence of a US or Chinese attack on the Soviet Union, Soviet statements indicate that the nuclear forces are assigned also an "active" deterrence role which relates to what the Soviets describe as "the external function of the Soviet armed forces," a function that has

recently been given a new and different emphasis. Whereas traditionally the function of the Soviet armed forces was said to be the defense of the Soviet Union and, subsequently, the "socialist community of states," it is now extended to encompass the prevention of Western attempts "to export counterrevolution," i.e., deterrence of imperialist policies and activities that stand in the way of the creation of favorable conditions for national liberation movements," and of impingements "on the peace and security of peoples, which objectively promotes the development of world revolutionary forces." First authoritatively suggested by Grechko in statements incident to the 24th Party Congress in 1971, the concept has been subsequently developed at high levels and particularly by Army General A. Yepishev, Chief of the Main Political Administration of the Soviet Armed Forces. Writing in 1972, Yepishev said that "in the present era . . . a deepening of the external function of the Soviet Armed Forces has logically taken place." Later he explained that "by its social nature and historical design, the army of the Soviet socialist state represents part of the international revolutionary-liberation forces . . . . Today the defense of the socialist fatherland is closely tied to giving comprehensive assistance to national liberation movements, progressive regimes, and new states who are fighting against imperialist domination." Further, an authoritative Soviet strategic study, *V. I. Lenin and Soviet Military Science,* which appeared shortly after the 24th Party Congress, directly related "the nuclear rocket power of the USSR" to the external function of the armed forces, saying that this power "reliably serves the interest of protecting not only our country but also the other countries of socialism and of all peace-loving peoples."

2. Soviet military might is credited with deterring the US from direct intervention in Cuba, for example, and with generally posing "the chief obstacle in the path of imperialist warmongers." Also, Soviet naval spokesmen emphasize the relationship between the rapid expansion of nuclear-armed Soviet sea power and the global deterrence purposes of the USSR. And some commentators have interpreted the "forced" agreement of the US to accept "the principles of peaceful coexistence" in relations between the US and the USSR as constituting a binding (and hence "legally" enforceable) commitment of the US to accept "deterrence" in its conduct toward all other countries and peoples, including particularly those "struggling for peace, independence and socialism."

3. So far Soviet authorities have not explained, or even discussed, the circumstance under which they might bring to bear their nuclear power to effect global deterrence, or the concrete steps they are prepared to take to this end. Instead, the matter has been put in such general terms as a

"realization that a nuclear war would be suicidal for capitalism," with the consequent effect of "neutralizing and paralyzing the forces of aggression."

National Prestige and Political Clout

1. Soviet leaders have long given every evidence of an acute awareness of the interrelation between military power and national prestige and have shown special sensitivity over deficiencies because of their claim to a superior social, economic and political system. Each step the Soviet Union has traveled along the nuclear path has consequently been utilized to the maximum to enhance the international standing of the USSR and to advertise at home and abroad the alleged advantages of its system. This was clearly overdone at the time of Khrushchev's missile-Sputnik bluff of the late fifties and early sixties, with consequent political embarrassment and humiliation for the regime. Even before Khrushchev was ousted, but with steadily increasing intensity thereafter, the Kremlin struggled with all available means to close the strategic missile gap as against the US. The success of these efforts was evident after 1968 and was crowned by Soviet attainment of admitted nuclear equality with the US at the Moscow Summit in 1972, all of which has, of course, dramatically altered the status of the Soviet Union in the world.

2. While the Soviet leaders show intense satisfaction over these great gains in prestige, their pronouncements and interpretations as to what has happened, and how and why, make clear that they consider the gains not in terms of the attainment of some sort of plateau where they can beneficially, or even safely, adopt a static overall relationship with the US, but in terms of a major advance within the framework of the dialectics of continuing competition and conflict between socio-political systems which are fundamentally and irreconcilably opposed to each other.

3. Assessment of Soviet commentaries makes clear that in Moscow's view gains in national prestige are important mainly in that they add to Soviet political clout and thus contribute to the USSR's ability to shift the balance of world forces in its favor. Thus the new superpower status of the USSR, and of course the accretion in the capabilities of Soviet nuclear forces that brought it about, are being utilized by Moscow to extend and intensify the trend toward globalism in Soviet foreign policy and to open and capitalize on new opportunities for an expansion of Soviet political and military influence on a world scale.

4. The Soviet line is that already the balance of world forces has moved irretrievably against the US and the capitalist world. It is in terms of this change, and only in terms of this change, that Soviet authorities explain the

succession of US "adjustments" in the interest of detente. And the authorities indicate a firm resolve on their part to continue with that which appears so far to have worked so well. If the build-up of Soviet nuclear forces to a level equal to those of the US produced such favorable results, there can be no thought, according to Soviet assertions, of any letdown in efforts to strengthen them further.

War Fighting

1. The basic purpose of Soviet nuclear forces, as explained in Soviet sources, is to provide the Soviet Union with a war-fighting and a war-winning capability. Soviet doctrine and military posture do not distinguish between deterrent and war-fighting nuclear capabilities, but appear to view them as "fused together" in dialectical unity. The better the Soviet armed forces are prepared to fight and win a nuclear war, the more effective they will also be as a deterrent to an attack on the Soviet Union; at the same time, the ability of Soviet forces to fight and win a nuclear war provides indispensable insurance against the failure of deterrence. Thus, Soviet statements tend on the one hand to laud the armed forces as effective guarantors of the security of the Soviet Union from nuclear attack, and on the other to warn persistently of the danger of nuclear war and of the necessity of being fully prepared to meet it.

2. Soviet authorities deplore the possibility of nuclear war. They contend that under current conditions its inception would be irrational in the extreme. However, such admonitions are pointed exclusively at the West, since in Soviet literature it is only the West which is aggressive and might dare to contemplate the precipitation of nuclear war. What the Soviet Union might or might not do is subject to an entirely different set of rules. By definition, any course it adopts would be in the interest of "peace and progress" of all the peoples of the world.

3. Meanwhile, Soviet authorities leave no doubt of their intended reliance on nuclear weapons if a general war should come, whatever its origins. All Soviet literature and statements dealing with Soviet military capabilities and Soviet strategy uniformly stress the central role that nuclear weapons, and more particularly nuclear rocket weapons, have been assigned in all phases of Soviet military planning and preparations. Importance continues to be attached to conventional weapons, though not as a substitute for but as a supplement to nuclear rocket weapons. The furthest that any Soviet spokesmen has gone with respect to reliance on conventional weapons is to concede that "along with" the nuclear rocket weapons which "will be the main and decisive means of waging conflict," such weapons "will also find use, and in

8

...rm in the disorienting claims of bourgeois ideologues that there will be no ...ctor in a thermonuclear world war." They contend that the end of a nuclear ...r will be the collapse of capitalism and the victory of the Soviet Union and ...cialism on a worldwide scale. "Let it be known to all," Brezhnev asserted ...early as 1967, "that in a clash with any aggressor the Soviet Union will win ...victory worthy of our great people." Indeed, Soviet leaders are probably ...e only ones among the leaders of the world today who speak of victory in a ...clear war.

7. Authoritative Soviet writers also criticize as "deeply mistaken" the ...im by Western "ideologues" that the concept of heroism in a nuclear war ...obsolete and that there will be only "victims but no heroes." Furthermore, ...viet civil defense officials persistently propagandize the feasibility of assur- ...g the survival of the population and of the economy if proper preparatory ...asures are taken in advance of a war, and criticize those who believe that ...th sides will refrain from using nuclear weapons in a possible future conflict ...well as those who think that no defense against such weapons is possible.

8. Soviet insistence on the continued possibility of nuclear war is accom- ...ied by emphasis on the necessity to further strengthen Soviet military ...abilities and war readiness, to press military R and D to the maximum ...ent feasible, to intensify domestic controls in the interest of security ...inst enemy machinations, to prepare the population and members of the ...ed forces for the actualities of a nuclear conflict, and to improve the ...vivability of Soviet society and the Soviet economy under conditions of ...lear war. With respect to this last point, it may be important to note that ...ch of the extensive current military discussion of new efforts to develop ...eria directly stresses its relevance for survivability of the Soviet economy ...r nuclear war conditions.

In sum, the Soviet views relative to fighting a nuclear war appear to be ...omplete consonance with preparing the USSR both psychologically and ...sically for such risk taking as may be necessary in consequence of the ...ed Soviet purpose of continuing to strive for a further and ever more ...sive shift in the balance of world forces in their favor.

Question of Priorities and Relative Weights of Soviet Purposes Regard ...s Nuclear Forces

There can be no doubt that Moscow is anxious to avoid ...
the US, barring a development that would give it a dec...
... though Soviet spokesmen predict a Soviet vict...
...ar war, they consistently acknowledge the en...
...t from such a war and hasten to deny t...
...wife" of revolution (although the now st...

certain circumstances, units and subunits might conduct cc
only conventional weapons.''

4. Soviet commentators, it should be noted, insist that
age has not ceased to be an instrument of politics, "as
overwhelming majority of representatives of pacifist, anti-
the bourgeois world.'' Significantly, Soviet spokesmen a
denounce as "bourgeois pacifism'' the view that both s
stroyed in a nuclear war and that there can be no victor i
point of view had long been a matter of sporadic debate
Union. Shortly after the death of Stalin, questions as to th
weapons on the outcome of war were debated at the h
example, in 1954, when Malenkov spoke of the "de
civilization.'' for which he was sharply criticized at the t
Chairman of the Council of Ministers by Molotov and
that time insisted that only the capitalist system would
war. Subsequently, Khrushchev to all intents and purp
Malenkov line, and treated it as a central issue in Sovie
Chinese in the early 1960's, although in some of his state
asserting that the Soviet Union would be victorious.

5. More recently, in 1965-1967, there was a renewal
over the possibility of attaining victory in a nuclear war.
was resolved in favor of those who still stressed the fea
winning such a war, and since 1967 public statements
on the possibility of "mutual destruction'' have becom
appeared in *Pravda* in December 1969 and asserted
America know that within a few hours such a confli
millions but could also destroy all that has been crea
labors.'' This statement was made in the context of
SALT negotiations in Helsinki, and dealt in part with
US intellectuals. In August 1973, G. A. Arbatov sa
Budapest's television: "The prevention of nuclear w
interests of the United States and the USSR, since
suicide to both.'' However, the main theme of the ir
growing prospects for further improvements in Soviet
specific exception was subsequently taken by Soviet
to Arbatov's "suicide'' reference.

6. Rare exceptions to the contrary, the main thrust
ements is that victory in war can still be attaine
ar war "can cause substantial detriment to the
tion, inhibiting the advance of the revolutiona
e Soviet spokesmen argue that "there is prof

9

certain circumstances, units and subunits might conduct combat actions with only conventional weapons.''

4. Soviet commentators, it should be noted, insist that war in the nuclear age has not ceased to be an instrument of politics, ''as is claimed by the overwhelming majority of representatives of pacifist, anti-war movements in the bourgeois world.'' Significantly, Soviet spokesmen also now generally denounce as ''bourgeois pacifism'' the view that both sides would be destroyed in a nuclear war and that there can be no victor in such a war. This point of view had long been a matter of sporadic debate within the Soviet Union. Shortly after the death of Stalin, questions as to the effects of nuclear weapons on the outcome of war were debated at the highest level, as for example, in 1954, when Malenkov spoke of the ''destruction of world civilization.'' for which he was sharply criticized at the time of his ouster as Chairman of the Council of Ministers by Molotov and Khrushchev who at that time insisted that only the capitalist system would perish in a nuclear war. Subsequently, Khrushchev to all intents and purposes picked up the Malenkov line, and treated it as a central issue in Soviet polemics with the Chinese in the early 1960's, although in some of his statements he persisted in asserting that the Soviet Union would be victorious.

5. More recently, in 1965-1967, there was a renewal of the public debate over the possibility of attaining victory in a nuclear war. The debate evidently was resolved in favor of those who still stressed the feasibility of waging and winning such a war, and since 1967 public statements by Soviet spokesmen on the possibility of ''mutual destruction'' have become relatively rare. One appeared in *Pravda* in December 1969 and asserted that ''both we and America know that within a few hours such a conflict could not only kill millions but could also destroy all that has been created by both people's labors.'' This statement was made in the context of the beginning of the SALT negotiations in Helsinki, and dealt in part with the anti-war views of US intellectuals. In August 1973, G. A. Arbatov said in an interview on Budapest's television: ''The prevention of nuclear war equally serves the interests of the United States and the USSR, since nuclear war would be suicide to both.'' However, the main theme of the interview dealt with the growing prospects for further improvements in Soviet-US relations. Further, specific exception was subsequently taken by Soviet military commentators to Arbatov's ''suicide'' reference.

6. Rare exceptions to the contrary, the main thrust of current Soviet public statements is that victory in war can still be attained. It is conceded that a nuclear war ''can cause substantial detriment to the development of world civilization, inhibiting the advance of the revolutionary process,'' but at the same time Soviet spokesmen argue that ''there is profound erroneousness and

harm in the disorienting claims of bourgeois ideologues that there will be no victor in a thermonuclear world war." They contend that the end of a nuclear war will be the collapse of capitalism and the victory of the Soviet Union and socialism on a worldwide scale. "Let it be known to all," Brezhnev asserted as early as 1967, "that in a clash with any aggressor the Soviet Union will win a victory worthy of our great people." Indeed, Soviet leaders are probably the only ones among the leaders of the world today who speak of victory in a nuclear war.

7. Authoritative Soviet writers also criticize as "deeply mistaken" the claim by Western "ideologues" that the concept of heroism in a nuclear war is obsolete and that there will be only "victims but no heroes." Furthermore, Soviet civil defense officials persistently propagandize the feasibility of assuring the survival of the population and of the economy if proper preparatory measures are taken in advance of a war, and criticize those who believe that both sides will refrain from using nuclear weapons in a possible future conflict as well as those who think that no defense against such weapons is possible.

8. Soviet insistence on the continued possibility of nuclear war.is accompanied by emphasis on the necessity to further strengthen Soviet military capabilities and war readiness, to press military R and D to the maximum extent feasible, to intensify domestic controls in the interest of security against enemy machinations, to prepare the population and members of the armed forces for the actualities of a nuclear conflict, and to improve the survivability of Soviet society and the Soviet economy under conditions of nuclear war. With respect to this last point, it may be important to note that much of the extensive current military discussion of new efforts to develop Siberia directly stresses its relevance for survivability of the Soviet economy under nuclear war conditions.

9. In sum, the Soviet views relative to fighting a nuclear war appear to be in complete consonance with preparing the USSR both psychologically and physically for such risk taking as may be necessary in consequence of the stated Soviet purpose of continuing to strive for a further and ever more decisive shift in the balance of world forces in their favor.

The Question of Priorities and Relative Weights of Soviet Purposes Regarding Its Nuclear Forces

1. There can be no doubt that Moscow is anxious to avoid nuclear war with the US, barring a development that would give it a decisive advantage. Even though Soviet spokesmen predict a Soviet victory in the event of a nuclear war, they consistently acknowledge the enormous damage that would result from such a war and hasten to deny that it can serve as a desirable "midwife" of revolution (although the now standard line is that in case a

nuclear war does come it will inevitably be global in nature and will result in the final and total destruction of the capitalist system thorughout the world.) Hence, deterrence of the US from either a nuclear attack or courses of action that might lead to a nuclear conflict is obviously of very great importance in Soviet thinking. At the same time, however, the evidence indicates that the leadership, with its peculiar world outlook and operating within the framework of its peculiar environment, has genuine reservations regarding realistic possibilities of assured deterrence, at least not without unacceptable costs to its own system and to the dynamism with which it feels it necessary to press its own world interests and objectives.

2. The Soviets are deeply interested in prestige, which is so intimately related to their claim of superiority for their system and their attempts to prove it. But prestige considerations as such cannot by any means explain the level of Soviet defense efforts or the present style of Soviet exploitation of its nuclear force capabilities. It is obvious that Moscow believes it derives far more benefit from its expanding global role and especially from willingness of the West European governments and the US to meet Soviet terms with respect to it. Actually, the Soviets appear interested not so much in prestige for its own sake, but as a demonstration and added source of capabilities that enable it to influence developments to an ever greater degree throughout the world, and consequently as a constituent element within the complex of forces by means of which Moscow is striving to effect an "irreversible" shift in the balance of world forces. The Soviets quite clearly would like, and hope, to be able to utilize this complex of forces without precipitation of war with the US, that is under conditions of effective deterrence. But the Soviets themselves constantly argue that this may not be possible, that Soviet successes may produce US reactions that can escalate into nuclear war or even take the form of a direct nuclear attack on the USSR. Yet Moscow gives no signs of any willingness to abate or give up its struggle against the US, despite possibly serious consequences with respect to the effectiveness of deterrence. Instead, it stresses its intention to continue and even to intensify this struggle by all means short of a resort on its own to the use of its armed forces against the US.

3. Given the foregoing, and in the absence of universal nuclear disarmament, the ability to fight a nuclear war, with maximal prospects of winning should it come, assumes for the Soviets basic importance. It would seem axiomatic, in fact, that the Soviets see the most fundamental purpose of their nuclear forces as related to war-fighting capability. Existence of this capability, as carefully distinguished from intention regarding its deliberate employment, is in Soviet thinking an essential for effectiveness of the Soviet deterrence posture given the sort of dynamism they appear to anticipate on

the part of both the US and the USSR. It also facilitates, in fact appears in Moscow's eyes to be fundamental to the attainment of Soviet objectives relative to further shifts in the world balance of forces. And conceivably most important in the Soviet view is that, due to the dynamics of history, a general war between the capitalist and communist worlds may turn out to be "unavoidable" after all, making it a matter of elementary prudence to be as ready as possible for such a contingency.

4. In connection with this last point, it is important to note that the current Soviet leadership has modified the emphasis that Khrushchev came to place on the possibility that a new general war can in fact be avoided. Khrushchev initially, that is at the 20th Party Congress in 1956, limited himself to the statement that a general war was no longer "fatalistically inevitable," and added a further hedge to the effect that if the "imperialists" went against all reason and brought on such war, forces existed "to give a smashing rebuff to the aggressors and their plans." As time passed, however, Khrushchev became more and more categoric. In a speech on March 26, 1959 he stated that "we consider, proceeding from a Marxist-Leninist analysis of the present situation, that war is not inevitable today." Subsequently the CPSU Central Committee, in a letter to the Central Committee of the Chinese Communist Party, asserted that in view of the growing strength of the socialist camp and its allies among the peoples, "it will become really possible to rule out the possibility of world war from the life of society even before socialism fully triumphs on earth, with capitalism still existing in a part of the world."

5. Khrushchev's successors have taken a different approach. They continue on occasion to repeat the original Khrushchev formulation to the effect that a general war is no longer "fatalistically inevitable." But they almost invariably preface this statement with the modifier "while" and then go on to add that because of this or that consideration war still may occur. More often, however, the custom has become simply to use a different and less reassuring formulation which stresses that so long as imperialism exists the "danger," and sometimes the "real possibility," of a new general war will continue.

HOW MUCH NUCLEAR STRENGTH, IN THE SOVIET VIEW, IS ENOUGH?

Conceptual vs. Practical Limits on Soviet Force Size and Composition

1. There is no evidence of a specific Soviet conceptual limit on the size of its nuclear forces. However, Soviet spokesmen constantly refer to dangers from both West and East, and the general Soviet view, especially among the military, seems to be that the "more the better." In principle, as now authoritatively stated at top military levels, Soviet nuclear forces must suffice

12

to (a) "reliably defend the socialist Motherland" and deter an attack upon the Soviet Union or its allies; (b) in the event of any enemy preparing an attack on the USSR or its allies, to "frustrate" the initiation of the attack and assure the "decisive defeat" of the enemy; (c) support Soviet foreign policy objectives by forcing the West to deal with the Soviet Union from a position of "realism" rather than "strength" and reducing the risks of a dangerous Western reaction to Soviet gains; (d) deter the West from "exporting counter-revolution" and otherwise to stand as an effective obstacle to "imperialist aggression" in the Third World; and (e) support "national liberation" struggles and defend "all peace loving peoples" (or "the cause of peace") throughout the world.

2. At the same time, it is stated that Soviet military doctrine and strategy and Soviet concepts on force requirements and employment must remain flexible in order to take account of the changing capabilities resulting from new weapons developments, Soviet projections of the character of future wars, and new opportunities that may arise for attaining "decisive results" in such wars. Current Soviet concepts insist, therefore, that although the nuclear forces constitute the "main" striking power of the Armed Forces and are capable of attaining victory in a short time, there is also a requirement for a balanced development of all arms and services in order to assure a capability to wage war at various levels of violence and with all types of means, nuclear and conventional. Furthermore, the Soviet view holds that even in a nuclear war there is a need for combined arms operations and forces to assure the "final defeat" of the enemy.

3. In practice, the size and composition of the Soviet Armed Forces are the result of compromises between various interests within the military establishment as well as between competing demands for resources by the military and the economy. Furthermore, they are said to be determined by Soviet economic and scientific-technological capabilities, the anticipated direction of the development of the "state of the art" in weapons technology, the leadership's perceptions of the state of Soviet relations with the outside world, the degree of threat of war, the existing and anticipated military and political capabilities of the Western countries and in particular the US, and the probable forms of war which may be waged by them. The Soviets insist that these factors are in "close dialectic relationship," a view which precludes a concept of fixed limits on force size and composition.

SALT and the Further Development of the Soviet Armed Forces

1. To date (i.e. April 21, 1974) Soviet public statements show no evidence of the SALT agreements having any noticeable influence on Soviet military or strategic concepts or on Soviet views on the need for further improvements of

13

Soviet military capabilities. The Soviet strategic concepts and requirements for decisive offensive operations in a war in order to capture the initiative pre-date the Moscow Summit and remain in force also at the present time. Although the danger of a possible enemy surprise attack is treated as somewhat diminished at the present time, the critical need for a Soviet capability to deal effectively with such a danger, as well as to maintain a strategy and capability for damage limitation which could assure the survival of the Soviet Union and the preservation of its essential war-fighting and national power capacity in the event of an all-out nuclear war, continues to be emphasized. While Soviet spokesmen call for an agreement on limiting the qualitative improvement of strategic weapons, and express concern over the danger of a breakdown of detente as a result of an "unrestricted development of the MIRV system in the United States," various Soviet civilian and military leaders urge greater efforts in the development and application of scientific and technological innovations for military purposes and stress a direct relationship between the growth of the Soviet economy and the further strengthening of Soviet military might. There is no indication of a Soviet willingness to subscribe to the Western concept of "mutual assured destruction," which is said to be inherently unstable in view of the possibility of new breakthroughs in weapons technology as well as for political reasons.

2. Although the Moscow and Washington Summit agreements were acknowledged by Soviet leaders to have provided for an interim system of "equal security" in the strategic area, General Secretary Brezhnev warned President Nixon in Moscow that the USSR would continue to strengthen its strategic forces except as specifically prohibited by the SALT agreement, and the agreement itself was immediately followed by a public campaign for the further overall strengthening of Soviet armed forces on the stated ground that, despite the present effectiveness of the Soviet deterrent capabilities, the danger of war will persist as long as imperialism survives, and that greater might is needed to prevent the US from returning to the Cold War policy of attempting to deal with the Soviet Union from a "position of strength." This campaign was endorsed by Brezhnev and the CPSU Central Committee in March 1973 and in a number of subsequent speeches by Brezhnev and other members of the Politburo, as well as by Defense Minister Marshal A. Grechko in a succession of post-SALT speeches in 1972 and 1973 and on January 8 and 29 and March 13, 1974 and in a *Pravda* article of February 23, 1974. Soviet statements at the highest level make it unmistakably clear that the Soviet Union still seeks to attain further improvements in its military capability viewing this as an "objective necessity" dictated by the laws of social development, and does not believe its present posture to be sufficient to meet Soviet long-term security or foreign policy requirements. Thus in his

speech of March 13, 1974 Grechko told a Kremlin All-Army Conference of Komsomol Organization Secretaries that, "As a whole the conditions of the contemporary international situation require . . . that the defense capability of the Soviet state be tirelessly increased, and that the armed forces be strengthened. In this our party sees one of its main tasks."

How Much Further Should Soviet Forces Be Strengthened?

1. In the current phase Soviet authorities call not only for quantitative increases and qualitative improvements in the weapons within the framework of the SALT agreements, but also for the development of "fundamentally new weapons." It is asserted furthermore that "a responsible task" of Soviet military science "consists in continuing to further develop new methods of conducting an armed struggle, taking into account the prospects for the development of military technology and armaments." Although a recent (February 1974) Soviet commentary directed toward US military R and D activities questioned the possibility of attaining significant advantage as a result of qualitative weapons improvements and pointed to the growing strain on the economy (referring ostensibly only to the US) as a consequence of the "geometric" increase in the cost of each new generation of weapons, military spokesmen at the highest level, beginning with Marshal Grechko, argue that despite detente, the "greater the combat ability of the [Soviet] armed forces" and "the more powerfully they are equipped" the better will be the prospects for peace (January 8, 1974), and persist in suggesting the desirability of attaining "military-technical superiority over the capitalist armed forces." These spokesmen also stress that in the event of a nuclear war between the US and the USSR "a decisive role in its outcome would be played by the correlation of the countries' nuclear missile potentials."

2. At the same time, however, Moscow is concerned to avoid a breakdown of its detente policy and to avoid provoking a greater US defense effort. Consequently, Soviet propaganda seeks to reassure the US and its allies concerning Soviet peaceful intentions and to minimize the military and political implications of the continuing efforts of the Soviet Union to further strengthen its own military might.

SOVIET VIEWS ON THE EMPLOYMENT
OF NUCLEAR WEAPONS IN WAR

Basic Concepts

1. Current Soviet strategic concepts, as throughout the past decade, focus on the "worst possible case," i.e., a general war between the US and the

Soviet Union. The concepts insist that such a war, because of its "class" character, will be an all-out struggle between the two opposing systems, aimed at the total and final defeat of the opponent with the final end of its system, and that consequently, nuclear weapons will constitute the key element in combat. In the Soviet view the war may begin with a surprise attack or as a result of escalation of a limited war. The first strike with nuclear weapons, especially if delivered by surprise, could "determine the further course and outcome" of the war; the war would be fought on a global scale; it would require the use of multi-million armies; and additional weapons production will be required to sustain the military forces if the war becomes protracted. It is also indicated that the number of strategic weapons on hand at the start of the war will be of great importance in determining the course and outcome of the war, as will also be the state of war readiness of the armed forces and the morale and psychological preparedness for war of the troops and of the entire population.

Specific Soviet Expectations Regarding the Use of Nuclear Weapons

1. Soviet doctrine holds that nuclear weapons form the main combat element not only of the strategic but also of the ground, naval and air forces and are capable of simultaneously solving strategic and tactical missions. Nuclear weapons, in the Soviet view, have made the attack the "decisive form of military action," and make it necessary to conduct defensive tasks by means of active defense, i.e., by means of nuclear strikes. The massive use of nuclear weapons and the factor of surprise are said to "assume prime importance." Furthermore, to assure the destruction of the enemy and the survival of the USSR, the doctrine calls for a Soviet first counter-force strike.

2. The public Soviet line is that in the face of possible war initiation by the US or the latter's attempt to resort to a surprise attack, the Soviet Armed Forces must be "ready and capable to destroy and annihilate" the enemy's forces. Soviet spokesmen indicate that they do not expect to succeed in destroying the entire US strategic force in a pre-emptive attack, and in particular appear to recognize the difficulty of dealing with the US submarine-launched ballistic missile (SLBM) capability, showing particular concern over the "Trident" and "Poseidon" programs, but they argue that counter-force attacks and active air defense, combined with a disruption of US command and control, can significantly reduce the weight of the US strikes on the Soviet Union and thus facilitate the solution of the problem of the latter's survival and ultimate victory. While presumably the Soviets would launch their strike on warning in an attempt to pre-empt the US attack, no clear distinction is drawn between pre-emption and a preventive war. Some Soviet military leaders publicly acknowledge an interest in a Soviet

16

surprise attack strategy and are critical of those who think of surprise as "mainly associated with an attack by the enemy" on the Soviet Union. Even so, the possibility of a US nuclear first-strike attack is not excluded, thus requiring the maintenance by the Soviet Union of an assured second-strike capability in the form of hardened ICBM sites and an SLBM force.

Targeting

1. Soviet doctrine holds that in an armed struggle between the opposing systems, victory requires not only the defeat of the "imperialist" enemy but his "destruction." Consequently, Soviet doctrine and leaders clearly state that the Soviet nuclear weapons will be used to destroy the enemy's "means of nuclear attack, his large troop formations and military bases . . . [his] defense industry" as well as his main administration, command and control, communications and transportation centers, in order to (a) weaken his retaliatory strikes and thereby assure the survivability of the Soviet Union, (b) disorganize his war effort, administration and controls and deprive him of his military-economic potential, and (c) hopefully bring about his military and/or political collapse. The doctrine therefore calls for simultaneous strikes against the enemy's vital military as well as civilian targets. The most valued military effects would be primarily the destruction of the enemy's strategic capabilities both for its impact on the war and in order to minimize damage to the Soviet Union. Furthermore, since in the Soviet view victory requires the Soviet Union to emerge from the conflict in a dominant position, capable of imposing terms on the enemy and preventing him from rebuilding his strategic forces, the Soviet Union must be capable, either by withholding some nuclear weapons or, as Soviet statements emphasize, by manufacturing new ones, to attain strategic superiority in the course of the war and, if necessary, to be able to attack any newly identified enemy targets.

Anti-Ballistic Missiles and the Question of the Protection of the Homeland

1. The ABM Agreement has not altered the stated Soviet view on its war strategy nor led to a subscription to the concept of mutual assured destruction. The persistence of the Soviet search for a war-fighting and war-survival capability suggests that Soviet adherence to the ABM Agreement was the result of technical difficulties in Soviet ABM development and concern that the US might achieve a technological breakthrough in its ABM program, which could negate Soviet hopes for a successful first counter-force strike, and, combined with a MIRV capability, might incline the US to adopt a first-strike strategy.

2. Current Soviet doctrine perceives the development of a damage-limiting capability in terms of a combination of counter-force strikes, improved air

17

defense and anti-submarine warfare, and passive defense measures. In this connection we should note that new Soviet civil defense programs, instituted in 1973, seek to upgrade the operational readiness of the large Soviet military and civilian civil defense forces, as well as to continue efforts to disperse and harden vital industries and to develop a capability for the protection of the essential labor force and for quick repair and restoration of damaged industrial facilities and services in order to maintain critical war production in the course of the war. Soviet spokesmen insist that civil defense can provide effective protection against a nuclear attack, claiming that the Soviet Union, because of the greater dispersal of its population and production facilities, is less vulnerable to destruction than the US.

Limited vs. Unlimited Use of Nuclear Weapons

1. Soviet strategic commentaries are primarily concerned with the problem of a general nuclear war involving the US and the USSR. The possibility of lower levels of conflict is acknowledged but not discussed in any detail. While it is said that the Soviet armed forces must be prepared to wage war by conventional as well as nuclear means and that the form of war initiation and the enemy's war aims, as well as the weapons he uses and the scope of military actions, will influence military decisions and weapons employment, Soviet analysts appear not to allow a realistic possibility of avoiding an escalation of any conflict directly involving the US and the USSR to full-blown nuclear proportions.

2. Soviet doctrine does not discuss the possibility of using nuclear weapons in a controlled, escalatory fashion, or for war bargaining purposes (except possibly in terms of a residual nuclear force either withheld or newly produced in the course of the war), and Soviet spokesmen are scornful of such Western theories, which they claim are intended to allow the West and especially the US the possibility of avoiding retribution and to establish rules which will facilitate the initiation of war. Soviet commentators, both military and civilian, also condemn all Western war strategies based on the use of "mini" nuclear weapons, arguing that this is merely intended to create a more "tolerant" public attitude towards nuclear warfare, and like the renewal of US interest in a "counter-force" option serves to justify new weapons production and encourage the arms race. According to a February 1974 analysis, "the idea of introducing rules of the game and artificial restrictions by agreement seems illusory and untenable. It is difficult to visualize that a nuclear war, if unleashed, could be kept within the framework of rules and would not develop into an all-out war."

3. Although the Soviets acknowledge that local wars do not automatically escalate, the Soviets persist in warning of such a possibility especially if the

18

nuclear powers become involved in a confrontation or nuclear weapons are used by one side or the other. Soviet spokesmen also point out that modern conventional warfare has become highly destructive and "may lead to the annihilation of entire nations," thus making it harder to impose any restrictions on the use of nuclear weapons. It is evident that at the present time the Soviet Union finds it advantageous to leave all its options open regarding local war situations, but at the same time wishes to exploit Western uncertainties about Soviet responses and fears of an unlimited nuclear conflict in order to add weight to Soviet political demands.

SOVIET VIEWS ON THEATER WAR

The Relationship of Intercontinental and Theater Forces

1. The stated Soviet purpose is defense against an attack because, by Soviet definition, the Soviet Union would never initiate an unprovoked war. Indeed, suggestions of the possibility of Soviet use of strategic surprise without reference to a presumed pre-emptive character of such initiation very rarely appear in Soviet public statements. Current Soviet theater war concepts, like its strategic concepts, pay greatest attention to the nuclear war case in which nuclear weapons would be used to destroy the enemy's theater nuclear capability, his large troop formations, fleets and weapons storage sites, and to "pave the way" for the rapid advance of Soviet troops. When on the defensive, Soviet forces would rely also principally on nuclear strikes to destroy the enemy attacking forces and in order to prepare for the launching of a Soviet offensive. These objectives will be accomplished by the combined use of the Strategic Missile Forces and Air Forces against distant targets and the employment of intermediate and medium range and tactical nuclear armed missiles by the Soviet Ground and Tactical Air forces. Here again emphasis is placed on the use of surprise in executing the counter-force strikes. Furthermore, spokesmen emphasize that nuclear weapons are fully integrated into Soviet theater forces and provide their main firepower for the purpose of "establishing firepower superiority over an enemy," even though "units and subunits" may carry out specific combat missions by relying only on conventional weapons.

2. Soviet publications discussing a theater war in Europe warn that the use of tactical nuclear weapons or of "nuclear warning shots" will lead most likely to an escalation of the conflict and argue that any armed conflict in Europe, given the present network of military alliances, "would inexorably involve all other states of the world in the orbit of a thermonuclear collision." At the same time, Soviet commentators take note of European views that the June 1973 US-Soviet agreement on the avoidance of nuclear conflicts signals

19

the collapse of the US "flexible response" doctrine, and are highly critical of all suggestions for the creation of a combined European nuclear force, which they describe as being utterly "unrealistic." Yet they persist in asserting that until complete nuclear disarmament is achieved, the Soviet Union will remain ready to "wage war with the use of any means of armed struggle." In this connection, a well-known Soviet military theoretician, Lieutenant General I. Zavialov, points out that an "important task" of the Soviet Armed Forces is to be ready for the "swift transfer from one mode of action to another," i.e., from fighting with conventional weapons to using nuclear weapons, and notes that "the complexity lies in the fact that it is difficult to foresee at what stage of the operation nuclear weapons can be employed." It is evident that both the doctrine and stated capabilities of the Soviet Armed Forces leave them the option of waging a theater war with or without nuclear weapons.

3. Moscow, however, has made clear that for a theater war involving only the Soviet Union and China, the USSR would make all necessary use of its nuclear force, that it would not hesitate to resort to a nuclear first strike, and that it would not fall into the trap of waging a protracted war of attrition which is so favored by Chinese military doctrine. It may be that despite suggestions to the contrary actual Soviet planning with respect to other possible theater wars of major proportions (e.g., in Europe or the Middle East) is along the same lines.

II
SOME BASIC CONSIDERATIONS

The purpose of this paper is to examine and analyze, on the basis of recent Soviet publications and statements, current Soviet views on the utility of Soviet nuclear forces, the limits to be placed on such forces, the modes of their employment in the event of war, and their relationship to intercontinental and theater forces, including the impact of SALT and of Western controlled-war concepts on Soviet military doctrine.

The advent of the nuclear age has radically altered the Soviet Union's power position and role in world affairs, as well as its views on its ability to compete with the West for predominance. Soviet development of a large strategic missile-nuclear force has propelled the USSR from the status of a self-proclaimed besieged fortress amidst the so-called "capitalist encirclement" to the rank of a world superpower, which it shares only with the United States. Nevertheless, this "military-technological revolution" has produced complexities for the Soviet leadership compared to the rather straight-line view of the world and its future that prevailed in pre-nuclear days. The Soviet military leadership has been wrestling with the new problems posed for Soviet military, strategic and tactical doctrines, force composition and organization, command and control and the requirements of sustaining and assimilating the race in weapons technology. At the same time, the political leaders have sought to come to grips with the implications of the nuclear forces for Soviet security, foreign policy and resource allocation, as well as for communist political doctrine. Both party and military leaders have made clear that they are keenly aware that the new weapons technology has radically altered previous concepts of the balance of power, the character of war should it occur, and Moscow's opportunities to achieve its immediate and long-term objectives.

Most basic, the revolutionary implications of the advent of nuclear weapons are reflected in the shift from the Soviet belief in the "fatalistic" inevitability of war among the capitalist powers and especially between the capitalist and communist camps, a belief long enshrined in Leninist and Stalinist dogma and one on which great reliance was placed for the ultimate worldwide triumph of the communist cause, to the new concept that communist goals may now be attained without war and under conditions of "peaceful coexistence."[1] The corollary to this development has been a shift from what was essentially a defensive Soviet stance pending the creation of

---

[1] See F. D. Kohler, M. L. Harvey, L. Gouré, R. Soll, *Soviet Strategy for the Seventies: From Cold War to Peaceful Coexistence*, Monographs in International Affairs, Center for Advanced International Studies, University of Miami, Coral Gables, Florida, 1973, *passim*.

revolutionary situations and opportunities via the automatic working of "immutable social laws" to a dynamic policy of Soviet global involvements and growing pressures on Western interests. While the style and tactics of the USSR's efforts to exploit its new power status for political gains have changed with time, leadership personalities, and military capabilities, the overall forward thrust of Soviet policy, initiated by Khruschchev's nuclear gamesmanship, persists.

Any analysis of Soviet public views on the utility, limitations and employment of nuclear forces must take into account the fact that the Soviet leaders approach this question dialectically and perceive it in the context of a dynamic competition with the West for predominance. It would be a profound error indeed to ascribe to these leaders attitudes, values and interests which in all important respects closely parallel our own, or to endow them *a priori* with growing "realism," in our sense of the term, growing out of either the danger inherent in new nuclear weapons or the increase in Soviet military power. Not only, as Brezhnev and other Soviet leaders continue to stress, is the struggle between the two systems—the capitalist and the communist —inevitable and irreconcilâble regardless of changes in weapons technology,[2] but the Soviet Union as the leader, and in the Soviet view prime beneficiary, of a world revolutionary doctrine and movement views the utility of military power differently from the West, which essentially is oriented to the defense of the *status quo*. Indeed, the Soviets see a fundamental conflict between the principles of peaceful coexistence, as propounded by them, and Western notions concerning the preservation of the *status quo* in the non-communist world as a way of maintaining stable East-West relations.[3] Thus, as Soviet public pronouncements make very explicit, Soviet military power serves not only the aim of assuring the security of the Soviet Union, but also as the primary factor in bringing about a radical shift in the East-West balance of power in favor of the USSR. Of course, the Soviets argue that such a shift serves the cause of peace and detente while a balance of power favoring the West would "without a doubt" lead to greater international tension and increase of Western propensities for aggression.[4]

Soviet public discussions of nuclear power show a remarkable degree of continuity of basic formulations and concepts over the past decade, especially as they apply to military aims, strategy and operational concepts. This is not

---

[2]For example, see Brezhnev's speech of December 21, 1972, *Pravda*, December 22, 1972, and M. Suslov's speech of July 13, 1973, *Pravda*, July 14, 1973.

[3]Staff of the Institute of Philosophy of the USSR Academy of Sciences, *Problems of War and Peace*, Moscow, Progress Publishers, 1972, p. 267.

[4]G. Arbatov, "Concerning Soviet-American Relations," *Kommunist* (Communist), No. 3, February 1973, p. 105.

to say that there have been no public and internal debates and disagreements among the military and within the political leadership on various issues, among them the size and composition of Soviet Armed Forces, resource allocation, command and control, troop training and indoctrination, requirements for a theater war, and the feasibility of victory in a general nuclear war. Moreover, the implementation of military and political thinking, alongside Soviet actions as they relate to publicly proclaimed Soviet objectives and assessments of the global situation, have by no means been entirely consistent. The inconsistencies have arisen and continue to arise as a result of various factors such as Soviet internal power politics and the competition between major interest groups for resources and influence, differences over policy priorities and objectives and estimates of what is realistically feasible, difficulties in accommodating conflicting policy requirements and lines, bureaucratic inertia, and the impossibility, despite a highly centralized decision-making apparatus, of achieving a perfect orchestration of all statements and actions. To this must be added changes, sometimes abrupt, in tactics or direction as the leadership perceives new priorities or opportunities, or finds it expedient to compromise on various issues. As a consequence, one observes such seeming inconsistencies as the Soviet simultaneous effort to negotiate detente with the US even while undertaking what appear to Westerners to be gratuitous provocative actions, as, for example, the attempt to develop Cienfuegos, Cuba, into a Soviet nuclear submarine base; the cessation of Soviet jamming of VOA and BBC broadcasts while simultaneously intensifying the domestic "vigilance" campaign against the penetration of Western values and ideology; the calls for further arms control while at the same time actively pursuing the development of new strategic weapons and the testing of nuclear weapons and asserting that the chance of war, while reduced, will persist "as long as imperialism survives"; and insistence on the elimination of the use of force in relations between states in accordance with the principles of "peaceful coexistence" while at the same time pledging support to national liberation and revolutionary struggles and becoming actively involved in local conflicts such as the October 1973 Middle East War.

It must be pointed out, however, that the inconsistencies often exist only in the eye of the Western observer, who assumes there is a single overriding Soviet objective at a given time and, therefore, expects a total orchestration of all Soviet actions in its support. Actually, as the Soviet leadership candidly points out, it sees no inconsistency in pursuing several parallel policy lines which may appear contradictory if they are consistent with Soviet long-range goals. Its approach is not to try to resolve these inconsistencies, which are inherent in the roles of the Soviet Union as a state and leader of a bloc of nations and as the head of a global revolutionary and anti-imperialist movement, but rather to manage each policy line and activity so as not to negate the other. This approach appears both justified and feasible to the Soviet leadership, especially in its foreign relations, because its fundamental assumptions concerning the unrelenting and protracted global struggle allow for compromise with the enemy when this seems expedient, in parallel with activities aimed at furthering his defeat.

Nevertheless, in the sphere of military strategy, there is a consistency of fundamental concepts which, as Harriet Fast Scott notes,[5] derives from a set of guidelines established at the highest level of the Communist Party. One consequence of this has been to give Soviet public discussions and formulations regarding military matters a highly repetitive and dogmatic character, a fact which has led some Western analysts to treat them as being mainly ritualistic in nature rather than reflecting actual Soviet views. It is true that the Soviets seldom engage in a public debate over the finer points and implications of their military thinking or the precise relationship of Soviet military capabilities to it. Furthermore, Soviet public statements must be analyzed according to the rules and techniques of Soviet communication. Thus, while Soviet open discussions provide an imperfect guide to Soviet immediate military goals, assessments of power relationships and capabilities and actual risk calculations, they remain, because of the need to inform, indoctrinate and pressure a complex bureaucracy and large numbers of people, an important source of information on what the Soviets are about and hope to achieve. Furthermore, one must note that the direction of Soviet weapons and force development has generally been consistent with Soviet military doctrine and the leadership's statements of interest (although such development has at times been reflected in Soviet capabilities only after considerable delay), as has also been the case for the tenor of instruction and indoctrination of the armed forces and of the general population.

---

[5]Harriet Fast Scott, *Soviet Military Doctrine: Its Continuity 1960-1970*, Stanford Research Institute, Technical Note SSC-TN-8974-28, June 17, 1971, p. 68.

III
THE UTILITY AND PURPOSES OF SOVIET NUCLEAR FORCES AS SEEN FROM THE KREMLIN

The Soviet nuclear forces have come a long way from a position of marked inferiority to the US in the 1950's and early 1960's, when the Soviet Union had at best only a minimum nuclear deterrence force, to the formal recognition by the US of mutual security based on the principle of "equality" at the May 1972 Moscow Summit Meeting. Even so, the Soviet Union has sought to capitalize on its nuclear forces from the moment it was able to demonstrate a nuclear weapons and intercontinental missile capability. It has done so sometimes noisily, as in the period of Khrushchev's missile bluff of the late 1950's and early 1960's, and sometimes in a less openly propagandistic manner, as has been the practice of the current leadership. In either case, Soviet spokesmen have been quite candid in their view of the utility of the Soviet armed forces and their "main" striking element, the nuclear forces. For example, an editorial article in the leading party-military journal, *Communist of the Armed Forces*, September 1972, asserted that

> The main objectives of the Soviet armed forces in the current stage consist of the following: to guard watchfully and reliably the peaceful work of the Soviet people . . . to defend unselfishly their native socialist fatherland; to assure together with the armies of the fraternal socialist countries the defense and security of the entire socialist commonwealth from the intrigues of imperialism and its accomplices; to serve as a support for freedom loving people in this struggle against imperialist aggressors, for their freedom and independence; to be an invincible stronghold for peace and security in the entire world; to provide by their very existence, their increased strength, a restraining influence on the imperialist warmongers.[1]

Soviet views on the utility of Soviet nuclear forces, therefore, must be examined in terms of a number of purposes, namely: deterrence, prestige, support for Soviet foreign policy, and war itself.

DETERRENCE

The importance of nuclear forces as a deterrent to a possible Western attack on the Soviet Union was recognized by the Soviet leadership from the start. As early as 1954 Malenkov claimed that such an attack would lead to the destruction of the West and of the capitalist system.[2] Khrushchev's revision at the 20th CPSU Congress in 1956 of the theory of "inevitability of war" with the capitalist West also rested largely on the deterrence role of

---

[1]Editorial Article, "The Defense of the Fatherland, Service in the Armed Forces—the High and Honorable Responsibility of Every Citizen of the USSR," *Kommunist Vooruzhennykh Sil* (Communist of the Armed Forces), No. 18, September 1972, p. 65.
[2]Moscow Domestic Service, March 14, 1954.

Soviet nuclear capabilities. Thereafter, Khrushchev kept reinforcing the Soviet deterrence image by escalating claims concerning Soviet strategic capabilities, an image which was given some credibility by initial successes in the Soviet space program and by the successful tests of an ICBM in 1957.[3] By the time of the 21st CPSU Congress, in January 1959, Soviet leaders were claiming strategic parity with the United States and asserting that as a result of this shift in the balance of power any Western attempt to overthrow the communist system by means of war was now highly unlikely, if not excluded altogether.[4] The capitalist encirclement was proclaimed to be broken, and in May 1959 Khrushchev asserted that

> The imperialists know our strength; to attack us is tantamount to suicide; one would have to be insane for this. I do not believe they are as stupid as all that; they understand the consequences which the unleashing of war against the socialist countries may have for them.[5]

Soviet claims to a superior strategic capability, blown up by Khrushchev's rhetoric, collapsed as a consequence of the U-2 incident (May 1960) and new US intelligence estimates (1961), and the actual US advantage in strategic forces was fully demonstrated by the Cuban Missile Crisis (1962). Despite this change, Moscow persisted in exploiting the deterrence role of its strategic nuclear forces. By the late 1960's the credibility of the Soviet deterrence capability was greatly enhanced by Soviet development of an assured second strike capability based on the hardening of Soviet ICBM silos and the construction of a nuclear powered SLBM force, as well as by Soviet progress toward parity with the United States in numbers of ICBMs.

Soviet public pronouncements in the late 1960's and early 1970's continued to emphasize the growth of Soviet strategic power and its capability to "reliably" assure the "peaceful labor" of the Soviet people. In his pamphlet *On Guard over Peace and the Building of Communism*, published in 1971, Marshal of the Soviet Union A. A. Grechko, USSR Minister of Defense, wrote:

> Imperialism, as before, is fierce and bloody, ready for any adventure. There can be no doubt that if it were not for the colossal defense might of the Soviet Union, the high state of combat readiness of its army and navy, imperialism would have long ago attempted to carry out its evil plans [i.e., to attack the Soviet Union].[6]

At the 24th CPSU Congress, Brezhnev assured his audience that "any possible aggressor knows well that should he attempt a missile attack on our· country, he will receive an annihilating retaliatory blow,"[7] while Grechko

---

[3]*Pravda*, August 27 and November 29, 1957.

[4]*Pravda*, January 29, 1959.

[5]*Pravda*, June 1, 1959.

[6]A. A. Grechko, *Na Strazhe Mira i Stroitel'stva Kommunizma* (On Guard Over Peace and the Building of Communism), Moscow, Voenizdat, 1971, p. 105.

[7]*Pravda*, March 31, 1971.

told the Congress that "jointly with other socialist states, the USSR is capable of countering force with a superior force."[8] The deterrence role of the Soviet armed forces continues to be emphasized at the present time.[9]

Soviet military power, and in particular its growing strategic power, is credited with forcing the US to abandon its attempts to deal with the Soviet Union "from a position of strength" and to accept not only the concept of strategic parity but also the Soviet principles of "peaceful coexistence." Soviet spokesmen have cited the US-Soviet agreements signed at the 1972 Moscow and 1973 Washington Summit meetings as evidence of growing Western "realism" based on the recognition of Soviet military might and on the realization that the US could not risk war with the USSR. According to Soviet doctrine, because of its class nature, the US can be compelled to restrain its aggressive character only by evidence of sufficient force in the hands of its opponent to threaten its survival. Thus, according to Professor Major General Ye. Sulimov,

> The reactionary circles of imperialism can only be forced into peaceful coexistence by making them renounce violent, armed methods of struggle. No considerations of morals, religion or international law and no consideration based on reason can halt the aggressive desires of the reactionary imperialist circles and the military-industrial complex if they sense their impunity and their superiority in strength.[10]

Similar views are expressed by non-military spokesmen. Thus, G. A. Arbatov, Director of the USA Institute of the USSR Academy of Sciences, argued in October 1973 that the US was deprived of its ability to make use of its military strength in support of its foreign policy objectives because

> Just when imperialism acquired, it seemed, the "ultimate weapon," which its most militant representatives had long dreamed of, the realm of the possible use of military force in US foreign policy began to diminish seriously. This happened primarily because the United States did not manage to maintain a monopoly on nuclear weapons . . . the growth of the defensive strength of the USSR and the entire socialist community canceled out the plans which had been built on US "decisive military supremacy" and on the possibility of using military force against the socialist countries with impunity or blackmailing them with this force.[11]

---

[8]*Krasnaia Zvezda* (Red Star), April 4, 1971.

[9]For example, see General of the Army A. Yepishev, Chief of the Main Political Administration of the Soviet Army and Navy, "Soviet Army's Historic Mission," *Soviet Military Review*, No. 2, February 1974, pp. 5-6.

[10]Major General Ye. Sulimov, "The Scientific Nature of the CPSU's Foreign Policy," *Krasnaia Zvezda*, December 20, 1973.

[11]G. A. Arbatov, "US Foreign Policy and the Scientific-Technical Revolution," *SShA: Ekonomika, Politika, Ideologiia* (U.S.A.: Economics, Politics, Ideology), No. 10, October 1973, p. 3. See also, Arbatov's articles, "The Impasse of the Policy of Force," *Problemy Mira i Sotsializma* (Problems of Peace and Socialism), No. 2, February 1974, p. 41; "Strength Policy Stalemates," *World Marxist Review*, No. 2, February 1974, p. 56.

27

These spokesmen argue that the "correlation of forces" in East-West relations changed with the Soviet deployment of nuclear weapons and missiles, but that "imperialist circles" in the US long resisted drawing the necessary implications from this fact. Consequently,

> A further strengthening of the positions of socialism in the world, including particularly the Soviet Union's military might, was required so that not just individual representatives of the US ruling circles but the overwhelming part of these circles recognized the futility of attempts to talk to the Soviet Union "from a position of strength" and to come to the conclusion that it was more sensible to build relations with the Soviet Union on the basis of a recognition of equality.[12]

In the same vein, Brezhnev said, in a speech in India on November 29, 1973, that to end the Cold War it was "necessary convincingly to persuade its sponsors of the fallacy of their hopes" of being able to defeat the Soviet Union, and the only way to achieve this end was to convert "world socialism and the national liberation movement into an irresistible force."[13] Only when this point was reached, when, as one Soviet analyst wrote, the US "grasped the physical impossibility" of waging a nuclear war against the USSR because of the "assured crushing Soviet retaliation," did it begin to show interest in the "rules of conduct of states in the international arena."[14] As Brezhnev said in Havana on January 30, 1974, "Finally the capitalist world had to face the truth. It had to recognize the impossibility of solving militarily the historical differences between capitalism and socialism."[15]

Overall, the tone of Soviet public pronouncements has tended to indicate increasing confidence in the effectiveness of Soviet nuclear deterrence capability. Soviet leaders and spokesmen frequently assert that because of the US recognition of the "suicidal" nature (for the US) of nuclear war, the focus of the continuing struggle between the systems is shifting to non-violent areas of competition, i.e., political, economic and especially ideological. Thus, on May 1, 1973, Brezhnev declared that "the security of the Soviet people is insured more reliably than ever before."[16]

In achieving what the Soviets claim to be a shift in the "balance of forces" in their favor, a major role is assigned to the growth of Soviet strategic

---

[12]K. M. Georgiev and M. O. Kolosov, "Soviet-US Relations at a New Stage," *SShA: Ekonomika, Politika, Ideologiia*, No. 3, March 1973, p. 14.

[13]Radio Moscow, November 29, 1973.

[14]G. A. Trofimenko, "The USSR and the United States: Peaceful Coexistence as the Norm of Mutual Relations," *SShA: Ekonomika, Politika, Ideologiia*, No. 2, February 1974, p. 8. See also, Yu. Molchanov, "The Leninist Policy of Peace," *International Affairs* (Moscow), No. 2, February 1974, p. 5.

[15]*Pravda*, January 31, 1974. See also, A. N. Kosygin's speech in Minsk on November 14, 1973, *Sovetskaia Belorussiia* (Soviet Belorussia), November 15, 1973.

[16]*Pravda*, May 2, 1973.

weapons capability. For example, Army General V. Kulikov, Chief of the General Staff of the USSR Armed Forces and First Deputy Minister of Defense, wrote in December 1972:

> The main striking power of the Soviet Armed Forces is made up of the Strategic Missile Forces equipped with modern weapons . . . these forces, which are constantly in a high state of combat readiness and in which is concentrated colossal destructive power, are capable of dealing a crushing blow to any aggressor. . . . The presence of the powerful Strategic Missile Forces has a sobering effect on all who may be tempted to kindle the fire of a new world war, and who contemplate encroaching on the peace-loving socialist countries.[17]

In February 1973, Army General I. Pavlovskii, Chief of the Soviet Ground Forces and Deputy Minister of Defense, asserted that

> The chief strike force of the Soviet Armed Forces and the main means for curbing an aggressor are the Strategic Missile Forces, which serve as a reliable nuclear missile shield for socialist countries and are capable of striking an instantaneous crushing blow at any aggressor.[18]

At the same time, writing in the leading CPSU journal *Kommunist*, Kulikov stated that

> The long range, high level of combat readiness and colossal destructive power of strategic missiles make it possible to regard the Strategic Missile Force as the most important means for restraining the imperialist forces' aggressive aspirations and routing the aggressor in the event of his attacking our country.[19]

In the May 1973 issue of *Kommunist*, Grechko wrote that "today it can be confidently said that any military adventures by imperialism against the USSR and against the socialist countries are doomed to failure."[20] Another recent Soviet claim is typified by a statement of a leading *Red Star* commentator, who noted the changes which allegedly have taken place in earlier US doctrine aimed at "rolling back or even destroying communism."

> Now, when the USSR's political, economic and military might has increased immeasurably, even the most inveterate "hawks" do not make such revelations and appeals. If they are sane, the military strategists of imperialism realize that an attack on the Soviet Union and the countries of the socialist community would be tantamount to the aggressor's self-destruction. It is this which forces them to remove from their arsenal the most aggressive doctrines of the cold war and to adapt to the new situation.[21]

---

[17]V. Kulikov, "Guarding Peaceful Labor," *Partiinaia Zhizn'* (Party Life), No. 24, December 1972, p. 40.

[18]I. Pavlovskii, "The Economy and the Armed Forces of the USSR," *Planovoye Khoziaistvo* (Planned Economy), No. 2, February 1973, p. 20.

[19]V. Kulikov, "The Soviet Armed Forces and Military Science," *Kommunist*, No. 3, February 1973, p. 78.

[20]A. A. Grechko, "On Guard over Peace and Socialism," *Kommunist*, No. 7, May 1973, p. 15.

[21]Colonel A. Leont'ev, "Advances and Fantasies," *Krasnaia Zvezda*, July 21, 1973. See also, F. Fyzhenko, "Peaceful Coexistence and the Class Struggle," *Pravda*, August 22, 1973.

Brezhnev expressed similar views in a speech on July 27, 1973. General M. Grigorev, First Deputy Commander of the Strategic Missile Forces, said in a broadcast on November 18, 1973 that the Strategic Missile Forces "have become the main strike force and the chief means of deterring the aggressor," and that

> Soviet achievements in the development of missiles and nuclear weapons, besides being the object of our national pride, are of great importance internationally. These weapons offer reliable protection to the peaceful life and security of the members of the socialist community and of all the freedom-loving people.[22]

Again, in a speech in Kazan on January 8, 1974, Marshal Grechko also appeared to believe in the reliability of the Soviet deterrence capability when he said:

> The lessons of history teach us that the imperialists heed only force, and they try to pursue their policy from a position of strength. But the Soviet Union can counterpose to their strength the no less formidable might of its own armed forces. Our strategic missile forces have a sufficient number of nuclear missiles of tremendous destructive power and a range of several thousand kilometers.[23]

Increasing claims are made also about the deterrent role of the growing Soviet naval power, whose main strike force is said to be submarine launched ballistic missiles (SLBMs) and long-range naval aviation carrying nuclear weapons. For example, the Commander in Chief of the Soviet Navy, Fleet Admiral S. G. Gorshkov, wrote in February 1973 that the Soviet navy's ability to destroy the enemy's military-economic potential "is becoming one of the most important factors in deterring his nuclear attack."

> In this connection, missile-carrying submarines, owing to their great survivability in comparison to land-based launch installations, are an even more effective means of deterrence. They represent a constant threat to an aggressor, who, comprehending the inevitability of nuclear retaliation from the direction of the sea, can be faced with the necessity of renouncing the unleashing of a nuclear war.[24]

Similarly, Marshal of Aviation I. Borzov, Commander of Naval Aviation, wrote that "the presence of Soviet military ships on the oceans serves as an imposing restraining factor for any attempts at sudden aggression against our state or socialist countries."[25]

Although the potential aggressor who must be deterred is usually identified as Western imperialism or specifically the US, the Soviet nuclear deterrence

---

[22]Radio Moscow, November 18, 1973.

[23]*Komsomolets Tatarii* (Komsomol of Tatar), January 9, 1974. See also, Grechko, "On Guard of Peace and Socialism," *Pravda*, February 23, 1974.

[24]Fleet Admiral S. G. Gorshkov, "Navies in War and Peace," *Morskoi Sbornik* (Naval Digest), No. 2, February 1973, p. 21.

[25]Marshal I. Borzov, "The Mighty Fleet of the Soviet Nation," *Vestnik Protivovozdushnoi Oborony* (Herald of the Anti-Air Defense), No. 7, July 1973, cited in JPRS *Translations on USSR Military Affairs: Soviet Naval Day*, No. 960, September 20, 1973, p. 13.

capability is also directed at China. In the 1969-1970 period China was identified by name in Soviet publications as a potential aggressor, but subsequently such pronouncements became more ambiguous, possibly because the Soviet leaders wished to avoid giving the Chinese further grounds for charges that the Soviet Union was planning an attack. For example, Marshal of the Soviet Union V. I. Chuikov, then USSR Chief of Civil Defense, wrote in a pamphlet published in 1969 that

> At this time it is difficult to determine how much nuclear capability the militaristic clique of Mao Tse-tung can accumulate and how quickly it can do so, but having in hand nuclear weapons and even more so strategic missiles, the Maoists can threaten any country with nuclear attack.[26]

In response to such a threat, Soviet broadcasts to China in 1970 warned that the Soviet Union would not hesitate to resort to a nuclear first strike and that it would not fall into the trap of waging a protracted conventional war of attrition, favored by Chinese military doctrine:

> In a nuclear war an enemy can deal very powerful nuclear strikes on the most densely populated areas of a target country at the outbreak of the war without sending troops to invade it. Can this [i.e., Chinese] military theory based on a defensive and deceptive action to lead an enemy into an unfavorable position provide any answer to such military operations by the enemy? No, it cannot.[27]

Since then, however, Soviet statements have generally used as their guideline with respect to the Chinese danger Brezhnev's formulation in his speech on the occasion of the Fiftieth Anniversary of the Revolution, to the effect that an attack "wherever it may come from—the north or the south, the west or the east—will encounter the all-conquering might of our glorious armed forces,"[28] and his statement at the 24th CPSU Congress asserting Soviet readiness to rebuff an attack "regardless of where it comes from."[29] Nevertheless, Moscow does show its uneasiness about China's intentions and its growing nuclear capability. For example, a Soviet newspaper noted in February 1972 that while Peking speaks of the need for defense preparations, the "majority of Chinese missiles are deployed near the northern border with the Soviet Union and Mongolia," and expressed concern that because of the power struggle between the Chinese military and the Party, there may not be "effective control over the weapons of mass destruction."[30] Highly pointed inferences relative to the Chinese nuclear factor continue to be voiced, as for example in a major article in *Krasnaia Zvezda* on August 14, 1973, in which

---

[26]V. I. Chuikov, *Grazhdanskaia Oborona v Raketno-Iadernoi Voine* (Civil Defense in a Rocket-Nuclear War), 2nd Edition, Moscow, Atomizdat, 1969, p. 6.

[27]Radio Moscow, January 13, 1970.

[28]*Pravda*, November 4, 1967.

[29]*Pravda*, March 31, 1971.

[30]"Peking's Nuclear Weapons," *Za Rubezhom* (Life Abroad), No. 8, February 18-24, 1972.

the author cautioned that until "the problem of nuclear disarmament of all states possessing nuclear weapons" is resolved "the need for readiness to wage war with any means of armed struggle will remain." The People's Republic of China was given a conspicuous place in the listing of such states.[31] At the same time, Soviet commentators ridicule Chinese claims that the Soviet Union is threatening China with a surprise attack, and note that Peking has rejected the Soviet offer of January 15, 1971 of a treaty which would prohibit the use of force, conventional or nuclear, by the two parties against each other.[32] At the same time, Soviet spokesmen accuse the Chinese of linking themselves with the most reactionary and aggressive "imperialist" circles and of pursuing policies which constitute "a serious threat to the peace and security of nations."

While the above reflects Soviet views on the utility of nuclear forces in what may be termed their "passive" deterrence role, i.e., deterrence of a Western or Chinese attack on the Soviet Union, Soviet statements indicate that the nuclear forces are also ascribed a broader or what may be called an "active" deterrence role. This pertains to what the Soviets describe as the "international" function of the Soviet Armed Forces, a function that has recently been given a new and different emphasis.[33] This function now as in the past encompasses a Soviet commitment to defend its European satellites and the People's Republic of Mongolia against Western and, in the latter case, Chinese attack. This commitment is formalized by the Warsaw Pact as well as by bilateral Soviet mutual defense treaties with these countries. In this respect, Soviet statements stress the need for close military cooperation between the armed forces of the "socialist countries" and the Soviet Armed Forces, which "vigilantly watch the aggressive intrigues of the imperialists and are ready at any time to come fully armed to the defense of the socialist achievements of the peoples of the allied states."[34] But beyond this, it is asserted that "in the present era . . . a deepening of the external function of the Soviet Armed Forces has logically taken place."[35] This is said to be the result of several factors. One is the upsurge of what the Soviets call the "anti-imperialist" national liberation struggle in the Third World directed against Western domination and exploitation. Another is the efforts of the

---

[31]See Colonel I. Sidel'nikov, "Peaceful Coexistence and the People's Security," *Krasnaia Zvezda*, August 14, 1973. As is discussed further below, the stress placed on this point by Sidel'nikov, as well as other elements of this article, have implications for the overall nuclear stance of the USSR that go beyond the matter of China.

[32]Speech by L. I. Brezhnev in Tashkent, Radio Moscow, September 24, 1973.

[33]See Kohler, *et al.*, *Soviet Strategy for the Seventies*, pp. 43-95.

[34]A. A. Grechko, "Military Collaboration among the Socialist States' Armies," *Kommunist*, No. 15, October 1972, p. 47.

[35]General of the Army A. Yepishev, "The Historical Mission of the Socialist State's Army," *Kommunist*, No. 7, May 1972.

32

West, and especially the US, to oppose and crush the liberation movement and the "progressive" countries waging this struggle, either through direct military action (*viz.* Vietnam) or by proxy (*viz.* Israel vs. the "progressive" Arab states). Finally, there is the tendency of the "imperialist" powers, because of their fear of a direct armed confrontation with the Soviet Union, to now seek their objectives by resort to limited wars and ideological subversion. In this context, the Soviet Union has a duty to protect its allies and clients and all "progressive" states and movements against Western aggressive designs and efforts at "exporting counterrevolution" by violent and non-violent means. Here also Soviet military power is called upon to deter such Western actions.

"We can boldly state," Grechko told the 24th Party Congress, "that the Soviet Army is an army of proletarian internationalism rendering aid to all those struggling against imperialism and for freedom and socialism,"[36] a view which was echoed by Army General Yepishev, Chief of the Main Political Administration of the Soviet Army and Navy: "Our armed forces have become a mighty factor for preserving peace and the security of the peoples, a factor which objectively promotes the development of the world revolutionary forces."[37] In a book published in 1973, General Yepishev wrote:

> By its social nature and historical design, the army of the Soviet socialist state represents part of the international revolutionary-liberation forces. . . .
> Today, the defense of the socialist fatherland is closely tied to giving comprehensive assistance to national liberation movements, progressive regimes, and new states which are fighting against imperialist domination. . . .
> This activity of our army, directed to cutting off the export of imperialist counterrevolution under current conditions, may with full justification be viewed as one of the most important manifestations of its external function.[38]

It is also asserted that the US agreement to the principles of "peaceful coexistence" (i.e., the Agreement on "Basic Principles," signed in May 1972) commits the US to refrain, in the words of Academician N. Inozemtsev, from "undertaking military intervention against any particular liberated state and from exporting counterrevolution."[39]

---

[36]*Pravda*, April 3, 1971.

[37]Army General A. Yepishev, "Invincible and Legendary," *Komsomol'skaia Pravda* (Komsomol Pravda), February 23, 1973.

[38]Army General A. Yepishev, *Mogucheye Oruzhiye Partii*, Voenizdat, Moscow, 1973, translated in JPRS *Mighty Weapon of the Party*, December 7, 1973, p. 14. See also, Yepishev in *Kommunist*, No. 7, May 1972; "The Great Victory," *Krasnaia Zvezda*, May 9, 1973; and his article in *Soviet Military Review*, No. 2, February 1974, p. 6.

[39]N. Inozemtsev, "A New Stage in the Development of International Relations," *Kommunist*, No. 13, September 1973, p. 97. (Inozemtsev is Director of the Institute for World Economics and International Relations of The USSR Academy of Sciences.)

Thus Soviet spokesmen credit the "increased power and solidarity of socialist states" with deterring the US from direct intervention to overthrow the Castro regime, and assert that "the defensive might of the Soviet Union was and is the chief obstacle on the path of imperialist warmongers."[40] In a similar vein, the US is said to have been "compelled" by the growing defensive might of the socialist community to give up its attempts to play the role of "world gendarme."[41]

Following the October 1973 War in the Middle East, Marshal Grechko asserted that

> It was precisely the change in the correlation of forces in favor of socialism and the process of the relaxation of tension taking place on this basis which prevented the dangerous eruption of the war in the Near East from assuming dimensions threatening universal peace.[42]

It is asserted, furthermore, that "the increasing danger of the escalation of local conflicts into a general nuclear war in which the aggressor may suffer a crushing defeat is exercising a growing restraining influence upon him and may do more to keep him from a rapid shift to the 'active stage' of a military clash."[43] Finally, one may note the remarks of A. N. Shelepin, a member of the CPSU Politburo, made in Havana on November 13, 1973:

> Displaying constant concern for the upsurge of the economy and the raising of the people's standard of living, our Party and Government are devoting daily attention to strengthening the country's defense capability and their armed forces to protect not only the Soviet Union but also our friends and the cause of peace throughout the world.[44]

The relationship between Soviet "active" deterrence and the changed policies of the US under detente was summed up in an editorial in the May 1973 issue of *Kommunist* which asserted that "imperialism"

> . . . is compelled to adjust to the new condition wherein the correlation of forces in the world arena has changed in favor of peace, progress and socialism. A considerable role in the strategy of the imperialist powers is also played by the realization that a nuclear war would be suicidal for capitalism. All this creates objective prerequisites for neutralizing and paralyzing the forces of aggression,

---

[40]V. V. Zagladin, editor, *Mezhdunarodnoe Kommunisticheskoe Dvizhenie:Ocherk Strategii i Taktiki*, Moscow, Politizdat, 1972. Translated in JPRS, *International Communist Movement: Sketch of Strategy and Tactics*, No. 57044-1, September 18, 1972, Part I, pp. 57, 58.

[41]Lieutenant General I. Zavialov, "The Creative Nature of the Soviet Military Doctrine," *Krasnaia Zvezda*, April 19, 1973.

[42]*Komsomolets Tatarii*, January 9, 1974.

[43]D. M. Proektor, "International Conflicts and Imperialism's Current Military Strategy," in V. V. Zhurkin and Ye. Primakov, *Mezhdunarodnyye Konflikty*, Moscow, 1972, translated in JPRS, *International Conflicts*, No. 58443, March 12, 1973, p. 19.

[44]*Trud* (Labor), November 14, 1973. See also, Molchanov, *International Affairs* (Moscow), No. 2, February 1974, p. 5.

preventing a world war, and influencing the international situation in a direction which favors the cause of peace.[45]

Although current Soviet pronouncements indicate an increased sense of security and confidence in the ability of Soviet military power to deter an attack, the Soviet public position continues to be one of concern about the stability of the East-West power balance and its reliability as a deterrence factor. A number of reasons are given to explain this concern. First, as will be discussed in greater detail in another section of this study, the Soviet view holds that the struggle between systems is unrelenting and while rules of behavior may be agreed upon, they may be violated if the "balance of forces" should shift to the advantage of the "imperialists." It is constantly stressed that the current "realism" of the West in accepting peaceful coexistence with the Soviet Union is in conflict with the class nature of Western societies and with the unchangeable essence of "imperialism," which "rightly sees in socialism its deadly enemy."[46] Consequently, such a shift in "imperialist" policies may be only of a temporary nature.[47] Second, it is argued that "imperialism" will continue to try to destroy the Soviet system and that it cannot be relied upon to act "rationally" at all times. Third, the rapid advances in science and technology continually threaten to destabilize the military power balance and to reduce the effectiveness of the Soviet deterrence capability.

Soviet spokesmen consistently reject the US concept of mutual assured destruction (MAD) as a reliable form of assurance of Soviet security. As a leading commentator wrote in February 1974, "the concept of deterrence itself cannot be defended—it is a concept of 'peace built on terror,' which will always be an unstable and a bad peace."[48] It is argued that an approach to international stability based on the "balance of fear" results in growing "arsenals of nuclear missiles" which in turn means the "perpetuation of the threat of war."[49] Another more explicit argument against the MAD concept was stated as follows:

> Peace based on atom bombs and missiles cannot be stable. First, the development of science and technology means constant improvements in existing types of weapons. Second, new scientific dis-

[45]Editorial, "On Behalf of Peace and the Friendship of the Peoples," *Kommunist*, No. 7, May 1973, p. 7. See also, Colonel V. Khalipov, "The Historic Offensive of the Socialist World," *Kommunist Vooruzhennykh Sil*, No. 12, June 1973, p. 19.

[46]*Sovetskaia Rossiia* (Soviet Russia), August 27, 1970.

[47]V. Petrov, "The Internationalism of the CPSU's Foreign Policy," *Pravda*, December 21, 1973.

[48]G. A. Arbatov, "The Impasses of the Policy of Force," *Problemy Mira i Sotsializma*, No. 2, February 1974, as cited in FBIS, *Daily Report: Soviet Union*, February 20, 1974, p. B-7.

[49]A. Bovin, "Peace and Social Progress," *Izvestiia*, September 11, 1973; D. Proektor, "European Security—Some Problems," *Mirovaia Ekonomika i Mezhdunarodnyye Otnosheniia* (World Economics and International Relations), No. 9, September 1973, p. 88.

coveries could lead to the creation of essentially new types of weapons, which could sharply upset the "balance of fear" and create a state of general instability. Third, as a result of the above-mentioned circumstances, a vicious circle of "action and reaction" is created whereby any step by one of the sides in the military sphere gives rise to a counter response from the other side. This inevitably leads to an arms race. . . .[50]

Brezhnev personally endorsed such views at the Moscow World Congress of Peace-Loving Forces on October 26, 1973, when he condemned the concept of a peace based on a stable balance of deterrence capabilities, because

> That kind of peace would differ but little from the cold war. It would be a "cold peace" that could easily revert to a tense confrontation depressing the consciousness and life of the peoples, and fraught with the danger of a worldwide conflict.[51]

One might note that even though G. A. Arbatov, Director of the Institute of the USA, in a recent article expressed doubts that a technological break-through in weapons development would provide either side with "any real or truly important advantage," he acknowledged that such a development would be destablizing and could "affect the strategic situation" and even engender "an illusion" of temporary superiority which an aggressor might be tempted to exploit.[52] The importance for the Soviet Union of not falling behind in weapons technology was underscored by Brezhnev in a speech in Minsk at the end of the "Dvina" maneuvers in 1970 when he warned that given the rapid rate of scientific and technical development "new types and systems [of weapons] are created sometimes not just within a year but even within a shorter period" and that any delays could therefore have "major consequences."[53]

Although Soviet public analyses pay little attention to the question of what Soviet actions may provoke the West, but tend simply to assume that given an opportunity the West may launch an unprovoked attack on the Soviet Union, it is recognized, nevertheless, that communist global successes can reinforce Western propensities for violent action. The danger of an unprovoked attack is underscored, furthermore, by the Soviet belief, as expressed in military writings, that major and possibly decisive advantages can be gained from a surprise nuclear attack. Thus, Soviet pronouncements that an assured second strike capability, even one which appears sufficient to

---

[50]Iu. Kostko, "Military Confrontation and the Problem of Security in Europe," *Mirovaia Ekonomika i Mezhdunarodnyye Otnosheniia*, No. 9, September 1972, pp. 19-20. See also, Lieutenant Colonel V. Bondarenko, "Military-Technical Superiority: The Most Important Factor in the Reliable Defense of the Country," *Kommunist Vooruzhennykh Sil*, No. 17, September 1966, p. 11; Colonel S. Baranov, "The Material Foundation of the Might of the USSR Armed Forces," *Krasnaia Zvezda*, March 5, 1971.

[51]*Pravda*, October 27, 1973.

[52]*World Marxist Review*, No. 2, February 1974, p. 61.

[53]Major General V. S. Riabov, *Dvina*, Voenizdat, Moscow, 1970, p. 6.

threaten an aggressor with unacceptable levels of damage, cannot be fully relied upon to deter an attack under all circumstances. The official Soviet line is that the only answer lies in total disarmament or at least in the absolute prohibition and elimination of nuclear weapons: In the absence of these conditions, the occurrence of a nuclear war cannot be ruled out, and the Soviet Union must have a capability not only to deter its potential enemies from attacking it but must also be prepared to wage a nuclear war and win it. (See the discussion under *"War Fighting"* below.)

GLOBAL PRESTIGE AND CLOUT
AS A SUPERPOWER

The Soviet Union like other nations is, of course, very conscious of the fact that military power is a major element of national prestige. For the Soviet Union, the matter of prestige is doubly important because until recently it has been clearly inferior to the other great powers and also because it lays claim to having a superior social, economic and political system and to leading the world communist and national liberation movements. Yet for all its undeniably great potential, the Soviet Union for most of its history has been engaged in a massive and costly effort merely to catch up with the more advanced industrial nations, particularly the US. The development of nuclear and missile technology has dramatically altered the status of the Soviet Union in the world. Although it remains inferior to Western countries in the standard of living of its population and decidedly inferior to the US in GNP and overall technological capability, the Soviet Union is, nevertheless, a superpower thanks to its nuclear forces, and consequently a major actor in the international arena, the only one capable of challenging the United States.

Having effectively laid claim to superpower status and being engaged in direct competition with the US for global influence, the Soviet Union is clearly intent upon never again falling behind the US in weapons technology. This issue affects not only the Soviet Union's global image but also such vital questions as the effectiveness of the Soviet deterrence posture and Moscow's ability to negotiate with the US from a position of equality, if not superiority. In the case of the latter, Soviet leaders have repeatedly demonstrated their reluctance to enter into serious arms control negotiations when the US held an edge in its nuclear capabilities and thus seemed able to deal with the Soviets from a "position of strength." Thus, in commenting on the May 1972 SALT Agreement, a Soviet spokesman wrote:

> The recognition of the principle of equal security in the sphere of the US-USSR strategic nuclear balance constituted a major victory for peace-loving Soviet foreign policy and reflects the growth of the Soviet Union's international authority, on the one hand, and the result of the tireless efforts of our party, government and people in

37

strengthening the Motherland's defense capability and creating a powerful deterrent nuclear missile potential reliably defending the interests and security of the USSR and the entire socialist community, on the other. Yet even quite recently—some five years ago—the US military-political leadership gambled solely on "strategic supremacy."[54]

Moreover, it appears that the Soviets were reluctant to discuss further strategic arms limitations until they developed their own MIRV capability.[55]

A major change, however, has taken place in the style of Soviet exploitation of its nuclear force capability for prestige purposes. Khrushchev found it necessary to noisily proclaim all demonstrations of Soviet nuclear and missile development, including Soviet space activities, in an effort to assert Soviet technological equality with the US and, on the strength of this, to advance highly inflated claims concerning Soviet strategic forces and their qualitative and quantitative superiority over those of the US. His successors have been less vocal and specific in this respect. They have chosen the effective approach of leaving it largely to Western intelligence to ascertain and Western leaders to publicize Soviet advances in the nuclear and missile fields.

In the course of the SALT negotiations and the drafting of the May 1972 Agreement, the Soviet authorities refused to disclose the number of their ICBMs or missile-carrying submarines, and instead used US estimates of Soviet strength as a basis for the SALT Agreement. One obvious reason for the change in Soviet public treatment of its nuclear forces is that, while Khrushchev had to persuade the world of the new Soviet power status and for political as well as security reasons attempted to bluff the West concerning Soviet strategic capabilities, the status of the Soviet Union as a nuclear superpower is now universally acknowledged. Furthermore, Soviet propaganda has been exploiting changes in US defense policies and in US attitudes toward relations with the Soviet Union as evidence of US inability to maintain military superiority over the USSR. Thus, Arbatov in the above cited commentary accused the US of harboring a lingering hope of breaking the "strategic stalemate" by qualitative improvements in its strategic weapons but stressed the futility of US efforts to "achieve decisive military superiority" because of the "growing economic, scientific and, as a result, the defense capacity of the USSR."[56]

This has, however, posed policy problems for the Soviet Union. The demonstration of new Soviet weapons capabilities in the course of test firings monitored by US intelligence has given rise to concern in the US that the Soviet Union may be seeking military superiority. Consequently, the Soviet

[54]G. Sviatov, "Strategic Arms Limitation: The Principle of Equal Security," *Krasnaia Zvezda*, July 28, 1972.
[55]*The New York Times*, August 18, 1973.
[56]*World Marxist Review*, No. 2, February 1974, p. 58.

Union has been put in a position of attempting, without denying US disclosures of Soviet capabilities, to rebut those officials who argue that as a consequence of continuing Soviet military build-up, the US should also strengthen its defense capabilities. For example, in a rebuttal to General A. Goodpaster's statement that it is "the constant growth of the military power of the Soviet Union which is throwing us into confusion," Colonel General N. V. Ogarkov, First Deputy Chief of the USSR Armed Forces' General Staff, said in an interview that such statements are intended to confuse public opinion and maintain the element of "Cold War," and went on to assert: "I can state with full responsibility that assertions concerning the growth of the armed forces of the Soviet Union do not correspond to reality."[57] Again, Soviet response to Defense Secretary J. Schlesinger's press conference of August 17, 1973, concerning Soviet testing of a MIRV capability, while making no reference to the new Soviet weapons development, accused opponents of detente of attempting to sow mistrust and of "cooking" up "facts" in an attempt to create an "imaginary Soviet threat" and added:

> Strange as it may seem, the gamble on the escalation of mistrust and tension sometimes finds influential backers even in official Washington circles. This is indicated, in particular, by the recent speech at a press conference by J. Schlesinger, the current head of the U.S. Defense Department, which clearly played into the hands of the military-industrial complex.[58]

The main Soviet public line, however, is that the Soviet Union harbors no aggressive intentions and consequently its military power, unlike that of the US, is intended to strengthen world peace. Thus, any increase in that power is said to have a beneficial effect, in that it further restrains US aggressive actions and serves to promote the acceptance of the principles of "peaceful coexistence."

At the same time, the Soviet Union has sought to conceptualize on, in the furtherance of its "Third World" national liberation policies, the position, first put forward by the US, that the two great powers bear a special responsibility for world peace, and that the state of their relations is critical for general international stability and for the security and survival of other nations. For example, the joint statement by the Politburo, Presidium of the Supreme Soviet, and Council of Ministers of the USSR on Brezhnev's June 1973 visit to the United States asserted that

> While in the course of postwar decades tensions in Soviet-US relations adversely affected the whole of the international situation, nowadays, on the contrary, the improvement in Soviet-US relations, the obligations undertaken by the two countries to abstain from the threat of force or its use against each other, against the allies of the

[57]*Krasnaia Zvezda*, July 10, 1973.
[58]B. Svetlov, "Whom Does It Benefit?," *Izvestiia*, August 29, 1973.

other sides and against third countries, the clearly formulated will by both countries to respect the rights and interests of all states will serve as an important element of a radical improvement of the International situation and open up great possibilities for constructive cooperation between all other countries.[59]

In a speech in Tashkent on September 24, 1973, Brezhnev said that "because of the military, economic and scientific-technological potential of the Soviet Union and of the United States, the state of relations between them objectively exercises an influence on the international state of affairs as a whole, especially as regards the resolution of issues of war and peace."[60]

Soviet spokesmen leave no doubt that they derive great satisfaction from the admitted equality the USSR now enjoys with the US in the nuclear field and as one of the two superpowers capable of determining the destinies of mankind. But the question arises as to whether this new prestige and world authority are enough from the Soviet standpoint. Given a place side by side with the United States at the pinnacle, as it were, will the Soviet Union rest content with its gains?

Opinion in the US appears heavily weighted in this direction: with neither side in a position to gain substantial advantage over the other in a direct power sense, why should not the Soviet Union as well as the United States give up the hard, as distinct from the ritualistic, elements of its contest with the other?

In contrast to American beliefs, however, the Soviets indicate that there is no place in their thinking for a static situation in their relationship with the US and other capitalist nations. In the field of these relationships, Soviet leaders conceive of national power, including of course military power, mainly in terms of class struggle, i.e., in terms of the dialectics of political competition and conflict between social-political ideologies and systems which are fundamentally and irreconcilably opposed to each other. As *Pravda* explained editorially in a July 1973 summation of the new agreements and understandings effected with the US and other Western states,

> Soviet foreign policy is a class, socialist, internationalist policy. Our party approaches each international problem from the viewpoint of the interests of socialism, the interests of the liberation, anti-imperialist struggle of peoples. . . . The policy elaborated by the 24th CPSU Congress has proved its correctness and its great vitality. The Soviet Union is filled with the firm resolve to continue proceeding consistently along this well-tried path. Our country will continue to strengthen fraternal relations with its friends and allies—the countries of the socialist community. It will continue to further develop ties and contacts with countries liberated from the colonial yoke and give assistance to all peoples struggling for peace, national liberation, democracy and socialism. As before, the USSR will con-

---

[59]*Pravda*, June 30, 1973.
[60]Radio Moscow, September 24, 1973.

tinue to deal a resolute rebuff to all the intrigues of those who oppose the relaxation of tension and advocate a return to the "cold war," who sow the seeds of enmity and mistrust among peoples. Beneath the banner of the peace-loving Leninist foreign policy we have achieved great victories which gladden the hearts of all honest people on earth. The CPSU spares no effort and energy in order always to bear aloft this glorious victorious banner.[61]

Earlier, CPSU Central Committee Secretary and alternate Politburo member D. Ustinov had described the wide range of utility of Soviet military power as follows:

The Communist Party always remembers Lenin's warning on the efforts of imperialism to settle international questions by means of force and does everything essential to strengthen and improve the defense shield of socialism. . . . Today our valiant armed forces are equipped with the most modern weapons and military equipment. The military preparedness of the Soviet Army and Navy is at a high level. And this, as we have had more than one occasion to convince ourselves, has a very sobering influence on all kinds of lovers of military adventures. . . . The defense power of the USSR exists only for the defense of socialism, the freedom and independence of the peoples, for the protection of the noble cause of democracy and peace.[62]

Thus, in addition to perceiving military power, and most of all nuclear military power, as essential to its security and survival and its ability to protect its allies and clients, the Soviet Union sees it as the critical factor in bringing about a lasting shift in the general or overall "balance of world forces" which is necessary finally to break down the resistance of the capitalist nations. The basic Soviet thesis is that the capitalists will not voluntarily make concessions, withdraw from positions they hold and ultimately depart the scene of history, unless and until they are faced by a combination of forces that make their position hopeless. Here it is important to note that in the Soviet view, a "balance of world forces" favorable to the USSR depends upon a number of elements in addition to military power. These include the growth of Soviet economic power; the cohesion and ideological dedication of the Soviet people; the upsurge of the workers' and national liberation movements in the world and the intensification and successes of the so-called global "anti-imperialist struggle" against the US; the success of Soviet foreign policy initiatives; US internal difficulties and the decline of US international economic and political influence and power; growing contradictions between the US and other advanced states; the increasing constraints on the freedom of action of the US; and so on. It is on the basis of the combination of these factors that Soviet spokesmen claim that the balance of power is irrevocably shifting in favor of the communist camp and that "in our time, the main

---

[61]*Pravda*, July 12, 1973.
[62]Radio Moscow, April 20, 1973.

41

content, the main direction and the most outstanding peculiarities of world development are determined by the Soviet Union, the fraternal socialist countries and all present revolutionary forces."[63] But at the heart of the matter is still Soviet nuclear power, for without this, Soviet spokesmen insist, other requisite elements would be quickly reversed through the use, or threatened use, of force by the "imperialists." Thus *Pravda* in July 1973, credited the growth of Soviet military power with forcing the US to recognize that it could not hope to achieve its foreign policy objectives by means of the use or threat of force.[64] Again, Politburo member F. D. Kulakov asserted in a speech on January 18, 1974 that

> Positive changes in the international situation became possible because of the increased might of the Soviet Union and all the countries of the socialist community and the consistent and coordinated activity of the CPSU and other fraternal parties.[65]

Thus, in the Soviet view, the state of the military balance is a critical factor in determining the character of US-Soviet competition on a world scale. Not only was the attainment by the Soviet Union of strategic parity with the US the essential prerequisite for US acceptance of the principles of "peaceful coexistence," but the continued preservation of equality, if not superiority, will be needed to overcome the "anti-detente" forces in the US and prevent the "imperialists" from "reverting to Cold War" and a "position of strength" policy vis-à-vis the Soviet Union.

In terms of the Soviet view of the world balance of forces, the development of Soviet nuclear forces has transformed the Soviet Union, for the first time, into a global military power, thus intensifying the basic trend toward globalism in Soviet foreign policy and providing new opportunities for an expansion of Soviet political and military influence on a world scale. Attempts at such expansion, however, increase the potential risk to the Soviet Union of confrontation with the US and other major powers, and thus can be undertaken with a reasonable degree of safety only if Soviet military power remains sufficient to dissuade the West from contesting Soviet advances by military means. The lack of such power in the past has repeatedly forced the Soviet Union or its proxies to withdraw from exposed positions when confronted by a determined show of force. Of course, the Soviet Union, like the US, has found it difficult to translate nuclear capabilities into direct political influence. Khrushchev's attempt at "missile diplomacy" failed to achieve the desired results. At the same time, however, Soviet nuclear forces

---

[63]Khalipov, *Kommunist Vooruzhennykh Sil*, No. 12, June 1973, p. 18. See also, M. Suslov's speech on the 70th Anniversary of the 2nd Congress of the Russian Social Democratic Workers' Party, *Pravda*, July 14, 1973.

[64]G. A. Arbatov, "Soviet-US Relations at a New Stage," *Pravda*, July 22, 1973.

[65]*Bakinskii Rabochii* (Baku Worker), January 19, 1974.

have provided an increasingly effective umbrella for reducing the risks of Soviet probes for new advantages in various parts of the world and of Soviet support for new client states and leftist regimes, by increasing US reluctance to take counteractions, especially in the form of military intervention. As one Soviet military analyst expressed it:

> The power of the Soviet army and navy represent an essential condition and guarantee for the most successful forward movement of the world revolutionary process.[66]

Similarly, General Yepishev wrote in 1974 that

> One cannot fail to see that the military might of the socialist community serves as an obstacle to the export of counterrevolution by the imperialists and thus *objectively promotes the development of revolutionary and liberation movements.*[67]

From the Soviet standpoint the May 1972 Moscow Summit agreements, especially those dealing with peaceful coexistence and SALT, represented an outstanding example of the influence of the shift in the balance of power, and especially of Soviet military power, on Moscow's ability to further its global objectives. At the time of the 24th CPSU Congress, Grechko wrote that

> The realization of the foreign policy program of the CPSU which was formulated by the Congress will depend in a large measure on the defense capability of the Soviet state and on the condition of its Armed Forces. The military might of the USSR . . . is one of the most significant factors assuring favorable foreign conditions for the building of communism in our country and the development of all socialist countries, for the struggle for independence of the peoples.[68]

The signing of the Moscow agreements was greeted with assertions that it reflected a major change in US policies, a change which was forced on the US by Soviet power. Thus, it was claimed that

> The strategic course of US policy is now changing before our very eyes from "pax Americana"—the Americanized formula of world domination—to a definite form of necessity for peaceful coexistence. But, we must clearly understand that this change is a forced one and that it is precisely the power—the social, economic and, ultimately, military power of the Soviet Union and the socialist countries—that is compelling American ruling circles to engage in an agonizing reappraisal of values.[69]

Similarly, the "successful negotiations with the United States" were described as reflecting an "important result" of Soviet efforts in "strengthening

---

[66]Lieutenant Colonel V. Khalipov, "The Present Stage of the Aggravation of the Basic Contradiction of Our Epoch," *Kommunist Vooruzhennykh Sil,* No. 9, May 1969, p. 25.

[67]Yepishev, *Soviet Military Review,* No. 2, February 1974, p. 6. [Emphasis in original.] See also, Molchanov, *International Affairs* (Moscow), No. 2, February 1974, p. 8.

[68]Grechko, *Na Strazhe Mira i Stroitel'stva Kommunizma,* pp. 16-17. Army General Pavlovskii repeated this view in a broadcast to Soviet servicemen on July 11, 1972.

[69]A. Pumpianskii, "A Triumph of Realism," *Komsomol'skaia Pravda,* June 4, 1972.

the country's economic and defense might."[70] In a speech on July 27, 1973, Brezhnev asserted that the West had used the Cold War "to play on the nerves of the Soviet people" and its allies and had sought to "frighten" them with the aid of nuclear blackmail. Consequently, according to Brezhnev,

> Together with our allies in the defensive Warsaw Pact we had to create a defensive strength that would make the leaders of the bourgeois states understand that we cannot be spoken to in the language of threats; that one must talk with us on equal terms, so to speak, in the language of reason, realism and mutual advantage.[71]

This line was expanded further to relate Soviet foreign policy interests to Soviet military might as one of the key factors in facilitating the attainment of Soviet global objectives. Thus, a leading political commentator, in an article in *Pravda* which appeared soon after the Moscow Summit meeting, asserted that

> The more powerful our Motherland becomes, the more opportunities it acquires for influencing the course of world events in a direction favorable to the peoples. Recent events confirm once again that the Soviet Union and the other countries of the socialist community are a force increasingly determining the course of world development.[72]

Similarly, another article by "a lecturer of the Central Committee of the CPSU," published in December of 1972, stated the view that

> The Soviet Union's rapidly growing economic might and defense capability are the key material factors ensuring the steady amplification of Soviet foreign policy's efficiency and influence on world developments. . . .
> The increased might of the USSR and of the socialist community and the intensified anti-imperialist struggle have become prime factors for averting another world war and compelling imperialist states to display certain caution and restraint in international affairs and give most serious consideration to Soviet positions on international questions.[73]

And a major article published in the May 1973 issue of *Kommunist* stated that

> The role of Soviet foreign policy, based on the USSR's might and on the balance of world forces, which has changed in socialism's favor, is growing increasingly tangible, and the very process of the changes in the international situation taking place under this policy's influence is developing in depth and breadth. . . .
> According to the valuations of Western politicians, the Soviet-American agreements reached during the Moscow talks in May 1972 have meant that the United States has finally recognized the actual correlation of forces in Europe and in Soviet-American relations.[74]

---

[70]G. Arbatov, "On Soviet-US Relations," *Kommunist*, No. 3, February 1973, p. 104.

[71]*Pravda*, July 29, 1973.

[72]V. Korionov, "Solidarity Is the Source of Strength of the Peoples," *Pravda*, July 23, 1972.

[73]Yu. Molchanov, "Soviet Foreign Policy, a Factor Promoting the Revolutionary Transformation of the World," *International Affairs* (Moscow), No. 12, December 1972, p. 5.

[74]V. Gantman, "A Policy That Is Transforming the World—On the Role of Soviet Foreign Policy in Present-Day International Relations," *Kommunist*, No. 7, May 1973, pp. 29, 35.

The Soviet bloc armed forces, it was argued "are a powerful factor in raising the international authority of the socialist states and their peace-loving policy."[75]

Soviet leaders have also used this theme to assert that Soviet might has forced the West, and in particular the US, to give up its Cold War doctrines and policies and become more willing to accede to Soviet demands. For example, Podgorny, in a speech on July 7, 1973, said:

Faced with the ever-growing might of socialism and its active foreign policy supported by working people all over the world, imperialism is forced to withdraw from action the most militant doctrines of the "Cold War" times. Its attempts to follow a "policy of strength" are gradually yielding to a more sober approach toward solving topical problems through negotiations.[76]

Again, Brezhnev, in a speech in Havana in January 1974, pointed out that the Soviet Union and the "world socialist system have become a powerful indomitable force" as a result of which "the capitalist world finally had to face the truth," and give up its attempts to solve the competition between capitalism and socialism by military means.[77]

As was noted above, Soviet spokesmen not only relate the detente in East-West relations to the growth of Soviet military might, but claim that detente facilitates the upsurge of the revolutionary and national liberation struggle, because Soviet power serves to "thwart" or "prevent" Western efforts to resist this process and to "export counterrevolution." At the same time, Soviet leaders assert that support of the "anti-imperalist" national liberation struggle, including national liberation wars, is a major element of Soviet foreign policy.[78] Thus, Kosygin said in a speech on July 3, 1972, that detente does not preclude the right of peoples to resort to armed revolutionary and national liberation struggle. "This right is holy and inalienable," said Kosygin," and the Soviet Union unfailingly assists people who have risen in struggle against the colonialists or have become victims of aggression."[79]

The Joint Party-Government Resolution on Brezhnev's June 1973 visit to the US declared that

---

[75]Captain 1st Rank N. Shumikhin, "Socialism and International Relations," *Krasnaia Zvezda*, September 13, 1973.

[76]N. V. Podgorny, Speech in Sofia, Bulgaria, on July 7, 1973, *Rabotnichesko Delo* (Sofia), July 8, 1973.

[77]*Pravda*, January 31, 1974.

[78]For example, see Brezhnev's speeches on June 5, 1972, *Pravda*, June 6, 1972; December 21, 1972, *Pravda*, December 23, 1972; October 26, 1973, *Pravda*, October 27, 1973; Kosygin's speeches on July 3, 1972, *Pravda*, July 4, 1972; November 14, 1973, *Sovetskaia Belorussiia*, November 15, 1973.

[79]*Pravda*, July 4, 1972.

We shall continue developing ties and contacts with the countries which freed themselves from the colonial yoke, to give assistance to the peoples fighting for peace, national liberation, democracy and socialism.[80]

Consequently, Soviet military power must serve as a means to deter Western military responses to the national liberation movement and at the same time allow the Soviet Union to support such movements without undue risks of confrontation with the Western powers. Therefore, as noted above, the Moscow Summit was followed by increased references by Soviet military spokesmen to the growing "external role" of the Soviet Armed Forces in support of these movements. Indeed, Soviet military power, along with its economic capabilities, is said to have become the "decisive factor" in the "world-wide liberation struggle against imperialism."[81] Significantly, directives on Soviet troop indoctrination point out that "it is important to stress such functions of the Soviet Armed Forces as the thwarting of the export of imperialist counterrevolution and the support of progressive national liberation movements,"[82] And more general Soviet formulations call on the Soviet Armed Forces to be "vigilant" and ready to "rebuff" Western attempts to "solve international problems by means of force."[83]

According to Soviet statements, the prospects for increasing restraint on Western and especially US resort to violence in international relations as a result of the growth of Soviet power and influence are becoming better all the time. In his speech to the World Congress of Peace-Loving Forces in October 1973, Brezhnev, while acknowledging that "acts of aggression are still being committed on earth," asserted that

> Never before have so powerful a state and such powerful public forces been set in motion for the purpose of stopping the aggressor, extinguishing the hotbed of war and consolidating the foundations of peace.[84]

Following the October 1973 Middle East War, Soviet spokesmen credited the shift in the "correlation of forces" in favor of the Soviet Union and the resulting detente with having prevented a dangerous escalation of the war into a confrontation of the superpowers. Even though Soviet actions in the course of the war had strained the US-Soviet detente and had violated specific

---

[80]*Pravda*, June 30, 1973. See also, Colonel Iu. Sumbatian, "The Developing Countries: Their Friends and Enemies," *Krasnaia Zvezda*, October 4, 1973.

[81]Molchanov, *International Affairs* (Moscow), No. 12, December 1972, p. 7.

[82]Unsigned article, "Methodological Recommendations for Seminar Instruction on the Theme: 'The 24th CPSU Congress on the Defense of the Victories of Socialism; Ways for Further Improving the Military and Political Training of Army and Navy Personnel,'" *Kommunist Vouruzhennykh Sil*, No. 6, March 1973, p. 23.

[83]For example, see the April 27, 1973 CPSU Central Committee Plenum Resolution, *Pravda*, April 28, 1973; Editorial, "Toward New Heights in Combat Readiness," *Kommunist Vooruzhennykh Sil*, No. 12, July 1973, p. 3.

[84]*Pravda*, October 27, 1973.

elements of the Moscow and Washington Summit agreements, Soviet statements suggested that the existing balance of power left the US with no other rational choice but to preserve the detente.[85]

Soviet spokesmen have made clear that as the Soviet Union succeeds in shifting the East-West balance of power, including as a necessary base the military balance, in its favor, this will result in a situation in which, in Brezhnev's words, "no question of any importance in the world can be solved without our participation, without taking into account our economic and military might."[86] Thus it might be said as an overall matter that Moscow's approach to the utilization of its nuclear armed forces to global political ends will correspond to a judgement once voiced by Winston Churchill, namely that, "The Soviet Union does not want war. But it wants the fruits of war."

WAR FIGHTING

Soviet military writings and military posture do not specifically distinguish between deterrence and war-fighting nuclear capabilities or postures, but appear to view them as one and the same. The Soviet assumption is that the better the Soviet Armed Forces are prepared to fight and, if possible, win a nuclear war, the more effective they will also be as a deterrent to an attack on the Soviet Union and as a support of Soviet foreign policy, while at the same time insuring that the Soviet Union can take care of itself in the event that a confrontation does in fact escalate into an armed conflict. Consequently, Soviet public discussions of military organization, development, weapons, training and indoctrination, and the continuing need for ever greater military strength are predominantly in terms of war fighting. This orientation is also clearly evident in Soviet programs to prepare the economy and the entire Soviet people for a possible nuclear war.

Soviet Views as to the Continuing Danger of Nuclear War

The official Soviet rationale for this position is that although war with the West is no longer "fatalistically inevitable," and indeed that the present correlation of forces has significantly reduced the danger of an attack on the Soviet Union, the possibility of the occurence of war cannot be completely discounted, either for the present or all the more so for the future. In view of the grave consequences of a nuclear war, the possibility that one will occur

---

[85]For detailed treatment see, Leon Goure, Foy D. Kohler, Mose L. Harvey, *The Soviet Union and the October 1973 Middle East War: Implications for Detente,* Monographs in International Affairs, Center for Advanced International Studies, University of Miami, Coral Gables, Florida, 1974.

[86]See Brezhnev's speech in Minsk on March 14, 1970, cited in Major General V. S. Riabov, *Dvina,* p. 8.

must be, according to Soviet authorities at all levels, taken seriously and thoroughly prepared for. Although at the present time, the Soviet Union believes that it has succeeded in deterring the West and in compelling it to accept greater constraints on its policies, the Soviet public position, as was noted above, argues that the stability of the deterrent, i.e., mutual assured destruction, cannot be relied upon due to the impossibility of compromise of the class objectives of the two systems and the rapid developments in weapons technology. Consequently, the present constraints on the West and especially on the US may not prove effective or sufficient in the future and the US may revert to a more hostile and aggressive stance. Thus, Soviet statements tend on the one hand to praise Soviet gains in deterring the West and protecting the Soviet Union from aggression and in strengthening peace and international detente, and on the other to persistently warn of the continuing danger of war and the possibility of failure of the Soviet nuclear deterrent.

The Soviets insist that the capitalist world recognizes communism and its main power base, the Soviet Union, as its "deadly enemy" and that it, as well as the USSR, is aware that detente "does not mean the end of the struggle of the two world social systems," which will be waged "right up to the complete and final victory of communism on a world scale."[87] Although Soviet leaders argue that this struggle should be waged without resort to nuclear war, it is assumed that the capitalist powers will not give up without resistance and without attempting to "reverse the course of history" by seeking to destroy their main enemy—the Soviet Union—if the opportunity presents itself. Thus, regardless of any international agreements to which the US has been forced to accede by the growth of Soviet power, the danger of war is said to persist as long as "imperialism" survives. The most common and frequently used Soviet expression of this idea is that "imperialism" is in its essence aggressive and warlike, and that communist ideology and histori-cal experience "teach" that "as long as imperialism exists, the danger of aggressive wars will exist."[88] Consequently, while struggling to make "peaceful coexistence" in US-USSR relations "irreversible," the Soviet Union must as a matter of necessity be ready for a reversal in these relations. The danger of such a reversal is a persistent Soviet theme, which serves to justify the leadership's call for constant "vigilance" as well as the need for

---

[87]Professor F. Ryzhenko, "Peaceful Coexistence and the Class Struggle, *Pravda*, August 22, 1973.

[88]For example, see the CPSU Central Committee Greetings to the Fifth Armed Forces Conference of Secretaries of Party Organizations, *Krasnaia Zvezda*, March 28, 1973; Brezhnev's speeches on June 27, 1972, in *Pravda*, June 28, 1972, and on January 30, 1974 in Havana, *Pravda*, January 31, 1974; Marshal Grechko's speeches on July 11, 1972, in *Krasnaia Zvezda*, November 8, 1972, on January 8, 1974, in *Komsomolets Tatarii*, January 9, 1974; Kosygin's speech on November 14, 1973, in *Sovetskaia Belorussiia*, November 15, 1973.

the further strengthening of Soviet military power. As Brezhnev asserted at the 24th CPSU Congress, when he said:

> The Soviet Union is ready to support real measures for disarmament, strengthening peace and not damaging our security. At the same time, we must also in the future be prepared for any reversals in the development of events.[89]

Immediately following the May 1972 Moscow Summit meeting, Soviet authorities stressed the increasing importance of the non-violent forms of struggle between the systems. Marshal Grechko, however, immediately warned that "imperialism constantly carries with it a threat of war."[90] While arguments regarding the continuing threat of war were most elaborately developed by military spokesmen, warnings to this effect were repeatedly voiced by all elements of the top leadership and were repeated and elaborated upon by non-military as well as military spokesmen. Brezhnev in a speech of June 27, 1972, that is in less than a month after the summit meeting with Nixon in Moscow, pointedly stated:

> We assess the present situation soberly and realistically. Despite successes in the easing of international tension, a difficult struggle yet lies ahead against the enemies of the cause of peace, of national and social liberation. Marxists-Leninists have no illusions about the anti-popular essence of imperialism and its aggressive intentions.[91]

And in a message greeting to the Fifth Armed Forces Conference of Secretaries of Party Organizations held on March 27-29, 1973 Brezhnev concentrated on the danger "imperialism" continued to pose to the USSR despite "the recent improvement in international relations."

> By efforts of the USSR, of the fraternal socialist countries and of the peace-loving forces of mankind, a marked improvement of the international situation has been achieved. However, aggressive circles of the capitalist world stubbornly resist the healthy process of relaxation of international tension and intensify the arms race. History teaches that while imperialism exists, the danger of new aggressive war remains. Therefore, all possible strengthening of the defensive capability of the country of the Soviets and of the combat might of its Armed Forces always has been and will remain the sacred duty of our Party, of the Soviet government and people.[92]
>
> Of course, the imperialists are not now deciding to make a direct military attack. They well understand that such a step would end in catastrophe for them. But they are still counting on achieving military supremacy, undermining the foundations of international peace and, at a favorable moment, resolving the international dispute between capitalism and socialism by military means.[93]

---

[89]*Pravda*, March 31, 1971.
[90]*Krasnaia Zvezda*, July 12, 1972.
[91]*Pravda*, June 28, 1972.
[92]*Pravda*, March 28, 1973.
[93]*Krasnaia Zvezda*, March 28, 1973. See also, A. A. Grechko, "Military Collaboration Among the Socialist States' Armies," *Kommunist*, No. 15, October 1972, p. 35.

That same month, an article in the journal *USA: Economics, Politics, Ideology* pointed out that

> One also must not leave out of one's reckoning the fact that, in addition to the trend towards realism in politics and adaptation to the changes occurring in the world, opposing forces are also continuing to operate in the United States. They do not like the current development of Soviet-US relations and would like to turn it back.[94]

Although the June 1973 Washington summit meeting, and especially the signing of the US-Soviet Agreement on "Prevention of Nuclear War," was hailed in the Soviet Union as a major step in the further consolidation of detente and reduction of danger of nuclear war, it was followed by increasing warnings about the possibility of a reversal in US-Soviet relations, and again by non-military as well as military authorities. For example, titular head of the Soviet state Podgorny declared on July 7, 1973:

> The turning toward detente, . . . should not—naturally—give rise to illusions. Reaction is under pressure, but it has by no means given up its aggressive intentions or laid down its arms.[95]

Similarly, Brezhnev, in a speech on July 11, 1973, asserted,

> The aggressive forces of imperialism will probably not lay down their arms for a long time yet; and there are still adventurists who, in the name of their own egotistic interests, are capable of kindling a new military conflagration. This is why we consider it our sacred duty to pursue our policy in such a way that nothing unexpected can catch us unawares. . . .[96]
>
> We can see that the struggle over prospects of developing relations with the socialist countries is still being waged in the capitalist world. This does not surprise us. We know that there are forces that still think in terms of the Cold War. They advocate the unconstrained growth of military budgets and an increase in the nuclear potential. It is they who turn away from realities, who give rise to unfounded fear, and who do not stop short of slander. It is they who would like to undermine the treaties and agreements that have been concluded. In particular, I have in mind certain West German circles that seek to impose on the FRG the former sterile course vis-à-vis the GDR.[97]

USA Institute Director Arbatov, wrote in *Pravda* July 1973 that "the possibility of a movement backward to Cold War has yet to be eliminated, even though every new success for the peace policy makes the changes which have occurred [in US-Soviet relations] increasingly firm and stable.[98] In August 1973, he noted in an interview that "while objective changes indeed have occurred and these, as indicated by their trends, are long-term and will last a long time," this "does not in the least mean that the changes have become

---

[94]Georgiev and Kolosov, *SShA: Ekonomika, Politika, Ideologiia*, No. 3, March 1973, p. 20.
[95]*Rabotnichesko Delo* (Sofia), July 8, 1973.
[96]*Pravda*, July 12, 1973.
[97]Brezhnev, Speech in Alma Ata, Radio Moscow, August 15, 1973.
[98]*Pravda*, July 22, 1973.

irreversible."[99] Also in August, a roundtable of political commentators warned of the activities of the opposition to detente in the US and of plans for technological improvements in US strategic weapons systems.[100] Neither then nor later did Soviet commentators acknowledge that the Soviet Union was developing and testing new missiles.

A. Bovin, a political observer of *Izvestiia*, wrote in September that "imperialist policy, which is distinguished by adventurism and aggressiveness, can create a threat of international conflicts evolving into a global thermonuclear war."[101] Again Arbatov wrote in September that

Many representatives of the U.S. ruling circles have so far not abandoned their hopes that future achievements of a military-technical nature will still be able somehow to turn back the course of events, providing the United States with the opportunity to make effective use of military force as the main instrument of foreign policy.[102]

In a speech in Sofia on September 19, 1973, Brezhnev said:

Obviously the class struggle in the international arena, the confrontation between socialism and capitalism continue; the diametrically opposed social systems and their prevailing ideologies still remain. The differences in approach to major political issues still remain and the forces opposed to detente, dreaming of plunging mankind again into the ice-age period of the cold war, have not laid down their arms by any means.[103]

The October 1973 Middle East War brought an increase in Soviet warnings of a possible failure of the new relationship with the US, even though Soviet leaders and spokesmen credited detente and Soviet military might with preventing the escalation of that war into a US-Soviet confrontation. The Soviet involvement in Arab war preparations, the Kremlin's failure to abide by the Moscow and Washington agreements concerning abstinence from exacerbation of local conflicts and the requirement to warn each other of possible local wars which could pose a threat to the stability of US-Soviet

---

[99]Budapest Domestic Television Service, August 5, 1973, cited in FBIS, *Daily Report: Soviet Union*, August 7, 1973, p. A-15.

[100]Radio Moscow, August 26, 1973. See also, Lt. Colonel M. Ponomarev and V. Vinogradov, "The Choice Facing NATO," *Krasnaia Zvezda*, August 19, 1973.

[101]*Izvestiia*, September 11, 1973.

[102]G. Arbatov, "U.S. Foreign Policy and the Scientific and Technical Revolution," Part I, *SShA: Ekonomika, Politika, Ideologiia*, No. 10, October 1973, p. 11. Concern over the machinations of various "reactionary" circles in the US and Western Europe were also expressed at that time in other publications. For example, see V. Pshenko, "With a Rusty Pen," *Izvestiia*, August 5, 1973; Colonel G. Armuanov, "From Positions of the Cold War Times," *Krasnaia Zvezda*, August 7, 1973; Lieutenant Colonel M. Ponomarev and V. Vinogradov, "The Choice Facing NATO," *Krasnaia Zvezda*, August 14, 1973; Colonel I. Sidel'nikov, *Krasnaia Zvezda*, August 14, 1973; G. Ratiani, "International Review," *Pravda*, August 26, 1973; I. Kirin, "The Infectious Virus of General Goodpaster," *Sovetskaia Rossiia*, August 29, 1973; Iu. Iakhontov, "Old Plans," *Pravda*, August 30, 1973; Radio Moscow, September 5, 1973.

[103]Radio Moscow, September 19, 1973.

relations, as well as Soviet military aid to Egypt and Syria in the course of the war, indicated that the Soviet Union was not adverse to straining the detente in order to exploit the opportunity for gains. The threat of a unilateral Soviet troop deployment to the Middle East on October 25 and the US alert of its forces in response created a confrontation situation, if only briefly, which demonstrated the fragility of US-Soviet cooperation in areas where both had major conflicting interests. Thus, despite Soviet and US claims that detente remained operative, Soviet statements concerning a reversal of this policy not only increased but also acquired a sharper tone.

Speaking at the Moscow World Peace Congress on October 26, 1973, Brezhnev warned that the "imperialists" were still seeking to suppress the national liberation movement, that the "process which represents the most material preparation for a world war is continuing and even intensifying," and, being "realists, we all well know that wars and actue international crises are far from being a matter of the past."[104] This was the first time since the May 1972 Summit that Brezhnev claimed that the US was preparing for a world war. Less than a month later, Kosygin said in a major speech that the struggle to make the principles of "peaceful coexistence" a universal norm is going to demand "strenuous" and "prolonged" efforts.

> Although they are taking account of the new disposition of forces in the world, the aggressive imperialist forces are continuing to pursue a policy which demands constant vigilance on our part. Militarist circles in the West will utilize any pretext to stifle the trend toward the relaxation of international tension and to give fresh impetus to military preparations. Militarism is even apparent in Europe, where revanchist and other reactionary forces are continuing their activity aimed against the normalization of socialist countries' relations with the FRG and against the successful conclusion of the Conference on Security and Cooperation in Europe, as well as at reanimating the military activity of the North Atlantic bloc. A similar policy is manifest in the events in the Near East, in Indochina, and in other regions of the world.[105]

Yet he also expressed the opinion that the US Government is "displaying a similar approach" as the Soviet Union "to the agreements which have been concluded." Other Politburo members also warned about continuing resistance to detente on the part of "reactionary" and "militarist" forces in the West, of Western efforts to promote subversion in the Soviet Union in the guise of "free exchange of ideas," and they cited the overthrow of the Allende regime in Chile and the October War in the Middle East as proof of the readiness of the "imperialists" to resort to violence and aggression.[106] In

---

[104]*Pravda*, October 27, 1973.

[105]*Sovetskaia Belorussiia*, November 15, 1973.

[106]For example, see address by V. V. Shcherbitskiy at the Kiev "Arsenal" Plant, November 17, 1973, *Pravda Ukrainy* (Pravda of the Ukraine), November 20, 1973.

his November 7, 1973, address in Moscow's Red Square, Marshal Grechko said that "we do not have the right to forget that reactionary imperialism exists and its forces actively operate in the world, that they encourage the arms race and that they try to restore the spirit of the 'Cold War.' "[107] Similarly, Brezhnev said in a speech in India in November that "detente has not eliminated forever but warded off the threat of a nuclear world disaster."[108]

These themes have persisted in Soviet pronouncements. For example, an editorial in *Red Star* on December 5, 1973 asserted that detente had not "changed the anti-popular and aggressive essence of imperialism" and that "the process of material preparation for a world war is continuing and even intensifying in the capitalist world."[109] Another article warned that the "disappearance of the fatal inevitability of wars in the contemporary epoch cannot be a one hundred percent guarantee of the fact that aggressive forces will not attempt to start a new war."[110] The December 1973 issue of the Soviet journal *International Affairs* carried an article which asserted that

> It would be utopian to assume that peaceful coexistence between countries with different social systems could at once rule out any armed clashes. So long as imperialism and armed adventurism exist, they will inevitably, if only by virtue of their own momentum, unleash armed actions against the liberation movement of oppressed classes and peoples. . . .
> That is why all talk about an end to the "era of wars" and the arrival of an "era of universal peace" is premature and dangerous.[111]

A similar view was published in *Red Star* on December 20, 1973 by a senior Soviet political officer.[112]

Despite assurances from President Nixon and Secretary of State Kissinger that the US wished to continue the detente and that in the nuclear age there is no alternative to peace among the great powers, the tone of Soviet statements did not change. In his New Year address to the Soviet people, Brezhnev asserted that much still remained to be done to "guarantee the conditions for broad peaceful cooperation and to give a rebuff to the intrigues of the aggressive forces."[113] Again, in his speech in Havana on January 30, 1974, Brezhnev discussed various Western activities which contradicted the detente

---

[107]*Krasnaia Zvezda*, November 8, 1973.

[108]Radio Moscow, November 27, 1973.

[109]Editorial, "The People's Power," *Krasnaia Zvezda*, December 5, 1973.

[110]M. Avakov and S. Chernichenko, "The Vital Force of Leninist Principles of Peaceful Coexistence," *Kommunist Vooruzhennykh Sil*, No. 23, December 1973, p. 25.

[111]P. Zhilin, "The Military Aspect of Detente," *International Affairs* (Moscow), No. 12, December 1973, p. 25.

[112]Professor Major General Ye. Sulimov, *Krasnaia Zvezda*, December 20, 1973.

[113]*Pravda*, January 1, 1974.

policy and which he said "cannot but alert us." He went on to assert that efforts to acquire a unilateral advantage over the Soviet Union were futile and then added:

It is much more serious if something bigger is concealed behind all this, that is the hope to impede the improvement of the international climate to return the world to the ill-famed times of the "Cold War" and to give new impetus to the arms race. . . .
There do exist forces that are dissatisfied with the strengthening of peaceful coexistence. These forces are still considerable and command certain influence. Imperialism has by no means changed its aggressive nature. . . . The stockpiling and perfecting of weapons, first of all of nuclear weapons, is continuing.[114]

Soviet military leaders significantly mention not only the danger of a return to cold war, but also the threat of a new world war. For example, Marshal Grechko, in a speech on January 8, 1974, warned that

Our Party teaches that in assessing the contemporary international situation not only factors of peace and progress but also the forces counterposing them be taken into account and considered. It warns against voluntary or involuntary attempts to underestimate the military danger stemming from imperialism and regarding it as something unimportant against the background of the might of the world socialist system.
The positive changes in the international climate must not blunt Soviet people's vigilance. We must always be ready for any unexpected turns, dangerous adventures, and provocations on the part of the reactionary forces of imperialism.[115]

In early February several major articles in *Red Star* also dealt with this theme.[116] Later in the month, the 56th anniversary of the Soviet Army and Navy provided a further occasion for Marshal Grechko to voice such views. Thus, in his Order of the Day to the Armed Forces on February 23, the Defense Minister said that while Soviet foreign policy has achieved a "favorable influence" on the international situation,

At the same time, it is impossible not to see that reactionary imperialist forces are still active, trying to oppose the relaxation of international tension, and are building up the arms race and preparing military adventures.[117]

Grechko was even more explicit in an article in *Pravda* on February 23, 1974:

The world has changed but the aggressive, misanthropic nature of imperialism has remained unchanged. The reactionary circles are furiously opposing the relaxation of international tension and are

---

[114]*Pravda,* January 31, 1974.

[115]*Komsomolets Tatarii,* January 9, 1974.

[116]Rear Admiral V. Sheliag, "Two World Outlooks—Two Views of War," *Krasnaia Zvezda,* February 7, 1974; Army General Ye. Maltsev, "Lenin's Ideas of the Defense of Socialism," *Krasnaia Zvezda,* February 14, 1974; Editorial, "A Powerful Guard of the Motherland," *Voennyi Vestnik* (Military Journal), No. 2, February 1974, p. 5.

[117]*Krasnaia Zvezda,* February 23, 1974.

intensifying the arms race and the preparation of world war. . . . The spearhead of imperialism's military preparations is aimed against our country and all the countries of the socialist community.[118]

Grechko had written a somewhat similar article on the occasion of the 1973 anniversary of the Soviet Armed Forces, but that article spoke of the danger of "new conflicts" and a return to the "cold war" rather than of "world war," as he said in 1974, and did not include the statement that US war preparations were aimed directly at the Soviet Union.

Grechko's theme was echoed by other Soviet military leaders. For example, Army General S. L. Sokolov, First Deputy Minister of Defense of the USSR, wrote that the US is intensifying the preparations for a world war and stockpiling and improving its nuclear weapons.[119] General Kulikov, Chief of Staff of the Soviet Armed Forces, said in an interview that the imperialists were "stepping up" their resistance to detente.[120] He also warned that "China's leaders are now going along with extreme reaction." Moreover, General of the Army Yepishev wrote that the "exhaust fumes of the imperialist vehicle of preparation for war" were poisoning the politicl atmosphere.[121]

Speaking to an All-Army Conference of Komsomol Organization Secretaries in March 1974, Grechko again added his authoritative voice, warning that the successes achieved in the detente must not "dull the revolutionary vigilance of Soviet people," and particularly of the Armed Forces, and be allowed to engender "feelings of complacency."

> The nature of imperialism has not changed and the aggressive and reactionary forces continue to operate in the world—forces which oppose the relaxation of tension, fight for the increase of military budgets and the continuation of the arms race, try to sow mistrust among the peoples and stoke anti-Sovietism and anti-communism.[122]

Similarly, Brezhnev, speaking on March 15, 1974 in Alma-Ata, said that the Soviet Union had expected to encounter "stubborn resistance" to its peace policy and warned that "wherever it can, reaction strikes to take the counteroffensive," and he reminded his listeners that "in the final analysis, foreign policy successes are defined by the results of internal policy, the level of our economic, scientific-technical and defense potential and the political and moral unity of our society."[123]

---

[118]Marshal A. Grechko, "On Guard Over Peace and Socialism," *Pravda,* February 23, 1974.

[119]Army General S. L. Sokolov, "Always on Guard and in a State of Combat Readiness," *Krasnaia Zvezda*, February 23, 1974.

[120]Radio Moscow, February 22, 1974.

[121]Yepishev, *Soviet Military Review*, No. 2, February 1974, pp. 4-5.

[122]*Krasnaia Zvezda*, March 14, 1974.

[123]*Pravda*, March 16, 1974.

Although Soviet leaders and spokesmen have themselves consistently called for the further strengthening of Soviet military capability and for raising the combat readiness of the armed forces, they have pointed with alarm to the US defense budget and plans for improvements in the US strategic nuclear capability. This has been reflected in their statements on the intensification of the arms race and US war preparations. No doubt this campaign is aimed in part at inhibiting further US and NATO efforts at strengthening their defenses, and possibly also as an insurance against loss of face in the event that the Soviet Union fails to attain some of the hoped-for benefits from its new relationship with the US. In addition, however, the campaign is used to justify the further build-up of Soviet military power.

Another Soviet argument for the need to take account of the possibility of war has been the view that as the communists gain increasing ground in the world the capitalists may resort to a general war in a desperate if irrational attempt to delay their collapse. For example, Grechko wrote in 1970 that

> The course of modern social development confirms the idea expressed by Lenin that the more substantial socialism's victory is, the more stubborn becomes the resistance of the imperialist bourgeoisie. Not wishing to reckon with the lessons of history, imperialist reaction seeks a way out in various kinds of adventures and provocations, and in direct use of military force.[124]

More recently, a series of articles in *Moscow Pravda,* under the title, "We and the Rest of the World," asserted that the "most aggressive and desperate" reactionaries, driven by hatred of the Soviet Union, are willing to "take the risk of the 'total' destruction of mankind," according to the slogan, "Better Dead than Red." Consequently, the author concluded: "One thing is true. The history of mankind in our times remains extremely explosive and inflammable."[125]

Some Soviet commentators also raise the issue of an unintentional outbreak of a nuclear war. For example, Arbatov pointed out in an interview in July 1973 that

> The grim fact is that in the conditions of international tension, with huge stockpiles of weapons, there may arise a situation setting off an escalation of events despite a sincere wish not to start a nuclear war. It would be extremely difficult to halt such an escalation, the course of events would simply head towards such a war. This is actually something of which we had a glimpse at the time of the Caribbean crisis, or as it is known in America, the Cuban Missile Crisis.[126]

---

[124]*Krasnaia Zvezda*, April 18, 1970. See also, talk by Lieutenant General P. I. Shuvyrin, Radio Kiev, January 21, 1970; A. A. Grechko, "The Unconquerable Shield of the Motherland," *Pravda*, February 23, 1971.

[125]E. Genri, *Moskovskaia Pravda* (Moscow Pravda), August 17, 1973.

[126]Radio Moscow, July 18, 1973.

Arbatov claimed, however, that the detente and the various US-Soviet agreements had reduced the likelihood of such an eventuality. An article in *Komsomol'skaia Pravda* a month later emphasized the benefits of US-Soviet agreements on the prevention of "accidental or unsanctioned use of nuclear weapons" in either country and went on to note that

> The fact is, under conditions of the existence of powerful nuclear means of mass destruction, any error, even the most insignificant, can be fraught with fatal consequences. The world already knows of a whole series of instances where mankind has almost found itself on the brink of nuclear catastrophe as a result of the careless and sometimes even irresponsible conduct of U.S. military personnel.[127]

It is important to emphasize once again that on the whole, Soviet statements indicate that at present the danger of war has declined and that the detente is exercising an increasing beneficial influence on the attitudes and policies of the Western powers vis-à-vis the Soviet Union. Soviet spokesmen generally express confidence in the current commitment of the Nixon Administration to the detente policy. Thus, the danger of a reversal of this policy and of a new threat of war is perceived mainly as a possible future contingency. Yet in a characteristic Soviet manner, even while claiming new gains for international peace and expressing optimism about the future, the Soviets at the same time assert that they must be prepared for sudden reversals, unexpected threats and unanticipated changes in their opponents' behavior and policies. Thus, in the Soviet view, nuclear war is at one and the same time increasingly unlikely and yet may occur at any moment. The US is believed to be deterred and yet a change in its political leadership, a breakthrough in weapons technology, a local crisis which leads to a confrontation, or an error in judgment on the part of either Washington or Moscow (although the possibility of the latter is not admitted) can unexpectedly lead to a nuclear war. Consequently, Soviet policy is said to pursue the twin aims of strengthening peace and averting a new world war, while at the same time preparing to wage war and crush the enemy. According to Grechko, "love of peace and readiness well and truly to repulse the aggressor are fused together in our policy," and he recalled that the 24th CPSU Congress had stressed that

> The comprehensive raising of the defense might of our Motherland and the education of Soviet people in a spirit of great vigilance and constant readiness to defend the great achievements of socialism must continue to remain one of the most important tasks of the party and the people.[128]

---

[127]Professor O. Bogdanov, "For the Sake of Peace on Earth," *Komsomol'skaia Pravda*, August 10, 1973.

[128]*Krasnaia Zvezda*, March 28, 1973.

Soviet Views Regarding War and Politics
and the Consequences of a Nuclear War

Soviet spokesmen devote considerable attention to a discussion of the relationship of nuclear war to politics and as an instrument of rational policies. In particular, they take issue with Western "sociologists and military writers" for their "highly fallacious, one-sided" and class-biased arguments which are "in fact attacking the Marxist-Leninist doctrine on war and politics and trying to prove that it is no longer valid in the nuclear age.[129] They reject the contention of some Western writers that war has ceased to be an instrument of politics, on the ground that Marxist doctrine asserts that all wars are an expression of the objectives and interests of the ruling classes. Soviet commentators point out that such Western arguments are not only wrong but harmful because they fail to distinguish between the aggressor and the victim of aggression and ignore the fundamental distinction between "just" and "unjust" wars.[130] They argue that nuclear war

> ... has ceased to be an instrument of politics, as is claimed by the overwhelming majority of representatives of pacifist, anti-war movements in the bourgeois world. This is a subjective judgment. It expresses merely protest against nuclear war. It objectively ... underestimates the danger of a nuclear war and in many cases gives rise to illusions about the "automatic destruction," the "self-negation" of nuclear war, and dulls the vigilance of peoples.[131]

Soviet spokesmen also deny the validity of contentions by Western analysts that "nuclear weapons have helped shake the traditional Marxist-Leninist doctrine concerning the connection between war and politics.[132]

At the same time, however, it is acknowledged that nuclear war may not be a rational means for achieving political objectives. Nevertheless, there appears to be some controversy on this question. The Soviet discussion of this problem is constrained by the official position which argues that the Soviet Union is not aggressive, does not regard war as an instrument of policy and does not "export" revolution by means of war. Consequently, the question is overtly reduced to the issue of whether nuclear war remains a rational

---

[129]*Problems of War and Peace: A Critical Analysis of Bourgeois Theories*, p. 93.

[130]For example, see *ibid.*, pp. 94-95. Lieutenant General S. Lotutskii, "The Classics of Marxism-Leninism on the Development of the Military Art," *Voenno-Istoricheskii Zhurnal* (Military Historical Journal), No. 9, September 1973, pp. 3-9; Colonel D. Volkogonov, "Peaceful Coexistence—An Alternative for War," *Kommunist Vooruzhennykh Sil*, No. 19, October 1973, pp. 10-18; Admiral Sheliag, *Krasnaia Zvezda*, February 7, 1974.

[131]Ye. I. Rybkin, "Leninist Principles of Sociological Analysis of Wars and Contemporary Problems," in N. V. Karabanov, *et al.*, *Filosofskoye Naslediye V. I. Lenina i Problemy, Sovremennoi Voiny (The Philosophical Legacy of V. I. Lenin and Problems of Contemporary War), Translations on USSR Military Affairs*, No. 930, July 29, 1973, p. 40; Admiral Sheliag, *Krasnaia Zvezda*, February 7, 1974.

[132]Colonel T. Kondratov, "War as a Continuation of Policy," *Soviet Military Review*, No. 2, February 1974, p. 8.

instrument of policy for the "imperialists." In view of the assertion that "imperialism" is not constrained by moral or other value considerations from resorting to war and that it is aggressive and warlike by nature, the question of the rationality of resort to nuclear war depends on its consequences. Arbatov has taken the line that the "prevention of nuclear war equally serves the interests of the United States and the USSR, since nuclear war would be suicide to both."[133] He also wrote that the present nuclear stockpiles provide for "several thousand tons of explosives in TNT equivalent for every person living on earth" and went on to conclude:

> It has become clear that this [nuclear] might is becoming progressively less usable as a political weapon. In the words of the well-known military theorist Clausewitz, it can be said that with the emergence of nuclear missiles "any correspondence between the political ends of the war" and the means was lost, since no policy can have the objective of destroying the enemy at the cost of complete self-annihilation. . . . The sphere of the "applicability" of military force for rational political ends is inexorably shrinking.[134]

The suggestion from Soviet spokesmen that nuclear war may spell suicide for all belligerents is not new. In 1954, Malenkov spoke of the "destruction of world civilization," for which he was sharply criticized by Molotov and Khrushchev, who insisted that only the capitalist system would perish. Khrushchev came close to repeating the Malenkov line in his polemics with the Chinese in the early 1960's, although in his statements addressed to Soviet audiences, he persisted in asserting that the Soviet Union would be victorious. Again, in 1965-1967 there was a renewal of the public debate over the possibility of attaining victory in a nuclear war.[135] The debate was resolved in favor of those who still stressed the feasibility of waging and winning a nuclear war. In September 1972, however, Grechko told the Presidium of the USSR Supreme Soviet in connection with the ratification of the May 1972 ABM Agreement that

> The Central Committee of the CPSU and the Government devote great attention to the problem of prevention of a nuclear war, which poses a deadly threat to the future of entire mankind.[136]

Such general statements to the effect that nuclear war poses a grave threat to mankind have been a major theme in recent years in support of the detente and the so-called Soviet peace policy. An article in the October 1973 issue of *International Affairs* warned that "available nuclear stockpiles are quite

---

[133]Budapest Radio, August 5, 1973.
[134]*World Marxist Review*, No. 2, February 1974, p. 56. See also, K. Simonov, "On the Other Side of the Ocean," *Pravda*, December 26, 1969; A. M. Rumiantsev, *Problemy Sovremennoi Nauki ob Obshchestve* (Problems of Contemporary Science on Society), Moscow, Nauka, 1969, p. 356.
[135]See Thomas W. Wolfe, *Soviet Power and Europe, 1945-1970*, (Baltimore: The Johns Hopkins Press, 1970), p. 454 and fn. 125.
[136]*Pravda*, September 30, 1972.

sufficient to transform the centers of world civilization into deserts,"[137] while another in the February 1974 issue asserted that

In the new condition, even elementary common sense reveals that the utilization of the colossal stockpiles of nuclear-missile weapons could result in a holocaust for human civilization and, at any rate, would give no advantages to the aggressor and end in his defeat and destruction.[138]

Although Brezhnev has not gone so far as to endorse the destruction of civilization argument, he has warned that a "new war in Europe" with the use of nuclear weapons "could lead to the destruction of a number of European states."[139]

Even so, the mutual suicide and no-victory line is now relatively rare in the Soviet Union. The weight of opinion, and especially as voiced by military authorities, is that while nuclear war "can cause substantial detriment to the development of world civilization, inhibiting the advance of the revolutionary process," and that it would result in the death of many millions of people and the destruction of some countries, "there is profound erroneousness and harm in the disorienting claims of bourgeois ideologies that there will be no victor in a thermonuclear world war."[140]

It is noteworthy in this connection that an article in *Red Star* in February 1974 appeared to take direct issue with the views expressed by Arbatov in his February 1974 article cited above. Its author, Rear Admiral and Professor V. Sheliag, a doctor of philosophical sciences, ostensibly criticized Western views which "asserted that mankind and world vicilization would die and everything living on earth would be destroyed in the event of a war."[141] According to the author, Marxist-Leninists "have always considered and do consider that war, and all the more so a thermonuclear war, is the greatest misfortune for people. But the mood of the communists is far from one of futility and pessimism." He went on to refer to the CPSU Program on this question and then added:

If arguments about the death of civilization and about there being no victors in a nuclear war are to be presented in an oversimplified manner, they are based on mathematical calculations. The authors of these arguments divide the quantity of the stockpile nuclear potential in the world by the number of people living on earth. As a result, it emerges that all mankind really could be destroyed.

This is an oversimplified, one-sided approach to such a complex socio-historical phenomenon as war. In order to understand its

[137]P. Zhilin and Y. Rybkin, "Militarism and Contemporary International Relations," *International Affairs* (Moscow), No. 10, October 1973, p. 23.

[138]Molchanov, *International Affairs*, No. 2, February 1974, p. 5.

[139]*Pravda*, July 27, 1973.

[140]N. V. Karabanov, "The Modern Era and Problems of War and Peace," in Karabanov, *et al., Filosofskoye Naslediye V. I. Lenina i Problemy Sovremennoi Voiny*, pp. 18, 19.

[141]*Krasnaia Zvezda*, February 7, 1974.

nature, course and results, it is not sufficient simply to have knowledge of, and to apply, merely mathematical formulas. For this it is essential to take into consideration the actual correlation of political class forces both in the international arena and also within the countries. Moreover, an indisputable fact exists . . . at least half of the world's nuclear potential is in the hands of the Soviet Union and consequently is directed not against mankind but serves as the means of defending mankind. If the imperialists nevertheless unleash a war against us, the modern weapons in the hands of the Soviet fighting men would be a means of routing the aggressor and consequently a means of defending civilization.

This statement appears to imply that the Soviet nuclear forces would be used in such a manner as to deprive the "imperialists" of their ability to threaten the destruction of either mankind or the USSR.

Along the same lines, the former Chief of the Strategic Missile Forces, Marshal of the Soviet Union N. I. Krylov, wrote in 1969:

The imperialist ideologists are trying to lull the vigilance of the world's people by having recourse to propaganda devices to the effect that there will be no victors in a future nuclear war. These false affirmations contradict the objective laws of history. . . . Victory in war, if the imperialists succeed in starting it, will be on the side of world socialism and all progressive mankind.[142]

Another military spokesman asserted in 1970 that

Marxist-Leninists are not panicked in the face of the terrifying danger created by imperialism nor do they depict it as the prelude to the "end of the world." . . . It is necessary to understand clearly that the bourgeois pacifists' arguments about the "end of the world" in such a war and the impossibility of victory benefit only the aggressor and the nuclear maniacs, who would very much like one or another of those against whom they are contemplating a nuclear attack to freeze in terror and lay down their arms.[143]

Soviet military writers also criticize as "deeply mistaken" the claims by Western "ideologues" that the concept of heroism in a nuclear war is obsolete and that there will be only "victims but no heroes."[144] Frequent articles stress the requirement for moral-political preparation of the Soviet armed forces and people to insure victory in a nuclear war.[145]

Nonmilitary as well as military authorities insist that a war between the two camps will inevitably end with the collapse of capitalism and the world-wide victory of communism. This assertion is based on two main arguments. One

---

[142]Marshal N. I. Krylov, "The Instructive Lessons of History," *Sovetskaia Rossiia*, August 30, 1969.

[143]Major General K. Bochkarev, "Nuclear Arms and the Fate of Social Progress," *Sovetskaia Kirgiziia* (Soviet Kirgizia), August 25, 1970.

[144]Major General L. Oshurkov and Colonel A. Barmin, "An All-Party and State Task," *Kommunist Vooruzhennykh Sil*, No. 13, July 1972, p. 23.

[145]See, for example, I. A. Seleznev in Karabanov, *et al.*, *Filosofskoye Naslediye V. I. Lenina i Problemy Sovremennoi Voiny*, cited in JPRS *Translations on USSR Military Affairs*, No. 930, June 29, 1973, pp. 13-29; Army General A. A. Yepishev, *Mighty Weapon of the Party, passim*.

is that the masses in the capitalist countries, when confronted by the horrors of nuclear destruction, will revolt against their leaders who have brought this catastrophe upon them.

> If the imperialists unleash a new world war, the toilers will no longer tolerate a system which subjects people to devastating wars. They will mercilessly and irrevocably sweep capitalism from the face of the earth. Of course losses may be extremely high in this decisive clash between two opposing forces. Much, however, depends on the activeness of the masses. The more vigorously and resolutely they oppose the actions of the aggressor, the less damage will be inflicted on world civilization.[146]

The assertion that imperialism will inevitably collapse as a result of a nuclear war is included in the CPSU Program and is often quoted by Soviet leaders. The other line of argument, as will be discussed below, is based on the professional military view that it is possible to attain victory if the Soviet Union possesses a superior war fighting capability, effective means to assure the survival of critical elements of the population and the economy, succeeds in initiating a preemptive strike, and manages to maintain a dominant military capability through the further production of weapons in the course of the war.

Indeed, Soviet leaders are probably the only ones among the leaders of the world who speak of victory in a nuclear war. For example, Brezhnev has proclaimed: "Let it be known to all that in a clash with any aggressor the Soviet Union will win a victory worthy of our great people, of the homeland of the October Revolution,"[147] and Grechko asserted in March 1973 that "we are firmly convinced that victory in this war would go to us—to the socialist social system."[148] More recently, Grechko said:

> We assure our Party and our people that the Soviet Army and Navy are always ready to fulfill any order of the Motherland. And if the imperialist aggressor risks encroaching on our country, he will be beaten everywhere—on the ground, in the air, on the water and underwater.[149]

As was noted above, the prevailing Soviet view rejects the notion of a stable mutual deterrence based on the capability of mutual assured destruction, which Arbatov appears to be endorsing even though he also warns of the instability of a "balance of terror." Furthermore, the Soviet view rejects what it calls "bourgeois pacifism," which condemns all wars on moral grounds or because of their possible escalation to nuclear war. "We are not pacifists," Brezhnev declared in Havana on January 30, 1974, "we are not for peace at any price and we are not, of course, for any freezing of social-

[146]Karabanov, *Filosofskoye Naslediye* . . ., p. 19.
[147]*Pravda*, November 4, 1967.
[148]*Krasnaia Zvezda*, March 28, 1973.
[149]*Krasnaia Zvezda*, March 14, 1974.

political processes taking place inside the countries,"[150] i.e., the revolutionary and natural liberation struggle which could lead to armed conflict and wars. Earlier, a similar line had been expressed in *Izvestiia*, which had asserted that "utopianism and lofty sentimentality of pacifism are alien to us," and that the question of war and peace is based on a "realistic" analysis of the correlation of forces.[151] Another *Izvestiia* article had been even more explicit in asserting that

> War can and must be banned as a means for resolving international disputes. But we must not "ban" civil or national liberation wars, we must not "ban" uprisings and we by no means "ban" revolutionary mass movements aimed at changing the political and social status quo.[152]

As was noted above, Soviet leaders have made strong public commitments of Soviet support to the national liberation wars, even though Soviet commentators acknowledge the danger of escalation of such wars into nuclear wars, unless the West can be restrained. What is more, the logic of the Soviet position leads it to endorse all "just" wars even while it condemns the "unjust" ones, i.e., those initiated or waged by the imperialists and, as was noted, one of the Soviet requirements of the policy of "peaceful coexistence" is a "constant readiness on the part of the armed forces of socialism to disrupt the aggressive actions of the imperialist circles."[153]

Soviet Views on War Fighting As Related to Action

The views outlined above are used by the Soviet leadership to justify further efforts to strengthen Soviet defense capabilities and to intensify domestic controls as well as to carry out various programs designed to prepare the population and the armed forces psychologically and in practical ways for a possible nuclear war. It is asserted that the Party and Government are "doing everything possible to ensure that our social-economic achievements are combined with the proper development of the country's military-economic, military-scientific, moral-political and purely military potential, in the interest of ensuring the most reliable armed defense of the country."[154] The seriousness with which the Soviet leadership views the need to prepare the Soviet Union and its armed forces for a possible war, despite the detente

---

[150]*Pravda*, January 31, 1974.

[151]F. Burlatskii, "The Dialectics of the Modern World," *Izvestiia*, November 22, 1973.

[152]Bovin, *Izvestiia*, September 11, 1973.

[153]Colonel D. Volkogonov, "Peaceful Coexistence—An Alternative for War," *Kommunist Vooruzhennykh Sil*, No. 19, October 1973, p. 17.

[154]Colonel V. Kozlov, "The Development of Soviet Society and the Strengthening of the Country's Defense," *Kommunist Vooruzhennykh Sil*, No. 22, November 1972, pp. 7-8.

in East-West relations and its assertions that the prospects for peace are greater than ever before, is reflected in the well-publicized drive to further raise the combat readiness and capabilities of the armed forces, especially of their nuclear components, to improve the operational readiness of civil defense and to intensify the "military-patriotic" indoctrination of the population to withstand "any wartime ordeals" and strengthen its will to fulfill its duties "under the most difficult conditions at the front and in the rear."[155] Efforts are also underway to improve the survivability of the Soviet economy under war conditions. Soviet propaganda is directed to instill in the population and the armed forces "class hatred" toward "imperialism" and the "enemies" of the Soviet Union and shape "a clear understanding of the sources and danger of the outbreak of war and of the need for vigilance and constant readiness to repulse aggression."[156] The sum total of these efforts is directed toward "maintaining the Soviet state's defense capability at a level insuring the rout of any aggressor."[157]

To date, Soviet strategic thinking continues to push in the direction of a search for a comprehensive war-fighting and war-survival capability. Such an approach is logical enough, given Soviet views on the aims and character of East-West competition, on military power as an instrument of Soviet policy, and on an assumed US search for a rational strategy which would allow it to use its military forces in a confrontation with the Soviet Union. Although there appears to be a debate on some issues in the Soviet Union, the evidence so far does not indicate any change in the basic Soviet views or in Soviet defense policies. Being dedicated to changing the international political environment and balance of power and to acquiring increasing numbers of clients and interests in areas of great Western sensitivity, Soviet leaders must inevitably take into account the possibility of confrontation with the West and especially with the US. They must also be prepared for a possible armed conflict with China. A nuclear deterrence posture, therefore, would not meet Soviet requirements since Moscow neither believes nor is interested in a world of stable power relationships.

---

[155]Grechko, *Kommunist*, No. 7, May 1973, pp. 22-23. See also, Leon Goure, *The Military Indoctrination of Soviet Youth*, New York, National Strategy Information Center, Inc., 1973.

[156]Yepishev, *Krasnaia Zvezda*, March 28, 1973; Seleznev, in Karabanov, *et al., Filosofskoye Naslediye . . .*, p. 296.

[157]Kulikov, *Kommunist*, No. 3, February 1973, p. 77; See also, Grechko, *Pravda*, February 23, 1974; Sokolov, *Krasnaia Zvezda*, February 24, 1974.

THE QUESTION OF PRIORITIES AMONG SOVIET PURPOSES
RELATIVE TO THE USE OF SOVIET NUCLEAR FORCES

The question of the relative weights which Moscow assigns to the various purposes that it seeks through development and utilization of its nuclear forces poses a number of difficult problems.

One is that, as has been said, the Soviet leaders approach this matter, like most others, dialectically and perceive it in the context of a dynamic and continuing competition with the West for predominance. Here the actual Soviet practice runs strongly counter to a general propensity in the US to see the Soviets as a mirror-image of ourselves. The fallacy lies in the assumption that for really important matters the Soviet Union is a "normal" state that faces situations and develops policies in the same way as other "normal" states, and more particularly the United States. There is a further assumption that decision-making in the Soviet Union involves a strictly "rational" process, which in its turn is seen as reflecting the same considerations and weights as influence decision-making in the US. Stanley Hoffman in his *Gulliver's Troubles or the Setting of American Policy* has described the situation which characterizes US observers: "There . . . calculations reveal clearly how they project their own mode of thought on the world and thus how they operate in a mental universe whose rationality is merely their own writ large—where opponents are supposed to either reason like Americans or to be in need of education bringing them up to this level." According to a recent special study by two well qualified students of US practices relative to Soviet decision-making, "It would be hard to exaggerate the influence of this [self] image on American thinking about the Soviet threat. It is perhaps safe to say that almost everything of consequence that has been written about Soviet military or foreign policy over the past decade or so has used this concept."[158] These students cite as especially noteworthy, and in their minds highly misleading, the development and acceptance of the "action-reaction" concept as a key to US interpretations of Soviet conduct over the past few years in both the strategic and foreign policy areas. Again, Professor Richard Pipes pointed out in a statement to a Congressional Committee on February 20, 1974 that the "perfectly reasonable premise" that the US and the Soviet Union "must at all costs avoid situations which may lead to a nuclear war . . . has been accompanied in the United States (but not in the Soviet Union) by a whole philosophy of detente which ascribes to the other party motives and intentions which bear no relationship to its traditions or political system,

---

[158]Matthew P. Gallagher and Karl F. Spielman, Jr., *The Politics of Power: Soviet Decision Making for Defense*, Washington, D.C., Institute for Defense Analyses, October 1971, IDA Paper, p. 774.

and which is not at all reflected either in Soviet theoretical discussions of international relations designed for party cadres or in the agitation and propaganda material issued for mass consumption.''

The essence of the matter is that while we in the West view the Soviets as motivated by "realism" as we understand that term, the Soviets see realism in a quite different way. They operate on the basis of an entirely different set of calculations and against a different environmental background than does the US or other Western countries. These calculations and this environmental background relate to the peculiar Soviet world outlook born of Marxist-Leninist assumptions regarding an immutable class struggle which necessarily influences the international policies and conduct of the USSR and other states adhering to socialism on the one hand and all imperialist states on the other. Beyond this they relate to a number of other considerations: the presumed innate superiority of the socialist system over the capitalist, and the driving necessity to demonstrate this superiority; the requirements incident to per-petuation of the monolithic rule exercised by the small minority of the population centering in the Communist Party of the Soviet Union and its hierarchy; the force and influence of deeply entrenched interest groups within the Soviet ruling structure; requirements incident to preservation of the "unity" of the Soviet-dominated "commonwealth of socialist states" and to Moscow's pretentions to leadership of the world communist and world liberation movements; and to the rival pretentions of Peking as well as the direct challenge of China to the USSR. They relate also to the special historic and geographical factors that have always heavily affected the outlook and purposes of Russian rulers; the unique ways in which the Russians have traditionally viewed their national security interests and needs; the dynamic sense of mission (or expansionism) that has consistently marked Russian conduct toward the outside world; the sense of unavoidable rivalry with the US, both as the only power capable of destroying the USSR and as the leader of one of the two world camps and the peculiar cultural factors and personal-ity traits that affect the Soviet leadership, both as a collective and as individuals.

A second and largely consequential problem is that the Soviets do not compartmentalize or distinguish among specific purposes which they pursue. While in Western eyes the purposes which Moscow seeks through its nuclear forces might seem conflicting or contradictory in nature, and under certain circumstances mutually exclusive, and hence bound by the laws of logic to some sort of priority ordering, in the Soviet way of thinking they are different aspects of the same thing, inseparable and indivisible, interdependent and interlocked, all parts of a dialectical continuum. The Soviets doubtless have preferences with respect to the *results* they may be able to achieve through

66

the simultaneous pursuit of these purposes, but they give no indication of a willingness to choose among the purposes themselves.

There can be no doubt that Moscow is anxious to avoid nuclear war with the US, barring a development that would give it a decisive advantage. Even though Soviet spokesmen predict a Soviet victory in the event of a nuclear war, they consistently acknowledge the enormous damage that would result from such a war and hasten to deny that war can serve as the "midwife of revolution," or that the Soviet Union is indifferent to the "fate of peoples."

> The conclusion that imperialism will suffer defeat if it forces a new world war on mankind does not in any way signify that we should strive toward a military confrontation. Precisely this position is taken by today's "leftist" revisionists [i.e., Maoists].[159]

Hence, deterrence of the US from either a nuclear attack or courses of action that might lead to a nuclear conflict is obviously of very great importance in Soviet thinking. At the same time, however, the evidence indicates that the leadership, with its peculiar world outlook and operating within the framework of its peculiar environment, has genuine reservations regarding realistic possibilities of assured deterrence.

The Soviets are deeply interested in prestige, which is so intimately related to their claim of superiority for their system and their aims to prove it. But prestige considerations as such cannot explain the level of Soviet defense efforts or the present style of Soviet exploitation of its nuclear force capabilities. What Moscow is really interested in is not the self-satisfaction that goes with prestige, but clout adequate to further its expanding global role and, especially, its influence on the Western European governments and the US to come to terms with it.

Although the Soviets quite clearly would like, and hope, to be able to expand their global power and influence without precipitating war with the US, that is, under conditions of effective deterrence, they themselves constantly argue that this may not be possible, that Soviet successes may produce US reactions that can escalate into nuclear war or even take the form of a direct nuclear attack on the USSR. Yet Moscow gives no signs of any willingness to abate or give up its struggle against the US, despite possibly serious consequences with respect to the effectiveness of deterrence. Instead, it stresses its intention to continue and even to intensify this struggle by all means short of a resort to the use of its armed forces against the US.

Given the foregoing, and in the absence of universal nuclear disarmament, the ability to fight a nuclear war, with maximal prospects of winning should it come, assumes for the Soviets basic importance. It would seem axiomatic, in fact, that the Soviets see the most fundamental purpose of their nuclear forces

---

[159]Karabanov, et al., *Filosofskoye Naslediye . . .,* p. 19.

as a war-fighting capability. Existence of this capability, as distinguished from any intentions regarding its use, is in Soviet thinking an essential prerequisite for effectiveness of the Soviet deterrence posture. It also facilitates, and in fact appears in Moscow's eyes to be necessary for, the attainment of Soviet objectives relative to further shifts in the world balance of forces. And perhaps most important in the Soviet mind is the consideration that, due to the dynamics of history, a general war between the capitalist and communist worlds may turn out to be "unavoidable" after all, making it a matter of elementary prudence to be ready for any contingency.

IV

THE SOVIET VIEW AS TO HOW MUCH NUCLEAR STRENGTH IS ENOUGH

The question of the future development of the Soviet Armed Forces and especially nuclear forces has become particularly urgent at this time when the Soviet Union has achieved strategic parity with the US. Until recent years, Soviet policy on force size and composition appeared to be aimed at closing the gap in strategic capabilities with the US while at the same time maintaining a sufficient theater force in Europe to assure in war the quick destruction of NATO forces and the conquest of that continent. Today, Soviet requirements have been complicated by the need to maintain an effective deterrent and war-fighting capability vis-à-vis the Chinese, as well as by the stated intention to maintain a capability sufficient to deter the US from "exporting counterrevolution" to less-developed countries and to support those countries in "anti-imperalist" national liberation struggles.

FACTORS DETERMINING SOVIET FORCE SIZE AND COMPOSITION

Open Soviet publications give no indication of the existence of any doctrinal or conceptual limits on the size of the Soviet Armed Forces or of the nuclear forces. What constitutes in the Soviet view "sufficiency" in military power is not spelled out but is relative to the ambiguous requirements of and a capability to (a) "reliably defend the socialist Motherland" and its allied communist states; (b) assure a "firm rebuff" to an attack on the Soviet Union and the "decisive defeat" of any enemy which dares to initiate war against the USSR; (c) provide effective support to Soviet global foreign policy, and deter the West from "exporting counterrevolution" and otherwise stand as an effective obstacle to "imperialist aggression" against Third World areas; (d) forestall any possibility of the West's gaining a significant advantage over the Soviet Union as a result of a technological breakthrough in weapons development.

In stating these objectives, Soviet authorities do not, as we do in the US, specify a capability to wage two-and-a-half or one-and-a-half wars, or otherwise spell out desired numerical limits for the Strategic Missile Forces, either in terms of numbers of warheads, missiles and missile carriers, or delineate megatons of nuclear explosives. Also, no mention is made of the implications for Soviet nuclear capabilities of the possibility of having either to fight a simultaneous war against the West and China or of the requirements for deterring one of these potential opponents while fighting the other. In fact, in their public communications Soviet secrecy is carried to the point where, as

69

was noted above, even during the SALT negotiations, the Soviet Union did not acknowledge the size of its strategic forces but used US estimates as a basis for the agreements and since then has refrained from publication of the agreed-upon figures in any communication to the Soviet population. Of course, the SALT negotiations inevitably tend to push the Soviet Union in the direction of defining what it considers to be the necessary or acceptable nuclear forces levels. Thus, Soviet leaders acknowledged that the number of strategic missiles authorized under the 1972 SALT Agreement, which made due allowances for the so-called asymmetries in the capabilities of the two sides, had established at least provisionally a state of "equal security" for the US and the USSR. Again, force size and composition and the balance of nuclear forces have been very much the topic of negotiations at SALT II and the Mutual Balanced Force Reductions (MBFR) talks.

This public stance, however, does not necessarily imply that Soviet decisions as to force size and composition are predetermined by clear-cut objectives or that actual Soviet capabilities can be rationalized either on the basis of arbitrary decisions of the leadership or haphazard circumstances and judgments. Instead, Soviet force development is said to follow strict "laws." It is said that "the development of the armed forces is determined by a set of economic, political, scientific-technical, and other factors which are in close dialectical interdependence."[1] The general direction of military development is said to be in accordance with Party guidelines, which in turn are said to take into account the nature of international relations, the character of a possible war and the likely forms of its initiation, the "state of the art" in weapons technology and its probable future development, the economic, social, political and moral strength of the Soviet Union as against that of its likely enemies, and so on.[2] According to Marshal Grechko:

> The party develops military affairs on the basis of a profound Marxist-Leninist analysis of the modern situation and the development of military-political forces in the international arena, taking into account the laws of social development and the achievements of science and technology. . . .[3]

Another Soviet formulation goes as follows:

> The forecasting of the international military and political situation, the overall distribution of forces in the world, the consequences of the scientific and technical revolution, and the military preparations

---

[1] Iu. S. Solnyshkov, *Ekonomicheskie Faktory i Vooruzheniye* (Economic Factors and Armaments), Moscow, Voenizdat, 1973, cited in JPRS *Translations on Soviet Military Affairs*, No. 931, June 29, 1973, p. 14.

[2] V. Kulikov, "High Combat Readiness Is the Most Important Condition of the Reliable Defense of the Motherland," *Kommunist Vooruzhennykh Sil*, No. 6, March 1973, *passim*.

[3] Grechko, *Kommunist*, No. 7, May 1973, p. 15. See also, General of the Army Ye. Maltsev, "Lenin's Ideas on the Defense of Socialism," *Krasnaia Zvezda*, February 14, 1974.

of the aggressive imperialist circles enable Soviet military science to predict the probable nature of a future war, the methods by which it will be waged, and the role of different types of armed forces, and branches of the forces in it.[4]

Scientific analysis and "prognostication" are said to help determine the development of new weapons and combat equipment and thus make it "possible to cut the time for producing new systems of weapons."[5] Soviet commentators also admit that the Soviet Armed Forces study foreign military developments and try to adopt their best features for their own use. Thus, it is said that "an immutable conclusion found in our Leninist legacy is that of carefully monitoring the development of bourgeois armies, studying their strategic and technical principles, weapons and equipment, and adopting only the best features into the armament of the proletariat."[6]

Probably the most obvious reason for the absence of a doctrinal or conceptual limit on the size and composition of Soviet nuclear forces, and the great difficulty the Soviets have in defining such limits, derives from the fact that the Soviet forces are not designed primarily for deterrence but for war-fighting purposes. Nuclear "sufficiency" for the latter purpose is far more dynamic than for the former and inevitably tends to push in the direction of efforts to achieve superiority, all the more so as the Soviet war-fighting posture entails also a search for a war-survival and war-winning capability. Thus, it is pointed out not only that "the decisive branch of the armed forces is the Strategic Missile Forces,"[7] but also that in a nuclear war "the decisive role in its outcome would be played by the balance of the missile-nuclear potential of both sides."[8]

Consequently, it is asserted that "Soviet military doctrine proceeds from the fact that a savage struggle is being waged in the international arena between two social systems—socialism and capitalism" and that the Soviet Union must "undertake the requisite measures to respond to force with *overwhelming* force in case the imperialists unleash a war against the nations of the socialist commonwealth."[9] Soviet military doctrine maintains that if such a war is initiated by the West it "will be a decisive collision of the two

[4]Lieutenant General I. Zavialov, "Scientific Prediction in Military Art," *Krasnaia Zvezda*, August 3, 1972; also by the same author, "The Creative Nature of Soviet Military Doctrine," *Krasnaia Zvezda*, April 19, 1973; "Scientific Provision in Military Art," *Soviet Military Review*, No. 1, January 1973, pp. 14-15.

[5]Zavialov, *Soviet Military Review*, No. 1, January 1973, p. 15.

[6]Colonel A. Timorin, "Leninist Doctrine of Defense of the Socialist Homeland and Modern Times," *Kommunist Vooruzhennykh Sil*, No. 22, November 1973, p. 13.

[7]Marshal of the Soviet Union A. A. Grechko, "V. I. Lenin and the Soviet State's Armed Forces," *Kommunist*, No. 3, February 1974, p. 22.

[8]Iu. Kostko, *Mirovaia Ekonomika i Mezhdunarodnyye Otnosheniia*, No. 9, September 1973, p. 19.

[9]Karabanov, *et al.*, *Filosofskoye Naslediye* . . ., p. 48. [Emphasis added.]

opposing systems," in which both sides would use all the weapons in their respective arsenals. Furthermore, it would be a global war, requiring the use of multi-million armies, and could be initiated by a surprise nuclear attack. It would appear, therefore, that the Soviets base their force requirements and composition on what may be termed the "worst possible case," and that their objective, as was noted earlier, is to achieve a capability to fight and win an unlimited armed struggle between the two systems. Thus, in a major book coauthored by a group of Soviet military leaders, which was published in 1972 after the Moscow Summit Meeting, Grechko wrote:

> The Communist Party and Soviet Government attach great importance to improving these forces [i.e., the Strategic Missile Forces] and day-to-day attention is also given to other branches of the Armed Forces and combat arms. They are being outfitted with all means of armed warfare needed to defeat any aggressor.[10]

In actual practice there is good evidence that the Soviet military posture reflects a compromise between interests and concepts as well as changing Soviet perceptions of US and probably Chinese military capabilities. The leadership must adjudicate the competition and conflicting demands for resources not only between the Armed Forces and various segments of the economy, but also among the various branches and services of the Armed Forces themselves. At the same time, it must assess not only the immediacy of a threat to the Soviet Union and the requirements of providing effective security but also take account of the need to deprive the US of any significant military or negotiatory advantage and of maintaining a military posture which will facilitate the attainment of Soviet foreign policy objectives. Furthermore, Soviet spokesmen recognize that the size and structure of the Armed Forces are influenced by the appearance of new weapons systems.

Although military spokesmen give the impression that they believe in the principle of "the more the better," and that "there can be no limit to the improvement of the combat readiness of troops and naval forces,"[11] they also recognize the critical importance of the country's economic capability and the level of its science and technology for the Soviet military position. It is said, therefore, that

> An important place in Soviet military doctrine is occupied by scientifically substantiated views on the role of the economy in war and its influence on the development of military affairs. . . . Our doctrine is based on the determining role of the economy and its ever-increasing influence on war.[12]

---

[10]Marshal of the Soviet Union A. A. Grechko, "We Serve the Soviet Union," *Armiia Bratstva Narodov* (The Army of Fraternal Nations), translated in JPRS, *Translations on USSR Military Affairs*, No. 919, May 30, 1973, p. 62.

[11]Kulikov, *Kommunist Vooruzhennykh Sil*, No. 6, March 1973, p. 19; Grechko, *Komsomolets Tatarii*, January 9, 1974.

[12]Zavialov, *Krasnaia Zvezda*, April 19, 1973. See also, Colonel S. Baranov, "The Material Foundation of the Might of the USSR's Armed Forces," *Krasnaia Zvezda*, March 5, 1971.

Or more simply that "the strengthening of the Soviet Union's defense might is inseparably connected with the growth of its economic, scientific and technical potential,"[13] and that "the further consolidation of the state's defense capability is possible only given the successful development of our economy, science and culture."[14] Consequently, it is claimed that

In the sphere of raising the defense capability, the party's main efforts are directed toward creating a well-developed military-economic base. . . .[15]

and that

In these conditions, the military-technological policy of the CPSU is directed toward creating and maintaining superiority of the socialist countries over the forces of war and aggression.[16]

The link between the growth of the economic power base and the strengthening of Soviet military capability and the priority given to the development of the economic power base as it relates to defense was emphasized by Grechko in a speech of March 13, 1974:

Guided by Lenin's principle of the unity of national economic and defense tasks, the party is purposefully implementing measures to raise the military-economic potential of the country. . . .
Under the conditions of the developed socialist society even broader opportunities are opened up for increasing our country's defense capability. This is assisted by factors like the presence of a powerful economic capability of supplying the armed forces with all modern types of weapons and combat equipment. . . .[17]

"Our country's growing economic potential," said Politburo member V. V. Shcherbitskii on January 15, 1974, "is a reliable guarantee for its defense potential."[18] Soviet spokesmen also note that in the arms competition, Western hopes to "wear out" the USSR economically have proven groundless.[19]

There is no reason to believe that the Soviet leadership is willing to accept all recommendations of the military concerning force size or investment in military capabilities. The persistent harping of the military on the danger of war is indicative of its belief in the necessity of maintaining pressure on the leadership in order to keep defense investments at the desired level. Even so, the Party from time to time openly admonishes the military on the latter's excessive focus on the quantitative aspects of military capabilities. Thus, an

[13]Colonel S. Bartenev, "The Economic Base of Defense Potential," *Soviet Military Review*, No. 8, August 1973, p. 3.
[14]Kulikov, *Kommunist Vooruzhennykh Sil*, No. 6, March 1973, p. 14.
[15]Grechko, *Kommunist*, No. 7, May 1973, p. 16.
[16]M. Gladkov and B. Ivanov, "The Economy and Military-Technological Policy," *Kommunist Vooruzhennykh Sil*, No. 9, May 1972, p. 12.
[17]*Krasnaia Zvezda*, March 14, 1974.
[18]*Pravda Ukrainy*, January 16, 1974.
[19]G. A. Trofimenko, *SShA: Ekonomika, Politika, Ideologiia*, No. 2, February 1974, p. 9.

article in the May 17, 1973 issue of *Red Star* by a senior member of the Military-Political Academy insisted that the military potential of a country is not made up by the quantity or quality of weapons alone.

> In some works by Soviet authors there are errors, for example, in the question of the essence and consequences of a nuclear missile war. The authors of these works have absolutized the quantitative analysis and arithmetical calculations of the destructive power of nuclear weapons. Whereas the dialectic approach to research into the nature of war and the question of victory in it, presupposes not only a quantitative but also a qualitative analysis of economic, scientific and technical, as well as moral and political factors and also the military factor proper.[20]

Indeed, Soviet spokesmen frequently refer to Lenin's statement to the effect that wars are won by the country which has superiority not only in military capability but also in economic, scientific, technical, sociological and moral fields.

SALT AND THE FURTHER DEVELOPMENT
OF THE SOVIET ARMED FORCES

The SALT Agreements signed in Moscow in May 1972 were said to be based on the principle of "equal security" which "gives neither side unilateral military advantages."[21] This interpretation of the agreements was publicly endorsed by the Soviet leaders, as, for example, by Kosygin[22] and Suslov.[23] While Soviet commentators have recognized that the agreements did not establish limits on qualitative improvements in the agreed numbers of missiles, they generally have taken the line that such improvements by the US would be "destabilizing" and might jeopardize the detente. For example, Arbatov wrote in the June 22, 1972 issue of *Izvestiia* that US efforts to "compensate for the restrictions imposed by the accords by whipping up the arms race in other fields" would adversely affect future efforts to expand the sphere of peaceful coexistence and disarmament.[24]

The general Soviet line is that it is up to the US to show its good faith and its willingness to abide not only by the letter but also by the spirit of the

[20]Major General A. Milovidov, "A Philosophical Analysis of Military Thought," *Kommunist Vooruzhennykh Sil*, No. 9, May 1972, p. 12.

[21]G. Sviatov, "Strategic Arms Limitation: The Principle of Equal Security," *Krasnaia Zvezda*, July 28, 1972; G. Trofimenko, "An Important Problem," *Pravda*, June 5, 1973. See also the Moscow Agreements on "Basic Principles" of May 29, 1972.

[22]A. N. Kosygin, Speech on May 26, 1972, U.S. Department of State, *Bulletin* Vol. LXVI, No. 1722 (June 26, 1972), p. 867.

[23]M. Suslov, Speech on May 26, 1972, at Joint Session of the Foreign Affairs Commissions of the USSR Supreme Soviet, *Pravda*, August 24, 1972.

[24]G. A. Arbatov, "The Strength of a Policy of Realism," *Izvestiia*, June 22, 1972. See also, his article in *Kommunist*, No. 3, February 1973.

agreements. Thus in his speech to the Supreme Soviet during the debate on the ratification of the Anti-Ballistic Missle (ABM) Agreement, Suslov warned:

It should be perfectly clear to all that the Soviet Union, proceeding from the interests of its own security, will attentively follow the attempts of certain US circles to distort the spirit and the letter of the Treaty and interim agreement which have been concluded and will take into account in its policy any changes which might emerge in the position of the US side.[25]

Similarly, an analysis of US-Soviet relations published in March 1973 points out that the further development of detente in East-West relations depends on the actions of the US.

A great deal here depends on how consistently what has already been achieved in these relations is implemented, how faithful the US ruling circles prove to be to the spirit and content of the agreements signed between the two countries and, finally, how far the United States is prepared to further develop and deepen relations of peace and mutual advantageous cooperation in both peoples' interests.[26]

Soviet public discussions of military buildup in the post-Summit period do not place the issue of performance on a clear *quid-pro-quo* basis, or in any sense convey a message to the US that "if you stop improving your military capability we will do likewise," although they do call for negotiations to make the interim agreement on strategic forces permanent and to devise some agreement limiting the race in qualitative improvements in strategic weapons. However, no specific mention is made of the recent improvements in Soviet strategic capabilities, and consequently all discussions in the US of the need for further strengthening of defense are treated as unilateral US efforts to gain an advantage and slow down the detente. For example, one of the senior staff members of the Institute for World Economics and International Relations of the USSR Academy of Sciences wrote in a book which was cleared for publication in August 1972:

The unchanging character of imperialism's aggressive nature and policies is creating the preconditions for the maintenance of a high level and the qualitative development of military strength, for strengthening militarism, and for the development of tendencies toward a further utilization of the achievements of the scientific and technological revolution for military purposes.

The author then went on to charge that within the US,

A process of the qualitative development of armed forces and weapons is in progress which is embracing all of the structural components of military strength—the strategic forces, general purpose forces, equipment for the strategic delivery of troops and reserves.

---

[25]*Pravda*, August 24, 1972.
[26]Georgiev and Kolosov, *SShA: Ekonomika, Politika, Ideologiia*, No. 3, March 1973, p. 20.

75

The author expressed special concern over an alleged US shift to a "naval strategy" designed to preserve a strategic nuclear strike capability in the event of a Soviet first counter-force strike.

A tendency is being revealed toward increasing the weight of naval strategy at the expense of land strategy and toward creating strategic systems which, since they will be dispersed in the world's oceans, should be able, in the opinion of Western strategists, to help weaken a retaliatory [sic] nuclear strike.[27]

Soviet spokesmen strongly criticize the US for its Trident program, which is said to be "incompatible with the spirit of the Soviet-American agreements,"[28] and for "thinking of creating new weapons systems as a 'bargaining card' to be used in dealings with the USSR."[29] A Soviet analyst wrote in *Pravda* that

. . . just recently military circles and the press close to those circles have raised a din—in accordance with the well-known prescriptions—about the United States' "military weakness" and about the need for a new round of the arms race. Blatant pressure is being brought to bear on Congress, which approves military expenditures, and attempts are being made to put some sort of brake on the next stage of SALT.[30]

A broadcast roundtable of members of the editorial board of *Za Rubezhom,* an important Soviet publication on foreign affairs, has asserted that "the opponents of international cooperation" in the US

. . . have immediately taken up arms against the Agreement on the Prevention of Nuclear War; and, in order to subvert it, the theoreticians of the Pentagon have made use of the thesis that an acceleration of the qualitative technological arms race without formal violations of the letter of the agreement will enable military and psychological pressure to be brought to bear on the Soviet Union. In Congress, the view has been expressed that military spending should be increased, rather than cut back, and that plans to create new and more destructive weapons should not be cancelled, but expanded. The weapons in question are new types of thermonuclear weapons, new missiles, new submarines and new bombers. In other words, let banned weapons remain banned, but create new ones which are not mentioned in the Soviet-American agreements.[31]

The panel members went on to condemn the "provocative nature of the thesis about creating new [weapons] systems as a means for putting pressure on the USSR." Soviet commentators also criticized Secretary of Defense

---

[27]Proektor, *International Conflicts*, p. 46.
[28]G. Sviatov, "A Gamble on 'Neptune's Trident,'" *Krasnaia Zvezda*, March 23, 1973.
[29]Trofimenko, *Pravda*, June 5, 1973.
[30]*Pravda*, August 26, 1973.
[31]Radio Moscow, August 26, 1973.

Schlesinger for asking Congress for increased defense appropriations on the ground of an alleged Soviet threat to the US.[32]

In the case of the ABM Agreement, Soviet spokesmen expressed themselves as being satisfied with the equal limitations on the number and deployment of missile launchers on both sides. The Soviet shift during the SALT negotiations from an initial focus on offensive strategic systems to agreement to limit ABM development and deployment has given rise to speculations whether this signaled a fundamental change in Soviet concerns about a defensive versus offensive posture and whether it indicated a growing Soviet willingness to embrace the principle of mutual assured destruction or merely reflected Moscow's technological difficulties with its ABM system and fears that the US may achieve a technological breakthrough in that area which, combined with the US MIRV capability, might incline the US to consider a first-strike strategy. Soviet public pronouncements, of course, have avoided any direct clarification of this question. They have merely argued that the large-scale deployment of ABM's might encourage an aggressor to launch a first nuclear strike and that the agreement prevented a dangerous spiraling race in new offensive and defensive weapons systems.[33] There is no indication in Soviet sources that the ABM Agreement as such signaled a shift in basic Soviet views on strategy and war. Since the early 1960's Soviet strategy has emphasized the critical importance of the first nuclear strike for the course and outcome of a war and the need for the Soviet Union to anticipate an enemy attack by launching a preemptive attack. Public claims concerning Soviet ABM capabilities, which had been prominent under Khrushchev, ended in 1967-68, but thereafter there was increasing mention of the role of Soviet strategic forces in a counterforce role and at the same time greater emphasis on various programs designed to increase the damage-limiting capability of the Soviet Union, notably civil defense, which Brezhnev personally urged be improved in 1966 and 1967. These basic views persisted after the signing of the ABM Agreement, and to date Soviet public statements have shown no inclination to accept the concept of a stable balance of mutual assured destruction. Instead the evidence indicates a continuing Soviet search for an effective war-fighting and war-survival capability.

Although the Moscow Agreements established the principle of "equal security" for both signatories, the Soviet leadership immediately served

---

[32]For example, see Radio Moscow, September 5, 1973; Lieutenant Colonel M. Ponomarev, "What Is NATO Worried About," *Krasnaia Zvezda*, December 8, 1973; B. Temnov, "The Pressure Continues," *Izvestiia*, January 27, 1974; Ponomarev and Vinogradov, "Maneuvers by the Opponents of Detente," *Krasnaia Zvezda*, January 20, 1974, Radio Moscow, January 27, 1974, February 4, 1974.

[33]For example, see the "debates" on the ABM Agreement by the Foreign Affairs Commissions of the Supreme Soviet of the USSR, *Pravda*, August 24, 1972.

notice that it would continue to strengthen its defenses. The essential justification was that the agreements, although diminishing, have not eliminated the danger of a nuclear war, and, consequently, the "Soviet Union and its allies will adopt all necessary measures to strengthen their defense capability, safeguard international security and thwart any and every intrigue by the enemies of peace."[34] The point stressed is that those responsible for Soviet defense cannot fail to take into account that "the aggressive forces of imperialism have not laid down their arms and evidently will not do so for a long time," and that various "adventurists" exist who are "capable of kindling a new war."

> Questions of the theory and practice of military building have been and remain a subject for the closest attention. Our military theoretical thought does not cease to develop the fundamental problems of Marxist-Leninist teaching on war and the army, including the problem of war, as a continuation of politics by different, violent means. This problem has always been one of the most acute. It acquired still greater acuteness in connection with the appearance of nuclear weapons. The military theorists and publicists are now returning to it. Many of them connect their interpretation of this problem with the relaxation of tension and the Soviet-U.S. agreement on preventing nuclear war. . . .
> It contains the countries' pledge to act so as to exclude the outbreak of a nuclear conflict between them and also between each of the sides and other countries. But this agreement still does not signify the end of nuclear weapons. Nor has the problem of the nuclear disarmament of all states possessing nuclear weapons—the USSR, the United States, the PRC, France, and Britain—yet been resolved. And our military theoretical thought believes that until this complex, difficult problem is resolved and as long as the aggressive forces of imperialism and various sorts of adventurists continue to exist, the need for readiness to wage war with the use of any means of armed struggle will remain.[35]

As a practical matter, Soviet military spokesmen have essentially ignored the Moscow Arms Limitation Agreements and Washington declarations on preventing nuclear war in their discussions of future requirements of the Soviet Armed Forces. Instead, they have continued to hammer away at the long-standard basic line of the Soviet leadership which has been affirmed and reaffirmed at all CPSU Congresses and by all other major policy pronouncements, i.e., the necessity for a continuing strengthening of the Soviet defense capability. In particular, commentators, including many not of the military, have persisted in citing Brezhnev's statement at the 24th CPSU Congress:

> Everything, comrades, that is created by the people must be reliably protected. To strengthen the Soviet state means to strengthen its armed forces, to increase the defense capability of our

---

[34]Sviatov, *Krasnaia Zvezda*, July 28, 1972. See also, O. Grinev and V. Pavlov, "An Important Step Toward Curbing the Arms Race," *Pravda*, June 22, 1972.

[35]Sidel'nikov, *Krasnaia Zvezda*, August 14, 1973.

country by every means. While we are living in a restless world this is one of the most important tasks. . . .

Fulfilling the will of the people, the Communist Party is constantly concerned with strengthening the country's defenses.[36]

Furthermore, the military has argued that "the constant strengthening of our army is a vital necessity, an objective, law-governed pattern for the successful building of socialism and communism. It ensues from the nature of modern social development and the specific features of the class struggle between capitalism and socialism."[37]

At the Moscow Summit Meeting, Brezhnev, according to Nixon, "made it absolutely clear" the USSR was "going forward with defense programs in the offensive area" which were not limited by the SALT Agreements.[38] And immediately after the Summit, military spokesmen intensified their campaign relative to the Soviet need for increased military strength. Thus Grechko, in an address on July 11, 1972 to graduates of Soviet military academies said,

Imperialism constantly carries within it a threat of war, and the surest way to prevent it, the most effective way of bridling the aggressors, is to strengthen our defensive might in every way.[39]

Chiefs of the several Soviet military services quickly began to echo Grechko's arguments.

The subsequent progression and outcome of this campaign is significant for assessing Soviet post-Summit policies. Grechko followed up his speech with an article in the October 1972 issue of the leading Party journal *Kommunist*[40] where he expanded the same line, and again repeated it in his address from the top of Lenin's mausoleum at the November 7, 1972 parade in the Red Square.[41] The latter speech was made in the presence of the entire Politburo and doubtless after its prior review and approval. Further evidence of leadership support was indicated by the keynote Anniversary of the Revolution speech by Politburo Member K. T. Mazurov on November 6, 1972, in which he warned of the continued aggressive intentions of the "imperialists," and said that

All this obliges us to display great vigilance to strengthen the Soviet Armed Forces, which stand firmly in defense of the gains of Great October and the security of the socialist homeland.[42]

---

[36]*Pravda*, March 31, 1971.

[37]Army General A. Yepishev, "The Historical Mission of the Socialist State's Army, *Kommunist*, No. 7, May 1972, p. 64.

[38]"President Nixon and Dr. Kissinger Brief Members of Congress on Strategic Arms Limitation Agreements, June 15, 1972," U.S. Department of State, *Bulletin No. 1724, July 10, 1972, p. 39. The President in reporting this position on the part of Brezhnev gave special emphasis to its import, introducing his remarks with the words, "I owe it to you and to the nation to say . . ."*

[39]*Krasnaia Zvezda*, July 12, 1972.

[40]Grechko, "Military Collaboration Among the Socialist States' Armies," *Kommunist*, No. 15, October 1972, p. 37.

[41]*Krasnaia Zvezda*, November 9, 1972; *Pravda*, November 8, 1972.

[42]*Pravda*, November 7, 1972.

In December 1972, the Chief of the General Staff and First Deputy Minister of Defense, Army General Kulikov, wrote in the CPSU journal *Party Life:*

> . . . our people have to reckon with the fact that as long as imperialism exists the danger of aggressive wars will remain. Although they have developed peaceful building on a large scale, they thus continue to regard the defense of the socialist Motherland and the raising of the might of the armed forces as their sacred duty.[43]

In February 1973, Kulikov came back to the theme in an article in *Kommunist:*

> Proceeding from Lenin's instructions that the existence of the socialist state in the face of world capitalism cannot be protected without strong national defense and a strong military organization, the CPSU has always regarded the task of strengthening the country's defense capability as one of the most important tasks in its acitvity. Priority attention is also devoted to its resolution under present-day conditions. . . . The reinforcement of the armed forces is combined with a system of collective measures to strengthen the defensive might of all the countries of the socialist community within the framework of the Warsaw Pact Organization.[44]

Also in February 1973, Army General Yepishev wrote about "the constant strengthening of our army" as being an "objective necessity" for the further development of Soviet society and the "building" of communism.[45] And in March Kulikov again repeated his call for the "further consolidation of the might of the armed forces," and warned that "any complacency or passive attitude toward the improvement of our military organization would consign to oblivion Lenin's behest on the defense of the socialist Motherland."[46]

Further evidence that the campaign by the military had the approval of the leadership as a whole came in March 1973 in the form of a Central Committee message signed by Brezhnev to the Fifth Conference of Armed Forces Secretaries of Party Organizations. The message made no specific reference to peaceful coexistence or to any of the agreements signed in Moscow in May, nor did it acknowledge the existence of a balance of deterrence, the existence of parity in strategic forces or the fear of capitalist nations of being destroyed in a nuclear war with the Soviet Union. Instead, as noted above, it asserted that as long as imperialism exists, the danger of aggressive wars will remain. Therefore, the all-round strengthening of the defense capability of the country of the Soviets and of the combat might of its armed forces always has been and will remain the sacred duty of our party, of the Soviet government and people.[47]

[43]Kulikov, *Partiinaia Zhizn'*, No. 24, December 1972, p. 39.
[44]Kulikov, *Kommunist*, No. 3, February 1973, p. 77.
[45]*Komsomol'skaia Pravda*, February 23, 1973.
[46]*Kommunist Vooruzhennykh Sil*, No. 6, 1973, p. 14.
[47]*Pravda*, March 28, 1973.

Subsequently this line was repeatedly reaffirmed by the military quoting either the Central Committee message or Grechko's speech at the same conference at which he too had asked for a further buildup of Soviet military might and had called for increasing vigilance by the Armed Forces "so that no devices of the enemy can rake us unawares."[48]

Thus, in his Order of the Day on the 1973 anniversary of V-E Day, Grechko stated that the Soviet people "are readily devoting their labor and knowledge to the cause of further strengthening the country's economic and defense might. The Communist Party and the Soviet Government are tirelessly taking pains to ensure that our armed forces have at their disposal everything necessary to reliably defend the socialist Motherland."[49] Also in May the Commander of the Warsaw Pact Joint Armed Forces, Marshal of the Soviet Union I. Iakubovskii, wrote that "the Communist and Workers' parties and governments of our countries constantly pay great attention to the comprehensive improvements of the organs of the defensive Warsaw Pact Organization."[50] Grechko, in turn, in the May 1973 issue of *Kommunist,* quoted Brezhnev's call for a further military buildup at the 24th CPSU Congress and added that "the building in the USSR of a developed socialist society signified the entry of our armed forces into an important new stage of their further development. ... The party displays tireless concern for strengthening the economic and defense capability of the country."[51] One should also note the joint resolution of the Politburo and government on Brezhnev's visit to the US, which ended with the following sentence: "The Soviet people by their selfless labor increase the power and might of the socialist Motherland and thus consolidate the foundation for durable peace and security of the peoples."[52]

Although Moscow claimed to see further evidence of the consolidation of detente and of the declining threat of a nuclear war as a result of the June 1973 Washington Summit meeting, this was followed, as was discussed above, by frequent warnings by Soviet leaders of the possibility of a reversal in US policies and that the danger of war while diminished still persists. These arguments in turn were used to justify the need for the continuing strengthening of Soviet military might. Thus, a major article in *Red Star* of August 14, 1973 repeated the line that "as long as the aggressive, reactionary forces of imperialism and various adventurists capable of kindling a new

---

[48]*Krasnaia Zvezda*, March 28, 1973.
[49]*Krasnaia Zvezda*, May 9, 1973.
[50]I. Iakubovskii, "An Alliance for Peace and Security of the Peoples," *Krasnaia Zvezda*, May 13, 1973.
[51]*Kommunist*, No. 7, May 1973, p. 14.
[52]*Pravda*, June 30, 1973.

military conflagration exist on earth, the all-round consolidation of the combat might and combat readiness of the USSR Armed Forces will make up one of our most important tasks."[53] Similarly, another article also published in August argued that the "forces of reaction and war" seek to "revive the notorious 'position of strength' policy":

> This is why the Soviet Union is forced to take all possible steps to increase its defense capacity and to improve its economic base.[54]

An editorial in *Red Star* on the occasion of the USSR Air Force Day in August noted the persistence of forces in the West opposed to detente and allegedly "in favor of the stepping up of war preparations and the escalation of military budgets," and concluded that "under these conditions the party teaches us to continue to be vigilant and strengthen the Soviet state's defense might and its armed forces' combat readiness."[55]

Military spokesmen were not the only ones to speak of the need for a further strengthening of Soviet military power. Thus, Politburo Member D. A. Kunayev declared in a speech in September that "we must not build illusions" and "forget that those forces hostile to us have not given up their intentions."

> This is why now, more than ever before, it is important to increase vigilance everywhere and with selfless and tireless labor strengthen the economic and defense might of our country.[56]

Speaking in Sofia on September 19, 1973, Brezhnev referred to the joint Soviet-Bulgarian efforts aimed at "raising the defense activities of our countries."[57]

In response to Chinese criticism which questioned the sincerity of the Soviet detente policy in view of the "constant strengthening of its armed forces," a broadcast by Radio Moscow asserted that "scientifically speaking, it is wrong to try to set the policy for peaceful coexistence between countries with different social systems against the necessity for the socialist countries to strengthen their national defense," on the ground that "imperialism" remains aggressive by nature and that Soviet might is needed to force the US to accept and abide by the detente.[58]

As on other such occasions, the Anniversary of the October Revolution on November 7 was used by various spokesmen to refer to the need for growing

---

[53]Sidel'nikov, *Krasnaia Zvezda*, August 14, 1973.

[54]Bartenev, *Soviet Military Review*, No. 8, August 1973, p. 2.

[55]Editorial, "The Motherland's Mighty Wings," *Krasnaia Zvezda*, August 19, 1973.

[56]D. A. Kunayev, cited in *Kazakhstanskaia Pravda* (Kazakh Pravda), September 8, 1973. [Emphasis added.] See also his speech on August 15, 1973, Radio Moscow, August 15, 1973.

[57]*Pravda*, September 20, 1973.

[58]Radio Moscow, September 10, 1973. See also, Captain 1st Rank N. Shumikhin, "Socialism and International Relations," *Krasnaia Zvezda*, September 13, 1973.

Soviet military strength. Thus, among the list of slogans prepared by the CPSU Central Committee for the November 1973 Anniversary of the Revolution, the fifth (out of a total of 61) stated:

Working people of the Soviet Union! Struggle actively for the implementation of the decisions of the 24th CPSU Congress, for the further strengthening of our Motherland's economic and defense might.[59]

On November 7, *Pravda* carried Grechko's Order of the Day to the Soviet Armed Forces in which he asserted that because "the imperialist circles continue their dangerous intrigues" and hinder detente, "the CPSU and the Soviet Government pay constant attention to the consolidation of the economic and defense might of our Motherland."[60] Grechko also used this theme in his address in Red Square during the November 7 military review,[61] and the line was echoed by other military leaders in their speeches on that day in various parts of the country.

During November, Shcherbitskii, in a speech in Kiev, said that "our supreme international and class duty lies in steadily strengthening the economic and defense potential of our country."[62] At the same time, a military spokesman again used the argument that the successes of the Soviet peace policy were the "result of the growing economic and defensive might of the Soviet Union and the entire socialist bloc," but because of the resistance of reactionary circles to relaxation of tension "the stronger the Soviet Union becomes from an economic and defense standpoint, the more reliable will be the defense" of the Soviet Union and of world peace.[63] This was followed by an editorial in *Red Star* which said that "a most important condition of this development [i.e., Soviet social and economic development] has always been and still is the strengthening of the country's defense capability."[64]

The New Year opened with a televised broadcast by Brezhnev to the Soviet people in which he said that "as the might of socialism is strengthening from year to year" Soviet world influence and the prospects for peace were gaining, and he went on to assert,

It goes without saying that in the future, too, we will have to take care of strengthening our country's defense, the security of the entire socialist community by acting in concert with the fraternal countries.[65]

[59]*Pravda*, October 14, 1973.
[60]*Pravda*, November 7, 1973.
[61]Radio Moscow, November 7, 1973.
[62]*Pravda Ukrainy*, November 20, 1973.
[63]Lieutenant Colonel A. Gromakov, "Scientific-Technical Revolution and the Soviet Armed Forces," *Sovetskii Patriot* (Soviet Patriot), November 21, 1973.
[64]Editorial, "The People's Power," *Krasnaia Zvezda*, December 5, 1973.
[65]*Pravda*, January 1, 1974.

Brezhnev also referred to the "heroic working class, whose skillful hands and high technical qualifications keep the powerful Soviet industry going—the basis of the fast-growing economic and military might of the country."[66] In his speech in Havana on January 30, 1974, Brezhnev again mentioned the further growth of Soviet military power by saying that "the Soviet Union's defense continues to strengthen on the basis of the general growth of the country's economic might. Our Party and our state see to it that the Soviet Army has everything necessary for a reliable defense of what has been created by the people."[67]

In the course of January and February, Soviet military spokesmen were also actively advocating the need for further strengthening of the armed forces. Thus, Grechko in a major speech in Kazan on the occasion of presenting the Tatar ASSR with the Order of the Friendship of the People, stressed that the Soviet Union does not rely "on the peace aspirations of the imperialists but on the real correlation of forces," and called for an open-ended strengthening of the "combat capability" of the armed forces and for "mightier" arms as the best guarantee of peace.[68] He followed this with a speech in Minsk on January 29 to a party conference of the Belorussian Military District during which, according to a Soviet report, he said that "we must proceed from the premise that, despite the thaw in the political climate in the world, efforts to strengthen the country's defense capability cannot be relaxed," and that the CPSU Central Committee demands that "we must still further strengthen the country's defense capability and raise the combat might of the army and navy so that lovers of military adventures are constantly aware that we are always on the alert."[69] A number of articles in *Red Star* and speeches by other Soviet military leaders echoed these views. So did a number of top political leaders. For example, Shcherbitskii in a speech on February 16 said that "the most important international duty" of the CPSU and the Soviet people was "to constantly foster our economic and defense potential,"[70] while Politburo Member Kunayev warned on February 18 that "international reaction" is becoming more aggressive and teacherous while China is pursuing a course "for the complete militarization of the country," and concluded: "This is why it is particularly important for our forces to maintain high vigilance and strengthen with all our might the economic and defense potential of our beloved Motherland.[71]

[66]*Ibid.*
[67]*Pravda*, January 31, 1974.
[68]Radio Moscow, January 8, 1974; *Komsomolets Tatarii*, January 9, 1974.
[69]Major General M. Loshchits and Colonel V. Trikhmanenko, "To Look Ahead, to Work with Perspective," *Krasnaia Zvezda*, January 30, 1974.
[70]Radio Kiev, February 19, 1974.
[71]*Kazakhstanskaia Pravda*, February 19, 1974.

The need for further military strength was a major theme in the celebration of the anniversary of the Soviet Armed Forces in February 1974. Grechko's Order of the Day on that occasion called on the Soviet people to "tirelessly strengthen the defense of the country and the combat capacity of the armed forces."[72] In his article in *Pravda* on February 23, Grechko spoke of the "unflagging concern" of the CPSU and the Soviet government for "the further strengthening of the country's defense capability and the raising of the Army's and Navy's combat might" and said that the armed forces were "mastering the science of victory."[73] Grechko's points were repeated in numerous speeches and articles by other military leaders. It should be noted that in their stress on added military strength Soviet military spokesmen have cited various statements by Brezhnev warning of the adverse activities by "imperialist" circles and their resistance to detente and disarmament. Soviet pronouncements along these lines continued after and independently of the celebration of Armed Forces Day. For example, Grechko, in a speech on March 13, said:

> As a whole the conditions of the contemporary international situation require that Soviet people maintain their high vigilance, that the defense capability of the Soviet state be tirelessly increased, and that the armed forces be strengthened. In this our party sees one of its main tasks.[74]

Two days later, Brezhnev, speaking in Alma Ata, underscored that "Soviet international achievements" are not only the result of efforts by statesmen and diplomats, but that in the "final analysis" these successes are due, among other factors, to Soviet "defense potential."[75] In the light of his warning in the same speech that there still is opposition to detente in the West and that "imperialist forces" strive to take the "counteroffensive," he appeared implicitly to endorse Grechko's argument that more military strength is needed to force the "imperialists" to abide by the principles of "peaceful coexistence."

The calls for additional strengthening of the Soviet military capability are to some extent at variance with the Soviet assessment of the present direction of US policy in relation to the Soviet Union, and especially of the Nixon Administration's commitment to detente. The arguments advanced by Soviet spokesmen to justify the need for more defense are generally quite vague, referring as they do to elements of the "US ruling circles" or to the military-industrial complex, which are said to still seek to promote the arms race and to find a way to use military power in support of US policies.

---

[72]*Krasnaia Zvezda*, February 23, 1974.
[73]*Pravda*, February 23, 1974.
[74]*Krasnaia Zvezda*, March 14, 1974.
[75]*Pravda*, March 16, 1974.

Specific evidence of the activities of these "reactionary," "militaristic" or "Zionist" circles is usually cited to include the demands by some US political leaders for a free flow of peoples and ideas between the countries, which Moscow denounces as an effort at subverting the Soviet system, the resistance in Congress to granting the Soviet Union a most-favored-nation status, such "aggressive" activities as the overthrow of the Allende regime in Chile and the "Israeli aggression" in October 1973 against Egypt and Syria, as well as the increases in the US defense budget.

It appears, therefore, that Soviet official calls for the further strengthening of Soviet military capability, which have persisted all along since the May 1972 Summit meeting, are not reactions to US defense activities or to any indications of growing hostility on the part of the US. Furthermore, it would appear that a major, if not the main, objective of Soviet criticism of US activities is not so much to justify the Soviet defense program, since this can always be done on the basis of the alleged immutable aggressive nature of "imperialism" and of the need for strength to assure the success of the Soviet peace policy, as to generate pressure on the US for unilateral restraint in making any improvements in the US defense posture. Fundamentally, the Soviet argument for greater military strength appears to be simply that "our military power has brought us this far, more power will bring us even further."

It should be noted that unlike the 1969-1970 period, public calls for greater military strength make only vague references to a Chinese threat to justify further Soviet defense requirements. Instead, the arguments presented are primarily in terms of the persistent threat of "imperialist" aggression, the need to prevent the West from backsliding to a policy of "position of strength" in dealing with the Soviet Union, and the latter's need to protect the national liberation movements and the "progressive" regimes in various Third World countries from US intervention. However, China is increasingly identified as an ally of the most reactionary "imperialist" forces, as virulently anti-Soviet and is accused of making war preparations and of advancing territorial demands on the Soviet Union. No doubt the Soviet leaders are very conscious of and concerned over the potential Chinese threat and the possibility of having to wage a war on two fronts, as well as the advantages the US may derive for its power position in the event of a Sino-Soviet war. It is uncertain, however, to what extent the requirement to deter and, if necessary, to fight a China increasingly armed with nuclear weapons and missiles affects the overall Soviet drive for the further build-up of its military capability and specifically, its strategic missile force. Obviously, from the Soviet point of view, it is still the US which potentially poses the greatest military threat to the Soviet Union, while China, even though it is becoming militarily more powerful, would not pose the same security problem for Moscow if US power could be reduced or neutralized and China was once again isolated.

VIEWS AS TO HOW MUCH FURTHER SOVIET DEFENSE SHOULD BE STRENGTHENED

A frequently propounded Soviet position is that the "constant strengthening of the armed forces is an objective necessity for the successful construction of socialism and communism." According to Soviet sources, the "further" strengthening of Soviet military capabilities includes improvement in existing weapons systems and the development of new weapons, increased combat readiness of the armed forces and especially of the Strategic Missile Forces, better command and control, the further development of strategic and tactical doctrines, and the psychological-political preparation of the Soviet military and of the civilian population for war. Soviet public sources, however, are seldom specific about the precise nature of these improvements or the characteristic of new weapons systems, and in fact either do not announce the existence of new weapons or do so only belatedly, usually after the West has become aware of their existence from other sources.

According to the Soviet view, a reliable defense "is unthinkable without the constant strengthening, renewal and improvement of the material foundation of military might of a state and its armed forces."[76] Numerous Soviet spokesmen, both military and civilian, have pointed out that the scientific-technological revolution in military affairs gives rise to rapid obsolescence of weapons systems and, consequently, generates a constant need to improve existing weapons and develop new ones. Soviet sensitivity to this question was reflected in Brezhnev's speech at the end of the "Dvina" maneuvers in 1970 when he urged Soviet scientists to push relentlessly the development of new weapons and equipment and not to fall behind similar developments in the West.[77] Furthermore, as has been noted, the strengthening of Soviet military capability is closely coupled with the growth of the relationship of economic growth to military power which was emphasized at the 24th CPSU Congress, as for example in the assertion that the new Five-Year Plan being launched by decision of Congress would provide the Soviet Armed Forces with "even mightier equipment and other improved means of armaments."[78] In his speech at the Congress, Premier Kosygin asserted that "the new

---

[76]Colonel S. Baranov, "The Material Foundation of the Might of the USSR's Armed Forces," *Krasnaia Zvezda*, March 5, 1971.

[77]Riabov, *Dvina*, p. 6.

[78]Editorial, "The 24th Party Congress on the Further Strengthening of the Country's Defense Capability and Raising the Combat Readiness of the Soviet Armed Forces," *Kommunist Vooruzhennykh Sil*, No. 10, May 1971, p. 75.

five-year plan will ensure the further strengthening of the defensive power of our state,"[79] and a commentary on his speech stated that

> The contemporary international situation and the interests of the security of our Fatherland, as comrade A. N. Kosygin said at the 24th Congress of the CPSU, require us, on the basis of the latest achievements of science and technology, to develop and organize the production of many new types of modern armaments, in order to improve the combat and technical qualities of weapons.[80]

At the same time, Soviet military publications underscored also the role of science and technology for improving Soviet defense capabilities.

> The acceleration of scientific progress is directly attributed to the defense industry, scientific workers, scientific institutions and the Armed Forces, which uninterruptedly are supplied with first class weapons and combat equipment. The Communist Party . . . constantly sees to it that the country's achievements in the area of economy and culture are combined with strengthening the defense might of the Soviet state and increasing its defense capacity. The present party program, moreover, will serve the interests of increasing the welfare of the people, strengthen defense and the development of the Soviet Armed Forces.[81]

Thus, an important feature of the current Soviet Five-Year Plan was said to be the further strengthening of Soviet military might "by all possible means."[82]

Following the Moscow Summit and the SALT Agreements, it was quickly emphasized that in the strategic weapons field the search for improvements could continue within the framework of the agreements, both in the way of qualitatively improving existing systems as well as in the direction of developing new weapons. The influential Director of the Institute of World Economics and International Relations of the USSR Academy of Sciences, Academician N. N. Inozemtsev, is reported to have predicted at a conference held in October 1972 in Bulgaria that "there will be a subsequent improvement of the armed forces and arms, particularly in qualitative respects," but he added that he expected these improvements to occur" on the general basis of a balance between the military forces of the states of the two systems, primarily the USSR and the US."[83] An important article in the December issue of the journal *USA: Economics, Politics, Ideology* pointed out that the 1972 SALT Agreement "did not close such paths for the qualitative improvement of strategic offensive weapons as, for example, increasing the

---

[79]*Pravda*, April 7, 1971.

[80]Colonel V. Kozlov and Captain 1st Rank A. Skryl'nik, "One of the Most Important Tasks of the Party and the People," *Kommunist Vooruzhennykh Sil*, No. 13, July 1971, p. 13.

[81]Editorial, "Decisions of the Twenty-Fourth Party Congress—In Practice," *Kommunist Vooruzhennykh Sil*, No. 10, May 1971, p. 8.

[82]For example, see Colonel V. Bondarenko, "Scientific Potential and the Defense of the Country," *Krasnaia Zvezda*, August 20, 1971.

[83]*Le Monde*, November 18, 1972.

accuracy of the multiple warheads of missiles, their reliability, invulnerability, and so forth, as well as the creation of new systems."[84]

The need to constantly improve missiles was emphasized in 1969 by the Chief of the Strategic Missile Forces, Marshal of the Soviet Union, N. I. Krylov, who warned that "military affairs do not tolerate stagnation" and that "consequently, missile weaponry will continue to improve steadily in the future."[85] After the Moscow Summit, a prominent military theoretician and spokesman, Lieutenant General I. Zavialov, wrote that "military science must look ahead and, in accordance with this, develop design targets for the creation of promising new combat equipment and weapons."[86] Subsequently, Army General Pavlovskii, a USSR Deputy Defense Minister and Commander of the Ground Forces, asserted that

> The leading heavy industry sectors should constantly ensure the rapid modernization of equipment and create fundamentally new weapons, which demands the constant improvement and expansion of scientific research and experimental design work.[87]

Again, in March and April 1973, Kulikov came back to this theme in two articles stressing the need for further improvements in Soviet armaments. According to him:

> The Communist Party is not only concerned about having a sufficient quantity of weapons, but also about replacing them in good time and not letting them become obsolete. Obviously, the fulfillment of these tasks is inconceivable without a developed industry and without the use of the latest achievements of science and technology.[88]

Kulikov was even more explicit in his second article, where he wrote that

> In order to ensure the reliable defense of the state, all branches of the armed forces and all types of weapons are being developed, taking into account the role that they will be called upon to play in a future war, with maximum attention being devoted primarily to improving active combat weapons.[89]

Speaking of the anti-air defense of the Soviet Union, Kulikov went on to assert that

> With regard to the status and potential of airborne attack weapons, it appears that today the trend is towards carrying out qualitative improvements on a new technical basis. . . . In order to ensure the effective struggle against an enemy's future weapons of airborne

---

[84]M. A. Mil'shteyn and L. S. Semeiko, "The Limitation of Strategic Arms: Problems and Prospects," *SShA: Ekonomika, Politika, Ideologiia*, No. 21, December 1973, p. 4.

[85]*Sovetskaia Litva* (Soviet Lithuania), November 19, 1969.

[86]*Krasnaia Zvezda*, August 3, 1972.

[87]*Planovoye Khoziaistvo*, No. 2, February 1973.

[88]*Kommunist Vooruzhennykh Sil*, No. 6, March 1973, p. 14.

[89]V. Kulikov, "Air Defense in the System for Protecting the Soviet State," *Vestnik Protivovozdushnoi Oborony*, No. 4, April 1973.

attack, further improvements must be carried out in one's weapons and equipments, new tacitcal methods must be mastered and, most important—improvements must be carried out in the training of the personnel.[90]

Of possible particular significance was his statement on the strategic importance of the anti-air defense system in ensuring the defense of the Soviet Union:

> Deployed and used for this purpose, the PVO Forces of the country must warn the country and the armed forces of an airborne or nuclear missile attack, it must inflict maximum damage upon an airborne enemy and it must prevent the enemy from carrying out strikes against important installations or military and naval forces.[91]

It is unclear, and perhaps deliberately so, whether Kulikov was suggesting the need for an ABM capability in order to "prevent" nuclear missile strikes against "important installations" or military forces. One may note, however, that in June 1973 Marshal of Aviation Ye. Ia. Savitskii, a Deputy Commander-in-Chief of the Air Defense Forces (PVO), wrote:

> The countries of the aggressive NATO bloc are perfecting their means of air-space attack, various types of missiles and missile-carrying aircraft, as well as an atomic submarine fleet, that is, the means of aggression which will permit the launching of attacks from the air on economic and administrative centers, as well as military targets.
>
> This is why the Party and the Government are obliged to devote unflagging attention to the further strengthening of the defenses of our country and its population from attacks from the air.[92]

Again, in November 1973 a Soviet broadcast to China made the ambiguous statement that the "long-range artillery and anti-aircraft rocket troops" shown at the November 7, 1973 military review in Moscow can, "together with other units, successfully accomplish their primary mission to protect the socialist countries from attacks by aggressors armed with conventional and space weapons."[93]

An article published in November 1973 noted that "combat improvements are being carried out in the missile equipment" but also pointed out that the Soviet Union was "striving to improve, strengthen and develop in every possible way all branches of the Armed Forces and all arms and services."[94] A Deputy Minister of Defense of the USSR, Engineer Colonel General N. Alekseyev, pointed out in February 1974 that

---

[90]*Ibid.*, p. 5.

[91]*Ibid.*, p. 4.

[92]Marshal of Aviation Ye. Ia. Savitskii, "Sentries of the Homeland's Skies," *Sovetskii Patriot*, June 17, 1973.

[93]Lavrov commentary, "The Soviet Armed Forces Are a Strong Fortress of Socialism," Radio Moscow, November 8, 1973.

[94]Gromakov, *Sovetskii Patriot*, November 21, 1973.

The Strategic Missile Forces, which are equipped with automated missile complexes, have been further developed in recent years. The branch of the forces with the largest numerical strength and the most diverse hardware—the Ground Forces—is also being constantly improved. Their saturation with every possible combat equipment and their high degree of motorization and mechanization enable the Ground Forces to resolve an exceptionally broad spectrum of missions under conditions of modern warfare. The Air Defense Forces and Air Force have acquired new combat qualities. The Navy today has awesome combat might. . . . The potential of various types of surface ships and missile-carrying naval aircraft has considerably increased.[95]

Other directions of improvements in Soviet defense capability were indicated in recent Soviet articles. For example, one of June 1973 stressed that

Before Soviet military science stand complex and responsible tasks, flowing from the decisions of the 24th Party Congress. At the center of attention is the development of effective ways and means of further raising the combat readiness of the Soviet Armed Forces for the decisive defeat of any aggressor. Therefore, it is important to continue to study the character and means of initiation and conduct of war by the most likely enemies. A responsible task consists in continuing to further develop new methods for conducting an armed struggle, taking into account the prospects for the development of military technology and armaments.[96]

Another article published in April discussed specifics as to the direction that these further developments should take:

Naturally, the level of military might achieved by the state cannot remain static. The armed forces continue to be further developed in conformity with the international climate and in keeping with scientific-technical progress. In the future this development will follow certain definite trends. The Strategic Missile Forces will be developed more from a quality standpoint, with improvements being carried out in their organization structure, control systems and equipment and in personnel combat readiness. In the Ground Forces, maximum attention will be devoted to improving missile flight ranges and accuracy. The Air Force is being developed along the lines of furnishing the aircraft with greater potential for destroying ground, sea and air targets and with increased speeds, ranges and altitudes. Similar improvements are taking place in all of the other branches and arms of service.[97]

According to Chief Marshal of Aviation P. S. Kutakhov, Commander-in-Chief of the Air Force:

. . . the Air Force units are being supplied with increasingly improved aviation equipment, arms and the most up-to-date flight control and support facilities embodying the highest achievements of

---

[95]Colonel General N. Alekseyev, "The Motherland's Mighty Guard," *Sotsialisticheskaia Industriia* (Socialist Industry), February 23, 1974.

[96]Lieutenant General G. Zavizion, "Concerning the Subject of Soviet Military Science," *Kommunist Vooruzhennykh Sil*, No. 12, June 1973, p. 32.

[97]Captain 1st Rank N. Shumikhin, "The Triumph of Leninist Doctrine Concerning Defense of the Homeland," *Kryl'ia Rodiny* (Wings of the Motherland), No. 4, April 1973, p. 2.

Soviet science and industry. . . . The speed, altitude and range of combat aircraft is increasing yearly.[98]

Thus, Grechko said in his November 7, 1973 speech in Moscow's Red Square, "the men of the armed forces are persistently mastering new weapons and equipment,"[99] First Deputy Minister of Defense, General of the Army S. L. Sokolov, wrote in February 1974 that the Soviet Armed Forces "embarked on a new stage of their development, . . . are constantly being furnished with the most up-to-date weapons and combat equipment" and that "this makes it possible to unswervingly raise their mobility, strikepower and firepower."[100]

An important element of current Soviet efforts to strengthen military capabilities is said to be improvements in the combat readiness of the Soviet armed forces and in particular the reactions of the Strategic Missile Forces for instant action. It is important to note that calls for greater combat readiness not only have persisted since the Moscow and Washington Summits, but appear to have intensified, even while Soviet spokesmen assert that the danger of a nuclear war has diminished and that the US is less likely than before to initiate a "suicidal" attack on the Soviet Union. For example, General Kulikov wrote in March 1973 that "one of the most important demands which the party makes on the armed forces is their maintenance in a state of high combat readiness," because of the persistent threat of a US surprise attack.[101] Similarly, Grechko said in January 1974 that "our task is to continue to raise our combat readiness."[102] Again, on March 13, 1974, Grechko asserted that the CPSU "is doing everything necessary to steadily increase the combat readiness of the armed forces."[103] In conjunction with these efforts, Soviet spokesmen refer to the resolution of the April 1973 CPSU Central Committee Plenum which had emphasized the need for constant readiness of the armed forces to "repel all intrigues" by the "imperialists."

According to Soviet sources, improvements in "readiness" include better troop training and the "mastering" by military personnel of new weapons and equipment, the solution of the problems of command and control under conditions of a nuclear war, a heightened state of training and readiness of the

---

[98]Chief Marshal of Aviation P. S. Kutakhov, "The Fighters of the Winged Formation," *Pravda*, August 19, 1973.

[99]*Krasnaia Zvezda*, November 8, 1973.

[100]General of the Army S. L. Sokolov, "Always on Guard and in a State of Combat Readiness," *Krasnaia Zvezda*, February 23, 1974. See also, Colonel M. Belov, "New Factors in the Development of Modern Armies," *Soviet Military Review*, No. 2, February 1974, pp. 10-13.

[101]Kulikov, *Kommunist Vooruzhennykh Sil*, No. 6, March 1973, p. 15.

[102]*Komsomolets Tatarii*, January 9, 1974.

[103]*Krasnaia Zvezda*, March 14, 1974.

civil defense forces, as well as the development and assimilation of new tactics by the armed forces and more intensive moral-political education of the forces so as to imbue them with greater loyalty and will to victory. For example, Grechko said in March 1974,

> The high quality of combat training is one of the important criteria of the troops' combat readiness. This year the main emphasis is being put on the qualitative standard of all combat and political training measures carried out in the Army and Navy. The requirements of the times are that the armed forces should keep abreast of scientific and technical progress and that in their activities our commanders and political workers should base themselves on the leading achievements of military science and military art, nurture and use everything new and progressive engendered by military theory and practice, and constantly renew and build up their arsenal of tactical methods and effective forms and methods of training and educating personnel. . . . It is essential persistently to improve existing tactics and to develop new ones.[104]

Soviet publications also specifically warn that despite the detente in US-Soviet relations and negotiatoins on arms control, the West should not expect the Soviet Union to relax its defense efforts. And Politburo Member A. P. Kirilenko pointed out on October 5, 1973 that constant work to increase Soviet defense capability is needed in order to achieve a "consolidation of the positive changes which have occurred in the international situation."[105]

Although Soviet spokesmen publicly urge an agreement with the US to limit qualitative improvements in strategic weapons, to date there is no indication in open Soviet publications that the Soviet Union may slow down its military research and development programs or that it intends to cease its efforts to improve its strategic weapons systems and to develop new ones. Since the SALT I Agreement Moscow has gone ahead with the testing of new missiles and given evidence of its acquisition of a MIRV capability. Possibly this was done in order to strengthen the Soviet negotiatory position at SALT II. But if so, the Soviets took the risk of alarming the US by demonstrating that, in the words of Secretary Schlesinger, they "are seeking a strategic advantage."[106] It is possible that if the Soviet leaders believe the US administration to be committed to the improvement of US-Soviet relations as a matter of political necessity, they may also believe that there is little risk of a major adverse US reaction to the new Soviet weapons capabilities, all the more so as Moscow has not publicly acknowledged their existence.

A crucial question at this time concerns the objectives the Soviet Union is pursuing in the further improvement of its defense capability. At present the

---

[104]*Ibid*. See also, General Maltsev, *Krasnaia Zvezda*, February 14, 1974.

[105]*Zaria Vostoka* (Dawn of the East), October 6, 1973. See also, Sidel'nikov, *Krasnaia Zvezda*, August 14, 1973; Grechko's statement of January 29, 1974, as reported by Loshchits and Trikhmanenko, *Krasnaia Zvezda*, January 30, 1974.

[106]*The New York Times*, August 18, 1973.

issue of how much capability and of what sort Moscow is trying to achieve is a subject of controversy among Western analysts. Soviet leaders have made clear that they want to attain a capability which would preclude the US from dealing with them from an overall "position of strength." Also, they have made clear that they are unwilling to allow the US any advantages in bargaining on arms control issues on the basis of the development of new weapons systems, such as Trident.[107] Furthermore, in the course of arms control negotiations, Moscow has demanded numerical advantages on the basis of alleged existing asymmetries in relative US-Soviet strategic require-ments but has resisted making any concessions when asymmetries favor the United States. There is consequently, a definite suggestion that the Soviet Union wishes to achieve something more than "equal security" as against the US, all the more so, as Soviet spokesmen insist, because the Soviet Union requires a capability to defeat any aggressor. The question as to whether the Soviet Union is actually seeking clear cut superiority over the US both in strategic weapons and in overall war-fighting and war-winning capability is at yet by no means demonstrable. However evidence provided in open Soviet sources, while sometimes ambiguous, tends on the whole to indicate such a purpose.

Claims to Soviet military superiority or indications of a desire to attain superiority have frequently appeared in speeches and articles since the days of Khrushchev's missile bluff in the late 1950's and early 1960's.[108] For example, Kosygin stated categorically in a speech in June 1970: "The defensive might of the Soviet state must be invincible in the full sense of the word."[109] Again, Army General S. Sokolov, First Deputy Minister of De-fense of the USSR, wrote in February 1971:

> We are all witness to the way the CPSU Central Committee takes care that in terms of military and technical facilities, we have unquestionable superiority over the armies of the most powerful capitalist countries. . . .[110]

In his pamphlet *On Guard Over Peace and the Building of Communism,* published in 1971 after the 24th CPSU Congress, Defense Minister Grechko asserted that the Soviet Union was capable of countering any aggressor with "superior force,"[111] and other similar statements were made in conjunction with the Congress. For example, an article in *Red Star* of March 5, 1971

---

[107]Trofimenko, *Pravda*, June 4, 1973.
[108]See Kohler, *et al., Soviet Strategy for the Seventies: From Cold War to Peaceful Coexistence,* Monographs in International Affairs, Center for Advanced International Studies, University of Miami, Coral Gables, Fla., 1973, pp. 88-89.
[109]Radio Moscow, June 10, 1970.
[110]*Sovetskaia Rossiia*, February 23, 1971.
[111]Grechko, *Na Strazhe Mira i Stroitel'stva Kommunizma*, p. 106.

noted the US-Soviet competition "in the interest of victory in war, in the quantitative and qualitative production of the latest armaments" and asserted that "the struggle for superiority in forces requires constant strengthening of the material foundation of an army's combat might."[112] Another article argued that

> The dialectics of the development of world events are such that it is impossible to preserve the peace necessary for developing a new society and not set the superior military power of the socialist countries against the military machine of imperialism.[113]

At the time of the Moscow Summit an article in a military journal argued that "the military-technological policy of the CPSU is directed towards creating and maintaining military superiority of the socialist countries over the forces of war and aggression."[114] The same month another article in a military journal claimed that "our military-technical superiority, superiority over any potential enemy will be reliably assured" by the current Soviet Five-Year Plan.[115]

Soviet discussion of the military superiority issue became somewhat more muted after the Moscow Summit but has persisted nevertheless. For example, in July 1972 an article asserted that

> The Soviet Army now has sufficient quantities of the most modern technology and maintains superiority over the armies of imperialist states. The Communist Party pays particular attention to the further development of the Strategic Missile Forces, which form the main combat might of the Armed Forces; it is also concerned with improvements of other types of forces, equipping them with the newest technical means.[116]

A book with the title *The Philosophic Legacy of V. I. Lenin and Problems of Contemporary War,* which appeared in the course of 1972, claimed that "the Soviet people not only built its own nuclear weapons in a short order, but subsequently ensured its superiority over the imperialist states in missiles and nuclear power."[117] The author went on to assert that the Soviet system and the higher morale and dedication of the Soviet people and its soldiers also contributed to Soviet superiority over its likely enemies. The September 1972 issue of *Communist of the Armed Forces* carried an article which contended that

[112]Baranov, *Krasnaia Zvezda,* March 5, 1971.

[113]Koslov and Skryl'nik, *Kommunist Vooruzhennykh Sil,* No. 13, July 1971, p. 11.

[114]M. Gladko and B. Ivanov, "The Economic and Military Technological Policy," *Kommunist Vooruzhennykh Sil,* No. 9, May 1972, p. 12.

[115]Major General M. Cherednichenko, "Military-Technological Progress and Tactics," *Voennyi Vestnik,* No. 5, May 1972, p. 16.

[116]Colonel S. Baranov, "The Formation of the USSR and the Strengthening of the Military Capability of the Country," *Voennyi Vestnik,* No. 7, July 1972, p. 11.

[117]Karabanov, *et al., Filosofskoye Naslediye . . .,* p. 63.

For the purpose of retaining military-technical superiority over a probable enemy it is necessary constantly to watch for development of the natural sciences, to take into account the achievements of basic research, especially those which are at the stage of completion.[118]

Soon thereafter an article by Marshal Grechko appeared in the October issue of *Kommunist,* dealing with the question of military cooperation of the Warsaw Pact states, in which he claimed that

Military-technical cooperation furnishes appreciable mutually beneficial results. It is aimed at ensuring the military-technical superiority of the socialist states' armies over the armies of likely enemies. This demands the continuous modernization of arms and combat equipment, and the development of new and improved models.[119]

Again, in March 1973 Kulikov claimed superiority for some unspecified Soviet weapons and equipment, writing that

The Soviet Army and Navy have the requisite number of all modern means of warfare. In terms of their qualitative indicators the majority of them are not only equal to but in numbers of cases surpass the weapons and equipment used by the armies of the imperialist states.[120]

Other claims to Soviet superiority in the quality of strategic weapons have been frequently varied. For example, Grechko said in a speech in Warsaw on October 11, 1973, that the CPSU and the Soviet Government "are doing everything so that Soviet Armed Forces are in possession of the best modern weapons."[121] Colonel General P. Gorchakov, Chief of the Strategic Missile Forces Political Directorate, wrote in November 1973 that "the missile forces are now equipped with the world's most powerful nuclear weapons and the most sophisticated means of delivering them to their targets,"[122] while on February 22, 1974, he said in a broadcast that the Soviet Army and Navy "are being supplied with the most modern weapons and military equipment" and that "the most powerful strategic missile forces have been established in the Soviet Armed Forces."[123] Most noteworthy, however, was Grechko's statement on January 8, 1974, in which he urged an open-ended further strengthening of the Soviet armed forces, on the ground that the "greater" their combat capability and "the more powerfully they are equipped . . . the more peaceful it will be on earth."[124]

---

[118]Lieutenant General G. Zavizion and Lieutenant Colonel Yu. Kirshin, "Soviet Military Science: Social Role and Function," *Kommunist Vooruzhennykh Sil,* No. 17, September 1972, p. 15.

[119]*Kommunist,* No. 15, October 1972, p. 48. (Emphasis in original.)

[120]*Kommunist Vooruzhennykh Sil,* No. 6, March 1973, p. 18.

[121]Radio Warsaw, October 11, 1973.

[122]Colonel General P. Gorchakov, "True Sons of the Motherland," *Krasnaia Zvezda,* November 18, 1973.

[123]Radio Moscow, February 22, 1974.

[124]*Komsomolets Tatarii,* January 9, 1974.

It is interesting to note that in calling for greater military strength, Soviet spokesmen often assert at the same time that the Soviet Union has sufficient weapons to assure its security. For example, Grechko wrote in *Pravda* on February 23, 1974, that "our Army and Navy now have everything necessary to rout any aggressor."[125] Similarly, Colonel General Alekseyev wrote on February 23, 1974, that the "Soviet Armed Forces are equipped with a sufficient quantity of nuclear weapons, missiles with various ranges and purposes" as well as other weapons.[126] Again, General of the Army Pavlovskii said on February 23, 1974, that "the Soviet Armed Forces have now turned into a reliable guard for the achievements of socialism and the peace and security of peoples."[127] However, these as well as other spokesmen who have expressed similar claims always hasten to add that every effort must be made to further strengthen Soviet military power.

As against the call by various military elements for attaining superiority for the USSR over the US some Soviet commentators, principally civilians, have argued that for the US to seek superiority over the USSR would be both vain and foolhardy. Conceivably these arguments were also intended as cautions to the Soviet military, although nothing said either directly or indirectly suggested that the arguments were intended to cut in two directions. Thus, several articles published in the course of 1970 denigrated the realism of any US hope of gaining an advantage from a new spiral in the arms race and warned that such an attempt would be "destabilizing" or, to put it simply would result in "the threat of thermonuclear war is increasing."[128] More recently a book by V. M. Kulish, *Military Power and International Relations,* published in 1972 after the Moscow Summit, while claiming that the US "is placing great hope on excelling the USSR in the development of strategic weapons," warned that

> The appearance of new types of weapons could seriously affect the balance of military forces between the two world systems. The degree and forms of this influence on the competition taking place between both systems and on the international-political situation depends not so much upon the actual properties and peculiarities of the new strategic weapons as it does upon the social and political situation existing in the world and also upon the overall strategic balance of forces in the world, particularly between the US and the USSR. Far-reaching international consequences would arise in the event that one side possessed qualitatively new strategic weapons which would serve to neutralize the ability of the opposing side to carry out effective retaliatory action.[129]

[125]*Pravda*, February 23, 1974.

[126]*Sotsialisticheskaia Industriia*, February 23, 1974.

[127]Radio Moscow, February 23, 1974.

[128]Unsigned article, "Between Helsinki and Vienna," *SShA: Ekonomika, Politika, Ideologiia*, No. 1, January 1970, p. 60. See also, "Observer" article, "A Serious Problem," *Pravda*, March 7, 1970.

[129]V. M. Kulish, *Voennaia Sila i Mezhdunarodnye Otnosheniia*, Moscow, 1972, translated in JPRS, V. M. Kulish, *Military Power and International Relations*, May 8, 1973, pp. 173-174.

Moreover, even a "relatively small" and temporary superiority by the US over the Soviet Union would have a "destabilizing influence on the international-political situation throughout the entire world." Similarly, as was noted above, Arbatov in his February 1974 article argued that any US success in its efforts to develop "new ultramodern weapons systems," while unlikely to confer a "real or truly important advantage," would nevertheless have a "destabilizing effect."[130] He also appeared to be saying that nuclear stockpiles had reached a level of "over-kill" and he claimed that "the value of this accumulated might as a policy weapon is steadily diminishing," a view which was later disputed by military spokesmen.

The question of sufficiency versus superiority depends on the purpose which the Soviet leaders see in military might. Arbatov's article appeared to argue that the existing strategic balance is sufficient to deter the outbreak of a nuclear war, especially if it is accompanied by an agreement limiting qualitative improvements in strategic weapons and that both the US and the Soviet Union will pursue their competition by non-violent means. At the same time, however, the military view, as was seen, categorically asserted that mutual deterrence based on the concept of a balance of terror or "mutual assured destruction" is essentially unstable. Nevertheless, the thrust of his article appears out of consonance with the simplified argument of the Soviet military that as long as "imperialism" exists the Soviet Union must have a capability to fight and win a nuclear war and that ever increasing military power is also needed to allow the Soviet Union to attain its foreign policy objectives without war. Be that as it may, however, from the standpoint of what appears to be settled Soviet military doctrine "sufficiency" is only relative, not absolute. Furthermore, because it is believed that the Soviet Union must always be prepared for the worst, the general tendency in Soviet practice has been to deploy whatever military technology is available, even if it is imperfect, rather than postpone such deployments in anticipation of developing better weapons in the near future. Thus, great importance has been attributed to quantitative indicators of military capability even while it is expected to upgrade its quality as new weapons come into production.

The Soviet view of what constitutes superiority is ambiguous. Public statements claiming Soviet superiority have tended to emphasize qualitative indicators such as Soviet advantages in the size of missiles or nuclear warheads, the quality of aircraft, or anti-aircraft missiles, and so on. The possibility of gaining an advantage as a result of a secret breakthrough in weapons development which the opponent would not be able to quickly counter has also been stressed, albeit usually in reference to what the US is

---

[130]*World Marxist Review*, No. 2, February 1974, p. 61.

up to. Yet, there is no doubt that great importance is also attributed to quantitative superiority in weapons and forces, especially in discussions of war-fighting and of the factors determining the outcome of a nuclear war. Furthermore, Soviet statements dealing with the question of how to attain superiority include such elements as strategic surprise, the effectiveness of counterforce strikes, the capability of the country to survive a nuclear attack and maintain essential war production, and the state of the morale and political cohesion of the population and of the armed forces. As has been noted, some Soviet analysts, civilian and military, have criticized writers who have focused primarily on the quantitative indicators of military power for ignoring Soviet political-moral superiority over the capitalist states.

The problem for the Soviet leadership obviously is that while it evidently perceives definite advantages in attaining strategic superiority over the US, it must balance this against the risks of scuttling the detente in US-Soviet relations and of initiating a new arms race. The leaders have been clearly concerned about the danger of an unrestricted arms race with the US—a race which the Soviet Union might well lose—and consequently have been wrestling with the problem of how to continue the Soviet military buildup without provoking such a race. It is possible, therefore, that the Soviet Union will become even more secretive about its military R & D programs, tone down its claims to superiority and reduce the "visibility" of testing of new weapons.

To date there is no indication in open Soviet sources that the SALT agreements have altered Soviet views on the size of Soviet nuclear strategic forces, and recent Soviet weapons tests suggest that warnings by Kulish concerning the destabilizing influence of any attempt to alter the strategic balance between the US and USSR are, in fact, meant to apply only to US efforts in that direction. While there appears to be no conceptual limitation on the size of Soviet forces, the data indicate that the leadership is influenced, on the one hand by economic and technological considerations, and , on the other hand, by estimates of US (and Chinese) capabilities and reactions. Furthermore, the size and composition of Soviet forces are said to be influenced by the characteristics of new weapons developments, which in turn influence Soviet strategy and the requirements for a war-fighting and war-winning capability.

In this connection, it should be noted that some interest has been shown in the Soviet Union in US methodologies for relating optimal military postures and armaments mix to economic and budgetary constraints and capabilities. A book published in 1973 entitled *Economic Factors and Armaments*, intended for "officers, generals and admirals of the Soviet Army and Navy" and students at military academies, described, on the basis of US materials, methods of systems analysis for ensuring "maximally efficient use of the resources allocated for military needs," the "rational composition of forces" and the calculation of the best armament mixes for the execution of various military missions.[131] No doubt the Soviet Armed Forces are in fact struggling with problems of effective resource allocation, growing costs, manpower problems, the efficient integration of new weapons and equipment into the forces, and so on. To what extent this situation is apt to lead to any changes in existing Soviet military doctrine and practice remains as of now highly problematical.

---

[131] Solnyshkov, *Ekonomicheskie Faktory i Vooruzhennie*, P. 14.

V
SOVIET VIEWS ON THE EMPLOYMENT
OF NUCLEAR WEAPONS IN WAR

Soviet military doctrine is largely determined by Soviet military capabilities as well as by the leadership's perception of likely future wars and forms of their initiation. As a consequence, the doctrine is far more explicit on the employment of nuclear weapons for some types of wars than for others. Soviet military leaders, however, assert that their doctrine is dynamic and creative rather than static and that it takes into account new developments in weapons technology as well as the character of East-West relations and the existing balance of power. Consequently, significant future changes in the doctrine cannot be excluded.

THE BASIC SOVIET VIEW

The predominant characteristic of Soviet public discussion of war is its overriding concern with a general nuclear war, although attention is also paid to other types of wars. The basic features of the Soviet view have remained essentially unchanged for more than a decade. They are:[1]

a. A world war, "if the imperialists succeed in unleashing it" (or "in the event that the imperialists dare attack the Soviet Union and other states of the socialist commonwealth"), will be a "decisive" collision of two opposing social systems. The war would bear an unlimited character because the war aims of each side would be the "total defeat" or "destruction" of the other.

b. The war will "inevitably" be a nuclear war in which the "main and decisive means" of combat will be nuclear weapons and the "main means of delivery will be missiles." This will be the case for both strategic and theater operations.

c. Even under conditions of a nuclear war, the possibility is not excluded that conventional weapons may find "wide application," and that "under certain conditions combat operations by units and subunits may involve only conventional weapons." Furthermore, while nuclear weapons will play the decisive role, final victory can only be achieved as a result of joint actions by all branches and services of the armed forces.

---

[1] See H. F. Scott, *Soviet Military Doctrine*; Marshal of the Soviet Union I. Kh. Bagramian, *et al.*, *Istoriia Voin i Voennogo Iskusstva* (History of Wars and Military Art), Moscow, Voenizdat, 1970; pp. 489-490; Major General I.Ye. Krupchenko, *et al.*, *Voennaia Istoriia* (Military History), Moscow, Voenizdat, 1971, pp. 340-342; Lieutenant General I. Zavialov, *Krasnaia Zvezda*, April 19, 1973; Grechko, *Na Strazhe Mira i Stroitel'stva Kommunizma*, p. 55; Karabanov, *et al.*, pp. 48, 85-96; Colonel V. E. Savkin, *Osnovnye Printsipy Operativnogo Iskusstva i Taktiki* (Fundamental Principles of the Art of Strategy and Tactics), Moscow, Voenizdat, 1972, p. 368, and "Characteristics of Modern Battle," *Voennyi Vestnik*, No. 3, March 1974, pp. 24-28.

d. Although nuclear weapons allow the attainment of the political and strategic aims of the war in a short time, the possibility is not excluded that the war may become protracted, requiring "enormous straining of efforts and resources" on the part of the warring countries.

e. The war may begin with a surprise nuclear attack or as a result of escalation of a limited war. But the character of modern weapons makes a surprise nuclear attack more likely and dangerous and requires, therefore, that the Soviet Armed Forces be ready at all times to reliably "repulse" (or "frustrate") the attack and to inflict a "crushing" or "annihilating" blow on the enemy.

f. In its scope the war will be a coalition war and consequently assume a global character, involving most, if not all, nations of the world.

g. The future war will require multi-million armies which must be ready to fight both with nuclear weapons and with conventional weapons.

h. The "first rule" of war is: "The course and outcome of a war, conducted with unrestricted use of all means of combat, depend first of all on the balance of existing military forces of the warring sides at the outbreak of the war, especially of nuclear weapons and their means of delivery. From this law flow a number of important principles of operational art and tactics, including surprise, concentration of main efforts in the decisive location and at the decisive time, troop mobility, etc."[2]

i. Because of the destructiveness of a nuclear war, one should not expect to be able to wage it with only the weapons in being at its outbreak, but one must be prepared to produce additional weapons and equipment in the course of the war. Consequently, the protection of the population and of critical elements of the economy is of strategic significance for the course and victorious outcome of the war.

WAR INITIATION: SURPRISE, FIRST STRIKE, PREEMPTIVE STRIKE

By Soviet definition, the Soviet Union never initiates war but only fights a war imposed on it by a foreign enemy. This dogma introduces a certain bias into Soviet formulations and leads to a certain confusion as to the precise Soviet meaning of surprise, first strike and preemption.

Soviet military authorities state that a war may be initiated by a surprise attack or as a result of the escalation of a local war, especially if the nuclear powers become involved in it. Furthermore, according to Grechko, war may begin "with either the use of nuclear or conventional weapons."[3] A war

---

[2] Savkin, *Osnovnye Printsipy . . .*, p. 368.
[3] Grechko, *Na Strazhe Mira i Stroitel'stva Kommunizma*, p. 55.

between the US and the USSR initiated with conventional weapons will in the Soviet view most likely escalate into a general nuclear war. While the Soviets require their armed forces to be flexible in the use of either category of weapons, they also argue that in view of the unlimited aims of both sides in a confrontation, the war is likely to lead to the use of all weapons. The Soviet view is reflected, for example, in the following statement by Grechko:

> At the present stage the Armed Forces must be capable under any conditions to frustrate a surprise attack by the aggressor with the use of *nuclear* as well as *conventional* weapons and with rapid, devastating blows to destroy his main missile-nuclear weapons and troop formations, thereby assuring favorable conditions for the further conduct and victorious outcome of the war.[4]

The question of escalation of local or limited wars into general nuclear war is treated more ambiguously. It is acknowledged that such wars do not *automatically* escalate into a general war, but it is also asserted that one of the "special features [of local war] is the danger of escalation of limited military conflicts into a general world war," as has happened in the past, and, consequently, that "this threat is not diminished but intensified by the imperialists' course toward unleashing small wars, which may detonate an unlimited armed conflict."[5]

Some Soviet spokesmen argue, however, that while the US has not "renounced in principle the use of conventional military means in its foreign policy,"[6] fear of escalation of local conflicts, "due to the globalization of international relations and military might," tends to create a situation in which an increase in the absolute strength of military force of the opposing systems is accompanied by a decrease in the possibility of its direct use in conflict and a greater importance of political solutions.[7]

Radio Moscow's military commentator, V. Berezin, while praising the June 1973 agreement on the prevention of nuclear war, commented that this "naturally reduces considerably the chances of local conflicts with the use of conventional weapons," and went on to assert:

> It should be remembered that modern conventional weapons are extremely sophisticated and highly destructive. Consequently, a conflict with the use of such weapons holds the danger of spreading and developing into a nuclear clash.[8]

---

[4]*Ibid.*, p. 64. [Emphasis added.]

[5]Colonel T. Kondratov, "The Reactionary Essence of the Theory of 'Limited Wars,'" *Krasnaia Zvezda*, September 28, 1972. See also, his articles in *Kommunist Vooruzhennykh Sil*, No. 21, November 1972, pp. 15-16, and *Soviet Military Review*, No. 2, February 1974, p. 9.

[6]Gromyko and Kokoshkin, *Mezhdunarodnaia Zhizn'* (International Affairs), No. 9, September 1973, pp. 94-95.

[7]Proektor, *International Conflicts*, p. 44. See also, M. Segatelian, "This Is a Totally Different War," *Literaturnaia Gazeta* (Literary Gazette), October 17, 1973.

[8]Radio Moscow, August 22, 1973.

Because the "tremendous increase in the power of conventional weapons" has narrowed the Soviet distinction between conventional and nuclear weapons, at least by implication Moscow appears to see the transition from the use of conventional to nuclear weapons as having become "easier." As Brezhnev has remarked, for example, conventional weapons can destroy entire countries. Soviet commentators cite the example of Vietnam, where the US Air Force is said to have dropped the equivalent in TNT of 650 atomic bombs of the type which struck Hiroshima.[9]

A major concern of Soviet military doctrine and discussion is the issue of a surprise attack. Commentators still frequently assert that the US is preparing to launch a surprise attack against the USSR in the hope of creating "favorable conditions" for a successful outcome of the war.[10] In an article published in March 1973, the Chief of the General Staff, Army General Kulikov, devoted considerable attention to this question. He asserted that the "imperialist aggressors are counting as before on the unexpectedness of their attack, in the hope of acquiring strategic advantages."

> Surprise attack has always been an important principle of military art and has frequently given the attacker decisive advantages in achieving victory. But while in the past surprise in attack was insured by the choice of time and unexpected targets for the first strike with a view to achieving the most effective results, new elements have now appeared in the arsenal of surprise, considerably influencing its significance. Among these can be numbered, in particular, the form and strength of the first strategic strikes, the ways of delivering them, and the use of new types of weapons and contact equipment.[11]

Another article discussing the need for the Soviet armed forces to be in a high state of war readiness pointed out that the "possibility exists of defeating the enemy without implementation of large preparatory measures and regrouping of troops."[12]

Although Soviet military commentators generally speak of a surprise attack as being initiated by the "imperialists," they treat the issue in such a way as to indicate interest in this strategy—and occasionally openly acknowledge this interest. For example, in a follow-up article, Rear Admiral A. Gontayev asserted that "surprise . . . must be understood as actions unexpected by the enemy in time, place, techniques and military means" and can be "strategic, operational or tactical." He criticized as a "psychological legacy of the last

[9]Colonel V. Bokarev, Rear Admiral V. Sheliat and Colonel M. Iasiukov, "Philosophy in the Ideological Struggle in the Modern Era," *Kommunist Vooruzhennykh Sil*, No. 24, December 1973, p. 26.

[10]Zavialov, *Krasnaia Zvezda*, August 3, 1972.

[11]*Kommunist Vooruzhennykh Sil*, No. 6, March 1973, p. 15. See also, Bagramian, *et al.*, *Istoriia Voin i Voennogo Iskusstva*, p. 500.

[12]Lieutenant Colonel N. Kostenkov, "The Social-Political and Psychological Aspects of Combat Readiness of Troops," *Kommunist Vooruzhennykh Sil*, No. 13, July 1973, p. 11.

war" the view "among some [that] surprise is mainly associated with an attack by the enemy on us, while aggressive operations of our forces, our fleet against the enemy are omitted."[13]

A major Soviet book on the *Fundamental Principles of the Art of Strategy* published in 1972, described the advantages conferred by a surprise attack as follows:

> The significance of the principle of surprise increases in accordance with the development of means of combat. Surprise allows one to forestall the enemy in the execution of strikes, to catch him unawares, to paralyze his will, sharply reduce his combat capability, to disorganize his command and control and to create favorable conditions for the destruction of even superior forces.[14]

Soviet statements concerning the danger of a US surprise attack are contradicted by the numerous claims that the balance of forces has shifted in favor of the Soviet Union and that the US increasingly recognizes that war with the Soviet Union would be tantamount to suicide. In this sense, Soviet leaders appear to believe that at present the existence of an assured Soviet second-strike or retaliatory capability makes a rational or deliberate US decision to launch a surprise attack highly unlikely. At the same time, public discussion of the question of an unprovoked Soviet attack on the US is politically prohibited, and Soviet views concerning it can only be ascertained by inference from statements on the advantages of strategic surprise. Quite properly, however, discussions by Soviet military spokesmen of war initiation and strategy do not predict the probability of a breakdown of mutual deterrence but consider the contingency when such a breakdown has occurred. Consequently, their discussion revolves around the issue of what the Soviet Union should be prepared to do *if* the "imperialists" initiate war either by means of a surprise attack or as a consequence of the escalation of a limited war.

According to the open Soviet literature, while recognition is given to the deterrence value of an assured second-strike capability and the need to be prepared to launch a retaliatory attack in the event that an enemy succeeds in launching a surprise attack, discussion concentrates primarily on the problem of developing a Soviet capability and strategy to "frustrate," "disrupt," "break up," or "forestall" an enemy attack. Although the term "preemptive blow" (*uprezhdainshchii udar*) is seldom used, the description of what this type of action is expected to achieve makes it fairly evident that in most cases reference is to a Soviet first counter-force strike. Nothing is said, however, concerning the circumstances or specific hostile actions by an opponent

---

[13]Rear Admiral A. Gontayev, "Surprise as a Category of Naval Art," *Morskoi Sbornik*, No. 3, March 1973, p. 30.

[14]Savkin, *Osnovnye Printsipy* . . ., p. 371.

which would motivate the Soviet Union to initiate such an attack, although the implication is that it would be merely attempting to beat the enemy to the punch and/or to blunt his nuclear strikes. Consequently, no clear distinction is drawn between Soviet "preemptive" and "preventive" actions. In the past, Soviet sources appeared to indicate that the leadership expected to obtain strategic warning from a variety of political as well as military indicators, because it was assumed that no country would initiate a war without a certain amount of political and military preparations. More recently, however, as was noted above, some Soviet military writers suggest that an attack may be launched without "large preparatory measures" which could serve to give warning, in which case political indicators may become especially important in anticipating the opponent's intentions. The literature does not indicate how much confidence the Soviet leadership has in the Soviet ability to preempt a US surprise attack, and it must be noted that there has been a decline in recent years in such claims by the highest political leaders.

Nevertheless, military spokesmen continue to deal with this problem, and it is used as one of the justifications for the emphasis currently being placed on the need to upgrade Soviet combat readiness. In their view, a Soviet first strike could not only significantly weaken or blunt an enemy's nuclear attack on the Soviet Union and thereby ease the Soviet war-survival problem but, by simultaneously destroying the enemy's defense industry and major industrial complexes, as well as his administrative, military-political command and control system and his vital communications and transportation centers, could result in his collapse or at least allow the Soviet Union to gain a measure of strategic superiority over him. Given such targets of a first nuclear strike, the Soviets hope that the attack would "determine the further course and outcome of the war" in favor of the Soviet Union. This latter expectation, however, suggests that one would be justified to read more into the Soviet meaning of "preemptive" than launch on warning of an enemy attack. The emphasis on capability and readiness for a first-strike strategy, whether called preemptive or preventive, is evident from the following:

a. Soviet military doctrine stresses the "offensive character of Soviet strategy" and the "primacy of the offensive type of military operations over defense." It is pointed out that

> War must not simply [be] the defeat of the enemy, it must be his destruction. This condition has become the basis of Soviet military strategy.[15]

---

[15]"V. I. Lenin and Soviet Military Strategy," *Voenno-Istoricheskii Zhurnal* (Military-Historical Journal), No. 9, September 1970, p. 5.

This would be especially so in a war between opposing social-political systems, which would be waged with "decisive political aims," i.e., the destruction of the opposing system. Consequently, "the offensive is the basic type of military operation and its goal is total destruction of the enemy."[16] Under modern conditions, defense is possible if it is "active defense," i.e., nuclear strikes would be used to destroy the attacking forces "even before the attack begins," and thereby create favorable conditions for resumption of the defense.[17] "Nuclear weapons," writes the military theoretician, Lieutenant General I. Zavialov, "have increasingly confirmed the role of attack as the decisive form of military actions and have given rise to the necessity of resolving even defensive tasks by active offensive actions."[18] It is asserted, furthermore, that a defensive strategy based on the concept of absorbing the enemy's first nuclear strike is wrong.

> The defensive, as a means of military operation, has lost its importance. In the face of an enemy possessing nuclear weapons and pinning his hopes on a first strike, a defensive strategy means to voluntarily subject a country and its armed forces to nuclear strikes, which is contrary to the concept of modern warfare.[19]

Although this particular statement was addressed to China, it appears to reflect the basic Soviet view on this question. Thus, another broadcast said that "it is no secret that the Soviet Union's Leninist defense plan calls for active defense instead of passive defense."[20] Furthermore, a frequent Soviet theme is that the Soviet Union has drawn the appropriate conclusions from the 1941 German surprise attack on Russia and its terrible consequences for the country and would never again allow itself to be caught unawares and permit the enemy to hold the initiative.

b. Soviet descriptions of the Strategic Missile Forces specify their significance in terms of their counter-force mission. For example, Grechko writes that

> The Strategic Missile Forces, which form the basis of the combat might of our Armed Forces, are intended for the destruction of the enemy's means of nuclear attack, his large troop formations and military bases, the destruction of the aggressor's defense industry, the disorganization of [his] state and military command and control, and of the operations of his rear and transportation.[21]

---

[16]Karabanov, et al., Filosofskoye Naslediye . . ., p. 54.

[17]Ibid.

[18]Krasnaia Zvezda, October 30, 1970. See also, Bagramian, Istoriia Voin i Voennogo Iskusstva, p. 499.

[19]Radio Moscow, January 13, 1970.

[20]Ibid., October 13, 1973.

[21]Grechko, Na Strazhe Mira i Stroitel'stva Kommunizma, p. 41.

Similarly, other Soviet military writers assert that

The Strategic Missile Forces have the combat ability which allows them in the shortest time to solve simultaneously the task of destroying the enemy's military-economic potential, to destroy his strategic means of nuclear attack, to smash his main troop formations. . . . Massive nuclear strikes by strategic weapons allow the attainment of the political aims [of the war] in a short period of time.[22]

Admiral of the Fleet Gorshkov, Commander-in-Chief of the Soviet Navy, also noted the counter-force role of the navy, whose mis'sion, he said, is to "participate in attacks of the county's [i.e., the USSR's] Strategic Missile Forces," and the "weakening of the nuclear attacks by the enemy's navy from the direction of the sea."[23] The counter-force mission of the Soviet Armed Forces was also expressed in a somewhat more ambiguous form in an article in *Red Star* on December 20, 1973, in which the author wrote that in view of the "material preparations for world war" by the imperialist states "the task is to restrain by any means the aggressive aspirations of the reactionary imperialist circles, including being ready and capable to destroy and annihilate those forces if they try to impose a new world war on socialism."[24]

c. Soviet discussions of how to "frustrate," "disrupt" or "break up" an enemy surprise attack, either explicitly or implicity, indicate that the basic concept is the ability of the Stratègic Missile Forces and Soviet missile-carrying submarines to carry out a counter-force strike. In the third edition of his book, *Military Strategy,* Marshal of the Soviet Union V. D. Sokolovskii wrote that "possibilities exist not to allow a surprise attack by an aggressor, to deliver nuclear strikes on him at the right time" and that "it is supposed that our retaliatory nuclear strike will considerably weaken the enemy's means of nuclear attack."[25] Earlier an article in the journal *International Affairs* had stated that

The first missiles and bombers of the side on the defensive [i.e., the Soviet side] would take off even before *the aggressor's first missiles, to say nothing of his bombers, reached their targets.*[26]

Various Soviet civil defense officials have underscored that Soviet counter-force strikes would play an important role in blunting the enemy's nuclear attack and thereby assure the effectiveness of the Soviet civil defense system.

---

[22]Bagramian, *et al., Istoriia Voin i Voennogo Iskusstva*, pp. 495, 489. See also, Krupchenko, *et al., Voennaia Istoriia*, p. 338.

[23]*Morskoi Sbornik*, No. 2, February 1973, p. 21.

[24]Major General Ye. Sulimov, *Krasnaia Zvezda*, December 20, 1973.

[25]Marshal of the Soviet Union V. D. Sokolovskii, *Voennaia Strategiia* (Military Strategy), 3rd edition, Moscow, Voenizdat, 1968, p. 361.

[26]L. Glagolev and V. Larionov, "Soviet Defense Might and Peaceful Coexistence," *International Affairs* (Moscow), No. 11, November 1963, p. 32. [Emphasis in original.]

For example, Lieutenant General Shuvyrin, a Deputy Chief of Civil Defense of the USSR, was very explicit when he wrote:

> . . . one must keep in mind that the aggressors will not be able to make full use for their purposes of their strategic means of attack. A portion of these means of weapons delivery will be destroyed or damaged before their launching while they are still on their launch sites, bases and airfields; another portion will be destroyed or damaged by the weapons of the Air Defense in flight at the approaches to the territory of the socialist camp; still another portion of the missiles and aircraft will fail to reach their targets for technical reasons [i.e., malfunction].[27]

Again, another senior Soviet officer wrote that

> Just as the Missile Forces will destroy the most important nuclear missile attack weapons of the enemy on the ground, the strike forces of the navy and particularly its nuclear submarine and naval missile carrying aviation, will destroy the carriers of nuclear missile weapons at sea and thus disrupt an enemy attack against our country carried out from the sea.[28]

Grechko, as quoted above, spoke about the readiness of the Soviet Armed Forces to frustrate a "surprise attack" and to destroy the enemy's main nuclear-missile weapons. This formulation was repeated in an article in the August 1972 issue of *Communist of the Armed Forces,* written as a guide for troop indoctrination.[29] In this connection, one should note Kulikov's statement that

> Military science devotes great attention to the quest for means of reliably repulsing a sudden attack by an aggressor and to the further elaboration of the most effective methods of organizing and implementing decisive military actions on varying scales. . . .
> The fulfillment of these tasks is inseparably linked with the further improvements of methods of studying the armies of imperialist states, their military-political and strategic concepts, and also the possible nature and methods of their unleashing and waging a war.[30]

d. In addition to their primary objective of bringing about the speedy defeat of the enemy, Soviet counter-force strikes are also treated as essential for assuring the survival of the Soviet Union in the event of a nuclear war, by preventing the enemy from saturating Soviet anti-air and civil defense systems, and destroying the Soviet Union. The above quote from Lieutenant General Shuvyrin is a case in point because the article argued that Soviet civil defense would only have to deal with the residual enemy force. Similarly, other civil defense officials have been asserting that

---

[27]Lieutenant General D. I. Shuvyrin, "A Reliable and Effective System," *Voennyye Znaniia* (Military Knowledge), No. 10, October 1968, p. 17.

[28]Vice Admiral V. D. Yakovlev, *The Soviet Navy*, Moscow, DOSAAF, 1969, cited in JPRS *Translations on USSR Military Affiars*, No. 692, April 5, 1971, p. 18.

[29]Colonel I. Forofonov, "The 24th CPSU Congress on the Mission of the Soviet Armed Forces in the Current Phase," *Kommunist Vooruzhennykh Sil*, No. 15, August 1972, p. 77.

[30]Kulikov, *Kommunist*, No. 3, February 1973, p. 86. See also, Krupchenko, *et al.*, *Voennaia Istoriia*, 341.

The most effective means of defending the county's population are effective actions aimed at destroying the enemy's offensive weapons both in the air and on the ground at their bases. Missile troops—the new type of armed force—play a major role in the destruction of the enemy's offensive weapons.[31]

Similarly, the book *Military History*, published in 1971, states that in a nuclear war "the actions of the Strategic Missile Forces and also of the PVO Forces [Anti Air Defense Forces] are of critical importance in frustrating the enemy's nuclear strikes."[32]

Generally explicit Soviet statements on how a first strike may be conducted have declined since the late 1960's and early 1970's. The expressions used most often are ambiguous, such as, for example, the following statement which appeared in a military journal in October 1973:

> Peaceful coexistence assumes a constant readiness on the part of the socialist armed forces to disrupt the aggressive actions of the imperialist circles. Combat readiness, that special quality of the military and naval forces that enables them to disrupt a surprise attack by an aggressor and defeat his forces, is being improved in a number of directions.[33]

Although Soviet statements appear to envisage that in the event of a threat of war the Soviet Union would attempt to deliver a first counter-force strike, there is no indication that the Soviet leaders have high confidence in being able to do so or that they believe that such a strike would in fact assure the survival of the Soviet Union. A recent editorial in *Red Star* suggests that the Soviet commanders are still wrestling with this problem, because, as the article states:

> The primary task of military science in the current phase is development of the problems of maintaining constant readiness to break up an attack and utterly defeat the aggressor under any conditions.[34]

While Soviet statements suggest that a first counter-force strike might destroy a substantial part of US strategic forces as well as of the economy and severely disrupt the administrative, control, communication and transportation systems, they do not indicate that such an attack is expected to completely disarm the US or to preclude some form of reorganization and of rearmament on the basis of surviving industries. It is argued, however, that the first strike could pre-determine the further course and outcome of the war and that it might lead to the organizational, and especially, the political,

[31]Radio Blagoveshchensk, August 5, 1970.

[32]Krupchenko, *et al.*, *Voennaia Istoriia*, p. 342.

[33]Colonel D. Volkogonov, "Peaceful Coexistence—An Alternative for War," *Kommunist Vooruzhennykh Sil*, No. 19, October 1973, p. 17.

[34]Editorial, "The Important Tasks of Military Science," *Krasnaia Zvezda*, December 23, 1973.

collapse of the US. Communist political spokesmen argue that given the sharply defined class nature of the war, the peoples in the capitalist countries will revolt against their leaders, who by their reckless policies would have brought this calamity upon them, while on the Soviet side the people would rally in support of such a "just" war and carry on with the struggle, regardless of sacrifices. While the party is waging a campaign to strengthen "Soviet partiotism" and prepare the population psychologically for a possible war, Soviet military leaders appear to rely more on conventional military wisdom and prefer to prepare for the eventuality that the enemy will not collapse politically and that the war may become protracted.

Once a war begins, the Soviet view does not appear to admit any possibility of war-bargaining through controlled use of nuclear weapons or de-escalation. Soviet spokesmen are generally highly critical of the various Western theories along these lines or of discussion concerning the possibility of restricting combat to conventional weapons (e.g., a European conventional war). They argue that all such theories are merely attempts by the "imperialists" to find a way of unleashing a war against the Soviet commonwealth without the risk of retribution, or that they are used to make the notion of an aggressive war more acceptable to the Western public. The general Soviet line remains that an armed confrontation between the opposing nuclear powers will almost inevitably be or will escalate into a general nuclear war.

Yet there are also some tantalizing hints in Soviet literature that the Soviet Union may want to keep its options open on this question and, for this reason, is maintaining a flexible posture and a capability to fight wars of varying intensity and scope. As was mentioned, Grechko wrote about war initiation with nuclear or conventional weapons. A major Soviet study of *The History of Wars and Military Art,* prepared under the supervision of a distinguished editorial commission headed by Marshal of the Soviet Union I. Kh. Bagramian, states that an "all-round analysis of all the changes occurring in the military field" has led to the conclusion that "the methods of conducting a missile-nuclear war will be different from those used in past wars and will depend on a number of factors. First of all, they will depend on the method used in initiating the war, what character it will acquire, what weapons would be employed, in what theater the combat actions will be conducted, etc."[35] It is also noteworthy that a major article on the Soviet view of the nature of modern war stresses that "in the conduct of a war, primary consideration must be given to the requirement of a law which states: the nature of the political goal exerts a decisive influence on the conduct of a

---

[35]Bagramian, *Istoriia Voin i Voennogo Iskusstva*, p. 500.

war" and, furthermore, that owing to the "tremendous destructive capabilities" of modern weapons, they cannot remain "outside political control."[36] There is also evidence that the Soviet conventional war capability has been tested in major maneuvers and exercises. Whether this implies that the Soviet Union might be willing to abide by self-limitations on war objectives, use of weapons, and scope of operations which its opponent may have imposed on himself is highly speculative. In any event, such thinking runs counter to the overwhelming body of Soviet literature on the question, which holds that war between the nuclear powers would most likely be nuclear and thus total.

Kulikov asserts, however, that regardless of the form of military action or the types of weapons used, the critical objective is the "decisive role of the offensive" and the capture of the "initiative."

> . . . military art now takes into account the need for and possibility of using various forms of military action. However, relying on the considerably increased capabilities of available types of weapons and combat equipment, it proceeds from the decisive role of active offensive actions, and the recognition of the very important significance of the struggle to gain time and to seize and hold the initiative.[37]

THE SUBMARINE-LAUNCHED BALLISTIC MISSILE (SLBM) PROBLEM

While it is self-evident that the Soviets view the blunting of a nuclear attack as preferable to having to absorb the total US strategic strike capability, current Soviet commentaries give no indication of the size of the residual US strategic force they expect to confront in the event that the Soviet Union were to succeed in delivering a first counter-force strike. In particular, Soviet sources, while recognizing the importance of the US SLBM capability, tend to be vague or ambiguous in discussing Soviet ability to deal with this threat.

Soviet navy spokesmen emphasize the greater survivability of missile-carrying submarines in comparison with land-based ICBM systems.[38] A book entitled *Anti-Submarine Weapons and Their Carriers*, published in 1973, states that

> The high combat stability of these boats [i.e., missile-carrying atomic submarines], attained by concealed sailing, unexpected use of weapons, great submerged speed, and ability to remain out at sea

---

[36]Major General V. Zemskov, "Some Questions on the Conduct of a War," *Kommunist Vooruzhennykh Sil*, No. 22, November 1972, pp. 15-16, 19.

[37]Kulikov, *Kommunist*, No. 3, February 1973.

[38]For Example, see Gorshkov, *Morskoi Sbornik*, No. 2, February 1973, p. 21; Captain 1st Rank K. Shitov, "Reconnaissance Missions and Forces on the Sea," *Morskoi Sbornik*, No. 9, September 1972, p. 58.

for a prolonged time in combat readiness, has made the atomic submarine a very difficult target for antisubmarine forces.[39] Consequently, Soviet publications express concern over the trend in the US of adopting a "sea strategy," according to which increasing emphasis would be placed on a sea-based strategic strike capability developed around the Trident system armed with Poseidon missiles. It is argued that the US is thereby violating the spirit of the SALT I Agreement, that it seeks to circumvent the agreement on "equal security" and strategic "parity" in order to attain nuclear superiority as well as to "divert" Soviet strikes from attacks against US territory.[40]

Soviet commentators argue that because the "imperialists place special hopes on their naval forces," in the event of a war "combat operations on the oceans will undoubtedly have a major effect on the outcome of the armed struggle as a whole."[41] Consequently, it is said that the Soviet navy must maintain a presence wherever US naval units are deployed in order to carry out "an immediate counterattack" should war break out.[42] However, while noting that the US Navy expects to "continuously track" enemy submarines after they leave their bases and to be able to destroy them immediately at the start of the war, Soviet sources do not specifically claim a similar capability for the Soviet Navy.[43] At the same time, Admiral of the Fleet Gorshkov stressed the importance of beating the enemy to the punch, by arguing that under modern conditions "delay in the employment of weapons in a naval battle or operation inevitably will be fraught with the most serious and even fatal consequences regardless of where the fleet is located, at sea or in port."[44]

Soviet sources discuss various forms and methods of antisubmarine warfare (ASW). For example, Marshal Sokolovskii wrote that

> Nuclear submarines with "Polaris" missiles can be destroyed in bases by strikes of the Strategic Missile Forces and long-range aviation, and while crossing the sea and in their patrol areas, by the operations of antisubmarine submarines, long-range aviation and other antisubmarine forces and means. . . . For successfully com-

[39]A. A. Kvinitskii, *Protivolodochnoye Oruzhiye i Yego Nositeli* (Anti-Submarine Weapons and Their Carriers), Moscow, DOSAAF 1973, cited in JPRS *Translations on USSR Military Affairs*, No. 988, December 4, 1973, p. 40.

[40]G. I. Sviatov, "The Naval Forces of the U.S.A.," *SShA: Ekonomika, Politika, Ideologiia*, No. 9, September 1972, p. 127; Shitov, *Morskoi Sbornik*, No. 9, September 1972, p. 58; Captain 1st Rank D. Fomin, "The Indivisibility of the Task of Strengthening Peace and the Defense of the Country," *Morskoi Sbornik*, No. 12, December 1973, p. 16.

[41]Admiral N. N. Amel'ko, Deputy Commander of the Navy, "The Oceanic Guard of the Homeland," *Voennyye Znaniia*, No. 7, July 1973, p. 6.

[42]Radio Moscow, January 13, 1970.

[43]Captain 1st Rank I. Vasil'ev and Captain 3rd Rank V. Mironov, "The Militaristic Exercises of the Combined Naval Forces of NATO," *Morskoi Sbornik*, No. 2, February 1974, p. 95.

[44]*Morskoi Sbornik*, No. 2, February 1973, p. 22.

batting them [i.e., enemy nuclear submarines], a reliable system of reconnaissance is necessary, which will ensure the timely detection of enemy submarines, particularly those carrying missiles, the exact determination of the coordinates of their location and guidance of active weapons against them.[45]

This suggests that the Soviet Union should strike first in order to destroy those enemy nuclear submarines which are in port. While reference is made to the importance of "winged missiles,"[46] mines[47] and hunter-killer submarines[48] for ASW, it is asserted that effective ASW requires the combined use of submarines, surface ships, planes and helicopters.[49] It is said, furthermore, that in addition to carrying out this strategic mission, the "main efforts of the fleets will be directed toward destroying nuclear missile-carrying submarines."[50] At the same time, Gorshkov criticized the failure of the Germans in World War II to provide air support and surface ship support for their submarines, apparently indicating that the Soviet Union would avoid this error and, in particular, that the naval air force would be used to destroy enemy ASW forces.[51] While not giving a clear assessment of Soviet ASW capability, it is significant that a recent statement cities "foreign press" sources to the effect that the US considers that "there still is much that has to be done before a sufficiently effective antisubmarine weapons sytem can be created."[52]

The question of whether the SLBMs would be used in a first strike or might be withheld for follow-on strikes in order to allow the Soviet Union to retain a residual nuclear-strike capability for bargaining purposes or to assure that it would have an effective strategic capability following the initial nuclear exchange is not specifically treated in Soviet publications. The point is repeatedly made that the primary mission of SLBMs is to strike enemy land-based targets in conjunction with the Strategic Missile Forces,[53] and that

---

[45]Marshal V. D. Sokolovskii, *Military Strategy*, 3rd edition, Stanford Research Institute, SSC-TN-8974-29, January 1971, p. 347.

[46]Admiral of the Fleet S. G. Gorshkov, "We Always Remember the Order of the Homeland," *Sovetskii Voin* (Soviet Warfare), No. 13, July 1973, cited in JPRS *Translations on USSR Military Affairs: Soviet Naval Day*, No. 960, September 20, 1973, p. 1.

[47]Captain 1st Rank V. Shchetinin, "Mine Weapons in War at Sea," *Morskoi Sbornik*, No. 5, May 1973, p. 26.

[48]Gorshkov, *Morskoi Sbornik*, No. 2, February 1973, p. 19.

[49]Captain 1st Rank G. Kostev, "Combined Action—the Most Important Principle of Utilization of Forces," *Morskoi Sbornik*, No. 2, February 1974, p. 33.

[50]*Ibid.*

[51]*Morskoi Sbornik*, No. 2, February 1973, p. 20.

[52]Kvinitskii, *Protivolodochnoye Oruzhiye* . . ., p. 41.

[53]Gorshkov, *Morskoi Sbornik*, No. 2, February 1973, pp. 19,21; Admiral S. Iu. Zakharov, *Istoriia Voenno-Morskogo Iskusstva* (History of Military-Naval Art), Moscow, Voenizdat, p. 562; Rear Admiral K. A. Stalbo, "The Development of Naval Science," *Morskoi Sbornik*, No. 12, December 1969, p. 33; Marshal of Aviation I. Borzov, *Vestnik Protivovozdushnoi Oborony*, No. 7, July 1973, p. 13.

they are well suited to carry out a surprise attack against such targets, as well as enemy naval formations.[54] At the same time, Gorshkov appears to assign to the Soviet SLBMs a second-strike role when he argues that missile-carrying submarines represent a threat of inevitable "nuclear retaliation," and thereby serve to deter aggression against the Soviet Union.[55] In all probability Soviet strategy in the employment of its SLBM capability will depend on a number of factors concerning which actual Soviet views are by no means clear. These probably include the questions whether the Soviet Union initiates the first strike or carries out a retaliatory second strike, what confidence it has in its ability to deploy its SLBM forces prior to the strike and without triggering a US first strike, whether the Soviet land-based ICBM capability is deemed sufficient to destroy all essential targets in a first strike or whether the SLBMs would be needed to deliver an "annihilating blow" which could bring about the enemy's collapse, and so on. It is conceivable, but not very likely, that withholding of the Soviet SLBMs could be used in an attempt to deter a US retaliatory second strike. One possible factor which might favor a Soviet strategy of withholding its SLBM capability is the apparent Soviet belief that the attainment of victory in a nuclear war will require the Soviet Union to retain a superior strategic capability which could be used either to prevent the US from rebuilding its military forces by follow-on strikes or to force the US to surrender under threat of such strikes. As will be discussed below, the Soviets insist on the need for war production in the course of the war to assure the replacement of destroyed or expended weapons and equipment and the attainment of superiority over the enemy. Whether this would include the production of ICBMs is not specified. It is evident, however, that the Soviet war objective of attaining the total defeat of the enemy and thus of gaining control over him would require the Soviet Union to have a residual capability to continue to threaten the US with further destruction, as well as an effective post-strike reconnaissance and surveillance capability to generate the intelligence necessary to identify new targets and monitor US military activities. Presumably, the Soviet anti-air and possibly also anti-satellite defense would be used to prevent the US from obtaining similar intelligence on the Soviet Union.

ABM AND THE QUESTION OF THE PROTECTION
OF THE HOMELAND

As was noted, the ABM Agreement of May 1972 does not appear to signal a growing Soviet willingness to embrace the concept of mutual assured

---

[54]Professor K. Zviagin, "The Fleets of the Great Powers in the Post-War Period," *Morskoi Sbornik*, No. 11, November 1973, p. 105; Kvinitskii, *Protivoldochnoye Oruzhiye . . .*, pp. 40, 55.
[55]*Morskoi Sbornik*, No. 2, February 1973, p. 21.

destruction. Soviet commentaries on the agreement claim to see in it an important step for arms control which prevents a spiral in the arms race resulting from efforts by both sides to develop new weapons to overcome the ABM systems.

The significance of the ABM Agreement for Soviet views on the employment of its Strategic Missile Forces and for the defense of Soviet territory against an attack is not a subject for public discussion in the Soviet Union. One may note, however, that the initial Soviet ABM deployment around cities rather than to protect Soviet missile sites may have been indicative of a Soviet view of ABM as reinforcing a Soviet preemptive strategy rather than reflecting a real concern over a possible US first counter-force strike. If this was indeed the case, the ABM Agreement would provide no reason for the Soviet Union to change its strategic concepts, but rather would be likely to lead it, as suggested by Soviet pronouncements, to place greater priority on the development of a preemptive counter-force capability. This appears reflected also in the current campaign to further raise the combat readiness of the Soviet Armed Forces, and especially of the Strategic Missile Forces, and in the assertions that the "main danger is the surprise use by imperialists of missile nuclear weapons" and that Soviet military science considers the "priority task" of the Armed Forces to be to "frustrate" an enemy surprise attack and "inflict on him a crushing blow."[56] Soviet military commentators, while frequently denying that an enemy would succeed in carrying out a surprise attack on the Soviet Union, persist in their view that a nuclear surprise attack can be decisive for the further course and outcome of the war and that it can significantly contribute to a country's survival in a nuclear war. At the same time, they note the increased US concern over the "growing difficulties in insuring the 'survival' of its land-based strategic offensive nuclear forces" and, therefore, the US interest in a mobile ICBM capability, such as the Trident system.

The ABM Agreement, furthermore, has not lessened Soviet interest in improving its active and passive defense capabilities and in finding ways to strengthen the survival capacity of the USSR. These activities predate the Moscow Agreements, but recent Soviet statements suggest that additional efforts are being made to further strengthen Soviet capabilities and readiness in this respect. Thus, there are persistent calls for an anti-aircraft defense capability which would make the Soviet Union impregnable to air attacks. According to Grechko, "the main mission of the Air Defense Forces is to repulse any surprise air attack by an aggressor and to ensure the uninter-

---

[56]Krupchenko, *Voennaia Istoriia*, p. 341.

rupted work of the economy, state organs, administrative and combat capability of the Armed Forces in the course of combat operations."[57] Similarly, Kulikov wrote about the Air Defense Forces as having become "a reliable shield designed to play a major role in defending the country and the Armed Forces against enemy air attacks."[58] In a speech on May 8, 1973, the Commander of the Air Defense Forces, Marshal of the Soviet Union Batitskii, expressed "certainty" that his forces were able to "ensure the impregnability of the air approaches to the Hero City—Moscow—to any aggressor."[59] An important military textbook published in 1973 states that

> At the present time the main task of PVO [i.e., Anti-Air Defense Forces] is to ward off a surprise air attack and to ensure the uninterrupted operation of the national economy, the organs of state control, and the combat capabilities of the armed forces during combat operations.[60]

In a major article which appeared in the April 1973 issue of the *Herald of the Anti-Air Defense*, Kulikov noted that

> It is essential to carry out complex measures aimed at protecting the territory of one's state, its cities and its most important economic centers against enemy strikes and to prevent the destruction of the population and also of troop formations and naval forces. In other words, the survivability of the country and of the Armed Forces must be ensured, regardless of the weapons and scale of attack employed by a probable enemy.[61]

How this could be accomplished without an effective ABM system Kulikov did not explain. He went on to assert that the Air Defense Forces play a major role in this regard, especially because "in a future war the scale and intensity of military operations in the air and also their influence on the course of the war will increase immeasurably," and he called for further improvements in weapons, equipment, tactics and combat readiness of the Air Defense Forces. Kulikov, furthermore, stressed the need for effective defense against air-to-surface missiles.

> The units and subunits of ZRV (SAM) and IA (Fighter Aviation) must be prepared to destroy those targets which are sharply changing their altitudes and flight course and speeds and which are resorting to anti-missile and anti-aircraft maneuvers. They must also learn how to confidently destroy targets having very small reflective surfaces, including pilotless aircraft and winged missiles. The crews of radar stations must be prepared to carry out their combat assign-

---

[57]Grechko, *Na Strazhe Mira i Stroitel'stva Kommunizma*, p. 46.

[58]Kulikov, *Partiinaia Zhizn'*, No. 24, December 12, 1972, p. 43.

[59]Radio Moscow, May 8, 1973.

[60]Major General V. V. Voznenko, *Nauchno-Tekhnicheskii Progress i Revoliutsiia v Voennom Dele* (Scientific-Technological Progress and the Revolution in Military Affairs), Moscow, Voenizdat, 1973, p. 108.

[61]Kulikov, *Vestnik Protivovozdushnoi Oborony*, p. 4.

ments under conditions involving the use by the enemy of self-homing anti-radar missiles and a large quantity of decoys.[62]

He also mentioned the need to develop effective methods against enemy attempts to jam "radar sets, radar sights and missile guidance channels," and other possible electronic warfare techniques.

THE NATURE AND IMPLICATIONS
OF CIVIL DEFENSE PROGRAMS

Great importance is also ascribed to passive defense measures, i.e., civil defense, as a means for ensuring the ability of the Soviet Union to survive a nuclear attack and for the attainment of victory. For example, it is said that

Civil defense is becoming a strategic factor which exercises a significant determining influence on the course and outcome of a modern war as well as on the post-war restoration of the economy.
. . .
In close coordination with the Soviet Armed Forces, the mission of civil defense is to protect the nation's strategic rear areas, to reduce to a minimum human and resource losses, thus making a major contribution toward victory over the aggressor.[63]

Colonel General A. Altunin, Chief of Civil Defense of the USSR and a Deputy Minister of Defense, wrote in a book published in 1974:

Under present conditions, when there has arisen the threat of wide use of means of mass destruction, and first of all of missile-nuclear weapons against the entire territory of the country, the preparation of the country's rear for defense against means of mass destruction has become, without a doubt, one of the decisive strategic factors ensuring the ability of the state to function in wartime, and in the final analysis the attainment of victory in war.[64]

The relationship of an effective civil defense to the attainment of victory in war has been asserted by many Soviet spokesmen who maintain that victory will belong to the country which is better able to ensure the protection of the people, economy, administration and transportation, as well as of food and raw material supplies.[65] Altunin writes that on the basis of the experiences in World War II and of studies conducted in the course of exercises, one can firmly conclude that

---

[62]*Ibid.*, p. 7.

[63]Karabanov, et al., *Filosofskoye Naslediye* . . ., pp. 85, 95.

[64]Colonel General A. Altunin, "Civil Defense Today," in K. A. Kondratiuk, ed., *Liudi i Dela Grazhdanskoi Oborony* (The People and Tasks of Civil Defense), Moscow, Voenizdat, 1974, p. 5. See also, Altunin, "The Main Direction," *Voennye Znaniia*, No. 12, December 1973, pp. 4-5.

[65]For a discussion, see L. Goure, *Soviet Civil Defense Revisited 1966-1969*, the RAND Corporation, RM-6113-PR, November 1969, and *Soviet Civil Defense 1969-1970*, Monographs in International Affairs, Center for Advanced International Studies, University of Miami, June 1971.

. . . on the state of civil defense, on the psychological and special preparation of the population for defense against weapons of mass destruction, on the timely execution of the entire complex of practical measures for the protection of the population and of the economy—on all these factors will depend in a large measure the course as well as the outcome of the war itself, and the further viability of the entire state.[66]

He states further that civil defense will be under a single military command, that it will operate in close cooperation with all elements of the armed forces and with the active participation of the entire population. Thus, in the Soviet view, civil defense is an integral part of Soviet military might and its war-fighting capability.

According to Soviet publications, civil defense by itself cannot solve the problem of effectively protecting large segments of the population and the essential sectors of the economy from destruction unless the armed forces do their part in blunting and reducing the weight of the attack by means of counter-force strikes and active air defense. Thus, the former Chief of the USSR Civil Defense, Marshal of the Soviet Union V. I. Chuikov, wrote in 1968:

It must be remembered that civil defense alone is not capable of solving all the tasks of defending the population and national economy; successful cooperation between units of the army and navy will ensure a considerable reduction of the destructive effects on people of weapons of mass destruction, thus assuring victory over the enemy.[67]

As was quoted above, Lieutenant General Shuvyrin was more explicit in claiming that a substantial part of the enemy's strategic forces would be destroyed on their launch sites and bases or in flight so that civil defense will face only the surviving enemy strike capability. In the same vein, Altunin points out in a recently published book the first counter-force strike mission of the Soviet armed forces and its relationship to civil defense:

While the Armed Forces take as their objective to prevent the use of destructive means against the rear of the country by the destruction of the attack weapons or the interception of the weapons on their way to their targets, Civil Defense, by carrying out protective measures and the thorough preparation of the population, seeks to achieve the maximum weakening of the destructive effects of modern weapons.[68]

It is furthermore asserted again and again that despite the destructiveness of modern weapons and especially of nuclear weapons, effective protection against them is possible. Some spokesmen also suggest that Soviet civil defense can contribute to the overall Soviet deterrence capability. Thus, a book published in 1972 asserted that

---

[66] Altunin, *Liudi i Dela Grazhdanskoi Oborony*, p. 6.
[67] *Rodina*, January 3, 1968.
[68] Altunin, *Liudi i Dela Grazhdanskoi Oborony*, p. 7.

Improvement of Soviet Civil Defense and an increase in its effectiveness constitute one more major obstacle in the way of the unleashing of a new world war by the imperialists.[69]

The author of this statement also claimed that "Soviet civil defense does not incite, does not promote and does not provide impetus to war."

The Soviet civil defense program has been in existence for a long time, but its specific adaptation to the requirements of the nuclear age dates from 1961, when control over it was vested in the Ministry of Defense. The program was given a personal impetus by Brezhnev at the 23rd CPSU Congress, where he called for the strengthening of Soviet civil defense, and it has gained a great deal of momentum ever since with the active support of party organizations at all levels.[70] Thus, a 1974 publication asserts that "the Communist Party and the Soviet Government assign great importance to civil defense and show constant concern for its strengthening."[71]

The Soviet civil defense program includes a whole complex of measures designed to (a) protect the population and especially essential industrial, transportation and communication workers, (b) protect vital industries and services in order to ensure continuous essential production and in particular production for the armed forces in the course of the war and (c) to facilitate damage limitation and the rapid repair and restoration of damaged industrial facilities and services.[72] In addition, the program includes a large-scale propaganda and indoctrination campaign to prepare the population psychologically and politically to bear the hardships of a nuclear war and to ensure its loyalty to the regime and its determination to fight and win. In his May 1973 article in *Kommunist,* Grechko wrote:

> Particular significance is attached to instructing the population in defense against weapons of mass destruction [i.e., nuclear, chemical and bacteriological weapons] and in the ability to rapidly liquidate the consequences of enemy nuclear strikes, promptly render extensive and diverse aid to the casualties, and secure conditions for the normal functioning of the facilities of the national economy and so forth.[73]

Essentially the objective of Soviet civil defense is to develop a significant damage limiting capability which, at least under relatively favorable circumstances, such as a successful Soviet first counter-strike and effective active defense, could preserve Soviet national power, including military power,

---

[69]Karabanov, *et al., Filosofskoye Naslediye . . .*, p. 96.

[70]For details see Goure, *Soviet Civil Defense 1969-1970.*

[71]M. N. Titov, *et al., Grazhdanskaia Oborona* (Civil Defense) "Vysshaia Shkola" (The Higher School), Moscow, 1974, p. 5.

[72]For details, see Goure, *Soviet Civil Defense 1969-1970, Soviet Civil Defense—Post-Strike Repair and Restoration*, June 1973, Center for Advanced International Studies, University of Miami.

[73]Grechko, *Kommunist,* No. 7, May 1973, pp. 22-23.

allow the Soviet armed forces to gain superiority in the course of a war and make it possible for the Soviet Union to recover more rapidly than its opponents.

Soviet insistence on the need to maintain war production in the course of the war is based on the view that because of the destructiveness of a nuclear war and the high rate of utilization of weapons, the war, especially if it becomes protracted, cannot be waged with only the weapons in being at its start. Additional weapons and equipment would have to be produced in the course of the conflict in order to sustain the armed forces. Furthermore, additional production would be needed to ensure rapid repairs to the economy. Thus, Marshal Sokolovskii wrote that

> . . . planning on conducting a war, no matter how short and swift moving, with only the reserve materials accumulated in peacetime, would be a mistake. It can be conjectured that in a future war, the role of the war economy will not only remain what it used to be, it will even increase in importance.[74]

Similarly, Marshal Chuikov argued that

> It is impossible to conduct war without the continuing supply of the armed forces with everything they need. . . . As noted, the supply- ing of the armed forces and of the population with everything necessary, the equipping of the civil defense forces with technical supplies for the successful execution of rescue and emergency repair work in the zones of devastation are only possible under conditions of sustained operation of the installations of the national economy in wartime.[75]

The importance of measures to limit damage to the economy and to make it possible to ensure the sustained operation of essential plants and services has been increasingly emphasized in recent years. Thus, according to the Chief of Staff of the Armenian SSR Civil Defense:

> Ensuring the stable [i.e., continuous] operation of facilities of na- tional economic significance in wartime is a most important task. It must be taken into account that in a modern war with the use of weapons of mass destruction, victory will be gained by the country having an economy which, despite losses and damage suffered in the course of the war, maintains the capability of supplying its armed forces with everything they require, and of supplying the country's population with food and basic necessities.[76]

Again, Altunin points out that "the survivability of the installations and sectors of the national economy will play an important role in satisfying the needs of the armed forces and of the population."[77]

[74]Sokolovskii, *Voennaia Strategiia*, 3rd edition, p. 272.

[75]Marshal of the Soviet Union V. I. Chuikov, *Grazhdanskaia Oborona v Raketno-Iadernoi Voine*, 2nd edition, Moscow, Atomizdat, 1969, pp. 32-33.

[76]Major General M. Muradian, "Raise the Readiness of Civil Defense," *Kommunist* (Yerevan), November 3, 1971, p. 4. See also, Baranov, *Krasnaia Zvezda*, March 5, 1971.

[77]Altunin, *Liudi i Dela Grazhdanskoi Oborony*, p. 12.

Soviet sources do not indicate what weapons and equipment it is believed essential to produce in the course of a war. There is no reason to believe, however, that this would not include the production of nuclear weapons and missiles, all the more so as Soviet military spokesmen emphasize the importance of attaining superiority in strategic weapons and because the Soviet Union will attempt to prevent new nuclear strikes by the enemy against its forces and territory.

Measures to ensure the viability of the economy in wartime include the sheltering and evacuation of the urban population and especially of the essential work force, the hardening and dispersal of industrial facilities and services, restrictions on the growth of large cities, urban planning designed to reduce the vulnerability of cities to attack, stockpiling of strategic reserves and vital repair materials and equipment and the organization of large, well-trained and equipped civil defense forces, both civilian and military, to carry out urgent repair and restoration of damaged plants and services. Under the Soviet plan, workers at essential plants and services will be dispersed from the target areas to commuting distance from their place of work so that one workshift at a time can remain at the plant. Industrial dispersal has received a great deal of attention in recent years. For example, Altunin writes that

> One of the decisive conditions for ensuring the survivability of the economy in wartime in addition to carrying out special measures to raise the hardness of each sector and industrial facility is the dispersal of the production forces on the country's territory.[78]

Soviet military spokesmen have repeatedly stressed the importance of industrial dispersal, some arguing that it should be carried out even at the cost of economic considerations. For example, an article published in 1970 said:

> . . . while the location of industry corresponds to the maximum considerations of economic expediency, industry must at the same time be adequately dispersed and protected and thus relatively less vulnerable to nuclear strikes . . . it is necessary to forego certain considerations of economic expediency for the sake of strategic interests dictated by the requirements of modern warfare. The strategic objective is now linked with the destruction not only of the armed forces of the enemy, but also of the objectives in the rear and its disorientation.[79]

Similarly, military theoretician Lieutenant General Zavialov wrote in 1973 about the need for "rationally sited production capacities," thus "insuring the survival of economic centers."[80] According to a member of the USSR

---

[78]*Ibid.*, pp. 12-13.

[79]Lieutenant Colonel V. Zubkov, "Leninist Principles of the Location of Production Forces and Defense," *Kommunist Vooruzhennykh Sil*, No. 17, August 1970, p. 15.

[80]Lieutenant General Zavialov, *Krasnaia Zvezda*, April 19, 1973.

State Planning Committee, in the years 1966-1970 almost 60 percent of some 1,300 new industrial enterprises were "sited in towns and settlements with a population of up to 100,000 persons."[81] Such dispersal of industry, it was pointed out, is not only advantageous from an economic point of view, but "is also of significance for defense."[82] It was said that a similar policy would be pursued in the current Five-Year Plan, with the major portion of new industry being built in small and medium sized towns, "especially in the Western Ukraine, Moldavia, the Republics of Central Asia and the Transcaucasus."[83] Special attention is being paid to the construction of new industrial centers in Siberia based on the development of new energy and mineral sources in that region. The US has been invited to invest in this development and to provide advanced technology for it. Referring to this shift of new industrial projects to Siberia, Grechko wrote that it "significantly increases the defense capability of the Soviet homeland and makes our industry less vulnerable in the event of a missile-nuclear war being launched by the imperialists."[84]

While the Soviet Union is thus said to seek to reduce the vulnerability of its economy to attack, Soviet spokesmen have repeatedly pointed out US shortcomings in passive defense preparations and in particular the alleged greater concentration and thus vulnerability of US industry. For example, it is said that many of the civil defense measures in the US exist only on paper and "are far from being realized" and that "foreign specialists themselves admit that the state of practical work aimed at raising the viability of the economy is far from being at the desired level."[85] It is furthermore asserted that

> The high concentration of industry, which is characteristic of the main capitalist countries, is in obvious contradiction to the requirements of a missile-nuclear war. It results in giving the economic regions the significance of major military industrial targets of strategic significance, the loss of which would undermine the economic capabilities of the state in wartime.[86]

---

[81]Interview with M. G. Pervukhin by V. Perevedentsev, "Production Forces, People and Rates, *Literaturnaia Gazeta*, February 17, 1971. See also, Colonel A. Sukhoguzov, "Problems of Viability of the Economy in Modern War," *Kommunist Vooruzhennykh Sil*, No. 3, February 1972, p. 12; N. Nekrasov, "The Economic Policy of the CPSU and the Distribution of Production Forces," *Kommunist*, No. 3, February 1972, pp. 69-70, and "The Future of Our Industry," *Trud*, June 15, 1972.
[82]Sukhoguzov, *Kommunist Vooruzhennykh Sil*, No. 3, February 1972, p. 12.
[83]Pervukhin, *Literaturnaia Gazeta*, February 17, 1971.
[84]Grechko, *Na Strazhe Mira i Stroitel'stva Kommunizma*, p. 38.
[85]Colonel L. Karzun, "Problems of Stability of Production," *Voennye Znaniia*, No. 10, October 1972, p. 27.
[86]Captain 2nd Rank B. G. Grigor'ev, *Ekonomicheskiye i Moral'nye Potentsialy v Sovremennoi Voine* (Economic and Moral Potentials in a Contemporary War), Moscow, Voenizdat, 1970, p. 76.

An article intended as a guide for political lectures about the United States as a part of Soviet troop indoctrination summarized its conclusions as follows:

> . . . it should be emphasized that there are a number of weak and vulnerable areas in the otherwise strong military-economic potential of the U.S.A., particularly the absence or shortage of certain important types of strategic raw materials, the dependence upon extended lines of sea communications with regard to both importing deficit raw materials and supplying finished goods to its allies, and finally, the concentration of industrial production (to include military production) in a comparatively small number of large industrial centers.[87]

No doubt the Soviets believe these US vulnerabilities to be significant, all the more so as Soviet military doctrine requires the destruction of the enemy's economic base in order to deprive him of his ability to continue to wage war. Furthermore, because of continuous efforts over the years to develop a capability to protect the population against nuclear, chemical and bacteriological weapons, Soviet military leaders may well believe that the US is less able than the Soviet Union to maintain war production and more vulnerable to follow-on attacks with such weapons for the purpose of disrupting or slowing US recovery efforts. Yet it must also be noted that for all the Soviet activities in passive defense, the Soviet population and industry remain far more concentrated than the Soviet military deem desirable. For example, according to the 1970 Soviet census, 75.6 million persons, or 55.5 percent of the total urban population, live in the 221 largest cities, most of which are also important manufacturing, administrative, scientific, transportation and communication centers. Furthermore, the pre-attack evacuation of urban populations poses a formidable problem especially if, as Soviet sources indicate, it is expected to be completed in 72 hours. It may well be within Soviet capability, however, to achieve a significant measure of protection if war threatens for what the regime would consider the more essential elements of the population and possibly also for some vital industrial facilities.

Present indications are that civil defense activities in the Soviet Union have not diminished, but rather appear to have intensified, since the Moscow Summit. For example, the appointment in October 1972 of Colonel General Altunin to the post of Chief of USSR Civil Defense was an upgrading in the status of the civil defense organization because Altunin is also a Deputy Minister of Defense. Since his appointment even greater emphasis has been placed on preparing industry to survive an attack, with Altunin claiming that "the important and complex problem of ensuring the stable work of the

---

[87]Colonel V. Kapalkin, "The USA—Largest Country of Modern Imperialism," *Kommunist Vooruzhennykh Sil*, No. 14, July 1973, p. 77.

national economy in the event of a war is being successfully solved in the country."[88] Furthermore, a new and expanded training program for the general population, including schoolchildren and civil defense formations, was introduced in 1973 on the "instructions of the CPSU Central Committee and the Soviet Government," designed to raise the "combat readiness" of civil defense. In addition, according to Altunin:

> Measures were taken for further improvement in administrative agencies, for organization of communications, for supplying the population, military subunits [i.e., military civil defense units] and nonmilitary civil defense formations with modern means of protection, and for equipping them with authorized property and technical equipment.[89]

Also of interest is the fact that despite international agreements increasingly restricting or prohibiting the use of chemical and bacteriological weapons in war, Soviet civil defense continues to prepare for defense against such weapons. The reason given is that in the event of an all-out war between the opposing systems, one must expect all weapons to be used. While in such a war nuclear weapons are expected to play a primary role, Soviet discussions suggest that chemical and bacteriological weapons may be used to increase casualties among the work force and to destroy the food supply and possibly to disrupt recovery efforts.

The present scope of Soviet civil defense activities has been described by the Chairman of the Council of Ministers of the Lithuanian Republic as follows: "In our country, there is not one economic branch or area of social endeavor that is not in one way or another associated with civil defense."[90]

SOVIET VIEWS ON NUCLEAR WEAPONS AND THEATER WAR

In the 1950's a sharp debate took place among Soviet military theoreticians concerning the role of nuclear weapons in a theater war and the utility of maintaining large ground forces. The new generation of missilemen argued for a reliance on nuclear weapons and a reduction in the size of "conventional" forces, asserting that such forces would not be able to operate or survive in a nuclear environment and that there would be little left for them to conquer. The "traditionalists" argued for large "conventional" forces, especially armored forces which would be able to exploit tactical nuclear strikes and consolidate the victory. Although Khrushchev leaned in favor of the former and instituted major reductions in the non-nuclear forces, the latter school

---

[88]A. Altunin, "At the Combat Post," *Krasnaia Zvezda*, October 4, 1972.

[89]Altunin, *Voennyye Znaniia*, No. 12, December 1973, p. 4.

[90]Iu. Maniushis, "For Defense of the Achievements of Peaceful Labor," *Sovetskaia Litva*, October 4, 1972.

prevailed in the end. Current Soviet doctrine insists that "final" victory can be achieved only by the combined efforts of all services, thus suggesting that victory is equated with physical military control of the enemy and the occupation of his territory.

> However great the role of the Strategic Missile Forces may be in war, a total victory over an aggressor can be achieved only as a result of joint operations of all branches of the Armed Services and with the active support and participation of the entire nation in achieving victory over the enemy.[91]

Nevertheless, the existence of nuclear weapons, as well as missiles of various ranges, has greatly altered the Soviet view of the character of a theater war and of combat operations therein. Although the possibility of waging operations without the use of nuclear weapons is recognized, especially as these apply to actions by regimental or smaller units, Soviet discussions focus primarily on a theater nuclear war. According to Soviet spokesmen, the theater forces rely primarily on nuclear force power in their offensive and defensive operations. Thus, Grechko wrote in 1971: "The main fire power of the ground forces is their operational [i.e., medium range] and tactical missile units."[92] Similarly, Marshal of Artillery G. Ye. Peredel'skii, the Ground Forces Commander of Missile and Artillery Forces, said in November 1973 that missiles "have come to constitute the Ground Forces' main fire power" and that "they play the decisive role in establishing fire power superiority over an enemy—something which largely predetermines the outcome of a battle."[93] Soviet military spokesmen furthermore assert that "modern combined forces operations will first of all be tactical nuclear strikes,"[94] and that nuclear weapons would be the primary means for breaching the enemy's defenses as well as for conducting "active" defense[95] and for achieving the "total defeat of the enemy in short periods of time and the seizure of important areas," by giving the attacking side the capability to destroy the enemy's main force groupings and his nuclear weapons.[96] It is also said that the Ground Forces, having their own nuclear weapons as well as a "large

[91]Gromakov, *Sovetskii Patriot*, November 21, 1973.

[92]Grechko, *Na Strazhe Mira i Stroitel'stva Kommunizma*, p. 43.

[93]Marshal of Artillery G. Ye. Peredel'skii, "A Shield of Fire," *Nedelia,* November 5, 1973. See also, Karabanov, *et al., Filosofskoye Naslediye. . .*, p. 53.

[94]Krupchenko, *et al., Voennaia Istoriia,* p. 343.

[95]Lieutenant General V. Reznichenko, "Maneuvering: Its Essence, Objectives and Forms," *Krasnaia Zvezda,* January 9, 1973. See also, "Combat Aggressiveness," *Krasnaia Zvezda,* June 5, 1973; "Features and Methods of Offensive," *Soviet Military Review,* No. 9, September 1973, p. 7-10; Colonel I. Kisin, "Increase the Speed of the Offensive," *Voennyi Vestnik,* No. 7, July 1973, pp. 36-39; Colonel V. Savkin, "Characteristics of Modern Battle," *Voennyi Vestnik,* No. 3, March 1974, pp. 24-28.

[96]Colonel A. A. Sidorenko, *Nastupleniye* (The Offensive), Moscow, Voenizdat, 1970, translated in U.S. Air Force, Soviet Military Thought Series, No. 1, US Government Printing Office, Washington, D.C., 1973, p. 221.

number of tanks" and other types of modern weapons and combat equipment, "are capable of independently solving the tasks of routing groupings of enemy troops on the ground theater of military operations,"[97] But it is noted that

Strikes by strategic missiles against major enemy installations will create favorable conditions for conducting offensive operations by the Ground Forces to a great depth and at a pace significantly exceeding the pace of a troop offensive during operations of the last war.[98]

As in the case of strategic operations, surprise strikes with nuclear weapons within the theater are considered as essential both to facilitate the offensive and in order to gain the initiative, and for the purpose of safeguarding one's own forces from enemy nuclear strikes. Thus, it is asserted that "the employment of nuclear weapons has greatly increased the role and significance of surprise in combat and has raised the requirement for its attainment."[99] It is also stressed that "heavy, surprise, simultaneous strikes make it possible to destroy manpower and equipment over a considerably larger area than was the case in the past."[100] The primary mission of these strikes will be to destroy the enemy's nuclear forces. For example:

Under modern conditions, destroying the enemy's means of nuclear attack acquires particular significance in a meeting engagement. The successful execution of this mission makes it possible not only to grasp the initiative but also to hold it firmly during battle.[101]

Or again, concerning the employment of aviation:

The main task of aviation is the struggle against the enemy's nuclear weapons by means of the destruction of launch sites, atomic carriers, cruise missiles, nuclear armed aircraft, missile ships and submarines, as well as nuclear weapons storage sites.[102]

The offensive operations will largely rely on nuclear fire power to prepare the way for the advance. "The principal means for conducting present-day offensive operations will be evidently the launching of nuclear strikes against the enemy and swift advance with the aim of attaining the total defeat of the enemy."[103] It is also asserted that "the path for the advance of the troops will be cleared by nuclear weapons."[104] Furthermore, it is said that "the em-

[97]Marshal Moskalenko, Sovetskaia Rossiia, February 22, 1974.

[98]V. V. Zoznenko and V. I. Matveyev, "New Means of Waging War and Methods of Combat Action," in Nauchno-Tekhnicheskii Progress i Revoliutsiia v Voennom Dele, Moscow, Voenizdat, 1973, as translated in Strategic Review, U.S. Strategic Institute, Winter 1974, p. 110.

[99]Krupchenko, et al., Voennaia Istoriia, p. 343.

[100]Karabanov, et al., Filosofskoye Naslediye . . ., p. 52.

[101]Reznichenko, Krasnaia Zvezda, June 5, 1973.

[102]Bagramian, Istoriia Voin i Voennogo Iskusstva, p. 496.

[103]Karabanov, et al., Filosofskoye Naslediye . . ., p. 54. See also, Krupchenko, et al., Voennaia Istoriia, p. 343.

[104]Krupchenko, et al., Voennaia Istoriia, p. 342.

ployment of modern weapons makes it possible to change the balance of forces quickly" and that victory in battle is determined by "who is first to deal an effective fire blow."[105] According to a book on tank warfare published in 1973:

> Above all, the use of nuclear weapons makes it possible to cause tremendous losses to the enemy in short amounts of time by destroying his human forces and technical equipment, and also destroying defensive installations behind his lines. Under these conditions, the ground troops have an important task: to take advantage of the results of the nuclear attacks on the enemy as quickly as possible. . . . Taking advantage of the gaps and breaks formed in the enemy's combat formations [by nuclear strikes], they can carry out bold encirclement and deep turning movements, attack the flanks and rear, and quickly move ahead so that the enemy cannot regroup and restore his destroyed defenses.[106]

These deep penetrations will also serve to destroy the enemy's reserves and his surviving means of nuclear attack.[107] In the view of the military theoretician Lieutenant General Zavialov, "the principle of concentration of the efforts of troops in a decisive direction" has given way to the "massing of nuclear strikes" which "assume primary importance," while the troops remain dispersed to avoid providing a target for enemy nuclear strikes.[108] It is noted, furthermore, that because of the reduced possibility of attaining surprise in a ground attack owing to modern reconnaissance and surveillance means, and the difficulty of achieving a breakthrough of enemy defenses "saturated" with antitank weapons, the surprise breakthrough must be by means of a "concentrated fire blow," with nuclear weapons, of course, being especially suitable for such a purpose.[109]

Because of the greater range of missiles as compared with conventional artillery, offensive and defensive operations can be supported by "maneuver by fire," which will consist of switching nuclear strikes from one sector of the theater to another without necessitating a preliminary redeployment of fire power as was the case in the past.[110] Defensive operations will also rely on nuclear weapons "to mount heavy strikes against the opposing enemy force even before it launches its attack."[111]

Soviet comments on various Western proposals to limit the scope or levels of violence of a possible war, as was noted above, have been largely negative,

[105]Reznichenko, *Soviet Military Review*, No. 9, September 1973, p. 10.

[106]Ye. A. Kosyrev, *Tanki* (Tanks), Moscow, DOSAAF, 1973, translated in JPRS *Translations on USSR Military Affairs*, No. 977, November 5, 1973, p. 57. See also, Savkin, *Voennyi Vestnik*, No. 3, March 1974, p. 25.

[107]Major General I. Skorodumov, "Swiftness of Action—the Guarantee of Success in Battle," *Voennyi Vestnik*, No. 5, May 1973, p. 15.

[108]Zavialov, *Krasnaia Zvezda*, October 30, 1970.

[109]Colonel A. Antonov, "Night Engagement," *Soviet Military Review*, No. 12, December 1973, p. 10.

[110]Reznichenko, *Krasnaia Zvezda*, January 9, 1973.

[111]Karabanov, et al., *Filosofskoye Naslediye . . .*, p. 54.

especially on all concepts involving the use of nuclear weapons, whether tactical or strategic. For example, a major book entitled *Europe and Nuclear Weapons,* by A. Ye. Yefremov, published in 1972, warns that the use of only tactical nuclear weapons in Europe is likely to lead to an escalation. The author asserts that "military conflict on European territory," given the present network of military alliances, "would inexorably involve all other states of the world in the orbit of a thermonuclear collision," and that the "threat to use some of the American tactical atomic weapons to carry out local actions in Europe, figuring that the use of 'warning atomic shots' will not lead to escalation and a global thermonuclear war," is obviously "dictated by propaganda rather than military considerations."[112] Soviet spokesmen ridicule the notion of arming NATO forces with "mini" nuclear weapons to reduce collateral damage and insist that the concept of waging limited wars with the use of nuclear weapons will continue to present the "threat of a rapid escalation of such a war, especially in Europe, into a general nuclear war."[113] In his February 1974 article, Arbatov asserted that the US is seeking to find "a way out of the strategic stalemate" and to find a way to "restore the full political 'applicability' of military force."

> Precisely this is behind the seemingly reasonable proposal to draw up "rules of engagement" for a future war, such as renouncing strikes against cities, the waging of hostilities only against the armed forces of the enemy, and so forth. In fact such proposals are a demagogic trick designed to reassure public opinion. . . .
> By itself, the idea of introducing "rules of engagement" and artificial restrictions "by agreement" is illusory and untenable. It is difficult to visualize that a nuclear war, if it is unleashed, could be kept within the framework of "rules" and would not develop into an all-out war.[114]

A Soviet discussion of the US doctrines of "flexible response," "differentiated responsibility" among US allies, "regional atomic war," and so forth, asserts that these theories assume that "in any of the 'responsibility' variants American armed forces would participate in the conflict at any level," and this means that "any partial military conflict" is likely to escalate into a general all-out war, all the more so as the US would not regard it as "mandatory to keep to a 'low level' of conflict."[115]

Soviet commentators are also highly critical of any concept for the creation of a West European nuclear force. They assert that "it is perfectly obvious

---

[112]A. Ye. Yefremov, *Yevropa i Iadernoe Oruzhiye,* Moscow, Voenizdat, 1972, translated in JPRS, *Europe and Nuclear Weapons,* March 14, 1973, pp. 329, 331.

[113]Iu. Iakhontov commentary, "Miniwar According to Goodpaster's Prescription," Radio Moscow, February 4, 1974. See also, Colonel N. Nikitin, "New Gambles by the Pentagon," *Voennyi Vestnik,* No. 1, January 1973, p. 116.

[114]Arbatov, *Problemy Mira i Sotsializma,* No. 2, February 1974, p. 46.

[115]Proektor, *International Conflicts,* p. 53.

that the plans of the supporters of 'Europeanizing' the nuclear partnership are in contradiction with the real situation."[116] They note European concern that the June 1973 US-Soviet agreement on the "Prevention of Nuclear War" signifies the abandonment of the US "flexible response" doctrine,[117] i.e., of assured US use of nuclear weapons in the defense of Western Europe, and ridicule NATO officers and other commentators who are fearful of a massive Soviet conventional offensive and who wish to rely on a nuclear defense of Western Europe. Soviet publications do take notice of the doctrine and exercises of the West German armed forces for limited conflicts based on the non-use of nuclear weapons, but they note that during exercises authorization was given for the use of tactical nuclear weapons against enemy penetrations of the defenses on the second or third day of the action and also against airfields and other targets within the zone of operations.[118]

Soviet sources persist in asserting that until nuclear disarmament is attained and while aggressive imperialist forces exist, the Soviet Union will have to remain ready to "wage war with the use of all types of means of armed struggle."[119] A frequent Soviet commentator on military affairs states the case as follows:

> For the happiness of all mankind, the communists do not spare their forces in order to prevent a nuclear catastrophe. At the same time, it would be premature to announce the limitation of the possibility of the use of nuclear weapons in case the aggressor unleashes a war. There are still no such objective social-class guarantees and a persistent battle must still be faced in order to achieve these.[120]

Nevertheless, Soviet spokesmen do not exclude the possibility that a theater conflict may begin with only the use of conventional weapons or that operations may be waged without the use of nuclear weapons. Thus, it is asserted that

> While working out the methods for waging combat under conditions of nuclear war, Soviet military science does not exclude the possibility of combat operations being waged with only conventional weapons.[121]

Some commentators appear to relate the scope and intensity of conflicts to the war objectives, although they insist that a war between the opposing

---

[116]V. F. Davydov, "The US-British Nuclear Partnership," *SShA: Ekonomika, Politika, Ideologiia*, No. 7, July 1973, p. 66. See also, Ponomarev and Vinogradov, *Krasnaia Zvezda*, August 19, 1973.

[117]Sidel'nikov, *Krasnaia Zvezda*, August 14, 1973. See also, A. Maslennikov, *et al.*, *Za Rubezhom*, No. 20, September 6-12, 1973, p. 3; M. Kudzin, "An Important Step Along the Road Toward Strengthening Peace," *Mezhdunarodnaia Zhizn'*, No. 9, September 1973, pp. 12-18; Iu. Iakhontov, "Old Plan," *Pravda*, August 30, 1973.

[118]Colonel A. Ryzhkov, "Without the Use of Nuclear Weapons," *Voennyi Vestnik*, No. 1, January 1974, pp. 112-114.

[119]Sidel'nikov, *Krasnaia Zvezda*, August 14, 1973.

[120]Colonel Ye. Rybkin, "The Leninist Concept of War and the Present," *Kommunist Vooruzhennykh Sil*, No. 20, October 1973, p. 27.

[121]Krupchenko, *et al.*, *Voennaia Istoriia*, p. 345.

systems will be waged without "compromise" to "total victory."[122] However, Soviet military writers usually indicate that the requirement for a capability to conduct conventional combat operations and the probability of such operations in wartime applies mainly to units of regimental size or smaller [i.e., in Russian *chasti* and *podrazdeleniia*], but leave it unclear whether the same holds true for larger troop units and operations. For example, it is said that

> In spite of the fact that nuclear weapons will become the chief means of defeating the enemy, their role and capabilities cannot be made absolute, especially in the attainment of goals of combat actions by *podrazdeleniia* and *chasti*. In a number of cases *podrazdeleniia* and *chasti* will have to perform various combat actions, including the attack, without use of nuclear weapons, using only conventional, organic "classic" means of armament. . . . Therefore, along with the development of the nuclear missile might of the Soviet Armed Forces, our party and government have attached and continue to attach great importance to the development and sophistication of these means of warfare, which have not lost their importance in any way whatsoever.[123]

A recent article on the "Characteristics of Modern Battle," dealing with theater operations, pointedly never refers to conventional operations except in the context of their being conducted by *chasti* and *podrazdeleniia,* and also emphasizes that these troops must always be ready for "actions under conditions of the use of nuclear weapons."[124] Other commentators have pointed out that "the conduct of military operations using nuclear weapons and the conduct of military operations using *chasti* and *podrazdeleniia* with conventional weapons are not isolated from one another, but are clearly interconnected and developed as a single whole."[125]

While Soviet spokesmen warn that a nuclear war in Europe would be a calamity for the peoples of the region, there is no public evidence of a special Soviet concern to avoid the use of nuclear weapons in a European theater in order to allow the Soviet Armed Forces to capture Western Europe with a minimum of damage. Soviet statements indicate that the overriding objective would be the destruction of enemy forces and in particular of their nuclear weapons and, consequently, that at least tactical nuclear weapons would be used throughout the conflict in order to facilitate the rapid advance of the Soviet forces and ensure their victory. Although Soviet spokesmen warn that even the limited use of nuclear weapons in a theater war can destroy entire countries and "wipe entire peoples off the face of the earth,"[126] the burden of

---

[122]Savkin, *Voennyi Vestnik*, No. 3, March 1974, p. 25.

[123]Sidorenko, *The Offensive*, p. 222.

[124]Savkin, *Voennyi Vestnik*, No. 3, March 1974, pp. 24-28.

[125]Baranov, *Krasnaia Zvezda*, March 5, 1971.

[126]For example, see Trofimenko, *SSha: Ekonomika, Politika, Ideologiia*, No. 2, February 1974, p. 4.

damage limitation is placed on the peoples of the opposing countries who, as was noted, are urged to take timely political action against their leaders to avoid devastation. Soviet sources also do not show any particular concern for avoiding damage to Soviet East European allies, apparently in accordance with their prevalent belief that a limitation on the use of nuclear weapons in Europe is unlikely, and that an armed conflict between the opposing alliances would most probably assume a "decisive" and, consequently, also an unlimited character.

The possibility of NATO de-coupling some or all of the Soviet European satellite states from a nuclear conflict by withholding nuclear strikes against them in the event that they do not actively participate in a theater war is ignored in Soviet public discussions. No doubt such an approach would be viewed by Moscow as a type of "imperialist nuclear blackmail" and as an attempt to divide the communist bloc, which would fail in the face of the "unshakeable unity of the Warsaw Pact countries." The Soviet line in this respect, as expressed by Grechko, is that

> Historical experience shows most convincingly that military cooperation is an objective necessity for the socialist states. . . . The essential class and political nature of military defense cooperation between the socialist states lies in the fact that it is directed against forces hostile to the cause of peace and socialism and is opposed to imperialism's attempts to restore capitalism in the socialist countries by military means. Hence the main arm of this cooperation—to ensure complete security for the countries of socialism under the conditions of the existence of two opposing social systems. . . . The most reliable way of preventing war and the most effective means of curbing the aggressor is to step up by all possible means the defensive might of our country and of the entire socialist community and to strengthen the combat cohesion of the member-armies of the Warsaw Pact Organization. . . . The combined military strength of the aggressive blocs of the capitalist states must be opposed by the combined military might and close alliance of the countries of socialism. Life itself dictates the need for cohesive collective action by the socialist states, and consequently, also for close combat cooperation between their armies. . . . The socialist countries have a single enemy—imperialism. . . .[127]

Grechko went on to note the continuous improvements in the weapons, equipment, training and indoctrination of the member states' armed forces and the growing effectiveness of these forces, as demonstrated by the various joint exercises and maneuvers. Similarly, Marshal of the Soviet Union I. Iakubovskii, Commander-in-Chief of the Warsaw Pact Joint Armed Forces, claimed that

> The military cooperation of the Warsaw Pact countries embraces virtually all aspects of the life and activities of the allied armies and is constantly intensified and strengthened each year.[128]

---

[127]Grechko, *Kommunist*, No. 15, October 1972, pp. 35, 37, 38, 40.
[128]Iakubovskii, *Krasnaia Zvezda*, May 13, 1973.

It is uncertain, however, how far the Soviet leaders would trust their allies in the event of a war and employ their forces in offensive operations against Western Europe. For the present these forces have not been issued nuclear weapons, although they receive some training in the use of tactical missiles.

No doubt Soviet denunciation of Western conflict-limitation theories reflects in part propaganda purposes. Moscow may well believe that a decline in the reliance of Western Europe on nuclear weapons for its defense would entail a reduction of US influence and presence in Europe, lessen the danger of West German "revanchism," and accelerate the area's drift toward an accommodation with the Soviet Union. It is thus to the Soviets' benefit to refuse to indicate their agreement to abide by any rules of warfare, all the more so as this would conflict with their main propaganda line of identifying Western, and especially US, imperialism as the main or sole source of danger of war, while at the same time proclaiming Soviet desire for peace and international security. From Moscow's point of view, it is far preferable to leave all options open. Essentially, however, in this particular as in others related to the use of nuclear forces, as long as the Soviet leaders believe in the irreconcilable and unavoidable struggle between the systems, the logic of such a viewpoint unavoidably leads them to believe in the necessity of preparing for the worst contingency.

APPENDIXES

APPENDIX A: Glossary of Principal Soviet Personalities Referred to in Text

Altunin, A., Colonel-General, Chief of Civil Defense of the USSR and Deputy Minister of Defense of the USSR.

Arbatov, G. A., Director of the Institute of the USA of the USSR Academy of Sciences.

Bagramian, I. Kh., Marshal, Member of Inspector-General Group of the Main Inspectorate of the Soviet Armed Forces.

Baranov, S., Colonel, Professor and Doctor of Historical Sciences at the Lenin Military Political Academy of the Main Political Administration of the USSR Armed Forces.

Batitskii, P. F., Chief of the Air Defense Forces (PVO) and Deputy Minister of Defense of the USSR.

Berezhkov, V., Chief editor of *SShA: Ekonomika, Politika, Ideologiia* (USA: Economics, Politics, Ideology), the monthly journal of the Institute for the USA of the USSR Academy of Sciences.

Berezin, V., Military Commentator for Radio Moscow.

Bochkarev, K., Major General, military writer and editor of important Soviet military books.

Bondarenko, V., Lieutenant Colonel, Candidate of Philosophical Sciences, and Instructor in the Department of Marxist-Leninist Philosophy of the Lenin Military Political Academy, of the Main Political Administration of the Armed Forces. Writes extensively in the military press on military-scientific subjects.

Brezhnev, L. I., Full Member of Politburo, and General Secretary of the CPSU Central Committee.

Chuikov, V. D., Marshal, former Commander of the Ground Forces, Deputy Minister of Defense, and Chief of Civil Defense of the USSR 1961-1972.

Gantman, V., Member of the staff of the Institute for World Economics and International Relations of the USSR Academy of Sciences.

Gorshkov, S. G., Admiral of the Fleet, Commander-in-Chief of the Soviet Navy, and Deputy Minister of Defense of the USSR.

Grechko, A. A., Marshal, Minister of Defense of the USSR and Full Member of the Politburo since April 1973.

Gromyko, Andrei A., Full Member of the Politburo and USSR Minister of Foreign Affairs.

Gromyko, Anatolii A., Member of the staff of the Institute for the USA of the USSR Academy of Sciences, and son of A. A. Gromyko, USSR Minister of Foreign Affairs.

Iakubovskii, I. I., Marshal, Commander-in-Chief of the Warsaw Pact Joint Forces and First Deputy Minister of Defense of the USSR.

Inozemtsev, N. N., Member of the Academy of Sciences, Director of the Institute for World Economics and International Relations of the USSR Academy of Sciences.

Khrushchev, N. S., Former Full Member of Politburo, First Secretary of the CPSU Central Committee, and Chairman of the USSR Council of Ministers.

Konev, I. S., Marshal, Member of the Inspector-General Group of the Main Inspectorate of the Soviet Armed Forces.

Kosygin, A. N., Full Member of Politburo and Chairman of the USSR Council of Ministers.

Krylov, N. I., Marshal, former Chief of the Strategic Missile Forces, and Deputy Minister of Defense.

Kulish, V. M., Colonel (retired), Doctor of Historical Sciences and Director of the International Relations Division of the Institute for World Economics and International Relations of the USSR Academy of Sciences.

Kunayev, D. A., Full Member of the Politburo and First Secretary of the Communist Party of the Kazakh SSR.

Leont'ev, A., Colonel, Military commentator who writes extensively in the military press on international affairs.

Maniushis, Iu., Chairman of the Council of Ministers of the Lithuanian SSR.

Mazurov, K. T., Full Member of the Politburo and First Deputy Chairman of the USSR Council of Ministers.

Milovidov, A., Major General, Professor at the Military-Political Academy of the Main Political Administration of the Soviet Armed Forces, under the CPSU Central Committee.

Molchanov, Iu., Doctor of Historical Sciences, lecturer for the CPSU Central Committee and for the "Knowledge" Society, which supervises the Soviet public lecturer and indoctrination system.

Ogarkov, N. V., Colonel General, First Deputy Chief of the USSR Armed Forces' General Staff.

Pavlovskii, I., Army General, Chief of the USSR Ground Forces, and Deputy Minister of Defense.

Podgorny, N. V., Full member of the Politburo and Chairman of the Supreme Soviet of the USSR.

Proektor, D. M., Staff member of the Institute for World Economics and International Relations of the USSR Academy of Sciences.

Reznichenko, V., Lieutenant General, Doctor of Military Science.

Savitskii, Ye. Ia., Marshal of Aviation, Deputy Commander-in-Chief of Soviet Air Defense Forces (PVO).

Savkin, V. E., Colonel, Candidate of Military Science.

Shcherbitskii, V. V., Full member of the Politburo and First Secretary of the Ukrainian CP Central Committee.

Shuvyrin, P. I., Lieutenant General, former First Deputy Chief of Civil Defense of the USSR.

Sidel'nikov, I., Colonel, Military commentator writing for *Red Star*, and editor of *Boyevoye Znamia* (Battle Flag), the newspaper of the Central Asian Military District.

Sidorenko, A. A., Colonel, Doctor of Military Sciences and a leading Soviet military tactician.

Sokolov, S., Army General, First Deputy Minister of Defense of the USSR.

Sokolovskii, V. D., Marshal, former Chief of Staff of the Soviet Armed Forces.

Suslov, M. A., Full member of Politburo and Secretary of the CPSU Central Committee.

Sviatov, G., Candidate of Technical Sciences who writes in the Military press on disarmament questions and on US military developments.

Trofimenko, G., Staff member of the Institute for the USA of the USSR Academy of Sciences.

Ustinov, D., Candidate member of the Politburo and Secretary of the CPSU Central Committee in charge of defense industries.

Yepishev, A., Army General, Chief of the Main Political Administration of the Soviet Armed Forces under the CPSU Central Committee.

Zagladin, V. V., Deputy Chief of the International Section of the CPSU Central Committee.

Zavialov, I., Lieutenant General, writes extensively on questions of military doctrine.

APPENDIX B: Glossary of Principal Soviet Publications Referred to in Text

Bagramian, I. Kh., *et al. Istoriia Voin i Voennogo Iskusstva.* (The History of War and of Military Art). Moscow: Voenizdat, 1970.

Chuikov, V. I. *Grazhdanskaia Oborona v Raketno-Iadernoi Voine* (Civil Defense in a Rocket-Nuclear War). 2nd edition. Moscow: Atomizdat, 1969.

Grechko, A. A. *Na Strazhe Mira i Stroitel'stva Kommunizma* (On Guard over Peace and the Building of Communism). Moscow: Voenizdat, 1971.

Grigor'ev, B. G. *Ekonomicheskie i Moral'nye Potentsialy v Sovremennoi Voine* (Economic and Moral Potentials in Contemporary War). Moscow: Voenizdat, 1970.

Iakovlev, V. D. *The Soviet Navy.* Moscow: DOSAAF, 1969.

Institute of Philosophy of the USSR Academy of Sciences. *Problems of War and Peace: A Critical Analysis of Bourgeois Theories.* Moscow: Progress Publishers, 1972.

International Affairs. Moscow: English-language monthly journal of the All-Union "Znaniye" Society.

Izvestiia. Moscow: Official daily of the Soviet Government.

Karabanov, N. V., editor. *Filosofskoye Naslediye V. I. Lenina i Problemy Sovremennoi Voiny.* (The Philosophical Legacy of V. I. Lenin and Problems of Modern War). Moscow: Voenizdat, 1972.

Kazakhstanskaia Pravda. Alma Ata: Daily of the Kazakh Communist Party and Government.

Kommunist. (Communist). Moscow: Major theoretical and political journal of the CPSU Central Committee, published 18 times per year.

Kommunist Vooruzhennykh Sil. (Communist of the Armed Forces). Moscow: Semimonthly military-political journal of the Main Political Administration of the Soviet Army and Navy.

Komsomol'skaia Pravda. (Komsomol Truth). Moscow: Daily of the Communist Youth League (Komsomol) Central Committee.

Kondratiuk, K. A., editor. *Liudi i Dela Grazhdanskoi Oborony.* (The People and Tasks of Civil Defense). Moscow: Voenizdat, 1974.

Krasnaia Zvezda. (Red Star). Moscow: Daily of the Soviet Ministry of Defense.

Krupchenko, I. E., *et al. Voennaia Istoriia.* (Military History). Moscow: Voenizdat, 1971.

Kulish, V. M. *Voennaia Sila i Mezhdunarodnyye Otnosheniia.* (Military Force and International Relations). Moscow: International Relations Publishers, 1972.

Kvinitskii, A. A. *Protivolodochnoye Oruzhiye i Yego Nositeli.* (Anti-Submarine Weapons and Their Carriers). Moscow: DOSAAF, 1973.

Literaturnaia Gazeta. (Literary Gazette). Moscow: Weekly newspaper of the Soviet Writers' Union.

141

Mezhdunarodnaia Zhizn'. (International Affairs). Moscow: Monthly journal of the All-Union "Znaniye" Society.

Mirovaia Ekonomika i Mezhdunarodnyye Otnosheniia. (World Economics and International Relations). Moscow: Monthly journal of the Institute of World Economics and International Relations of the USSR Academy of Sciences.

Morskoi Sbornik. (Naval Digest). Moscow: Monthly journal of the Soviet Navy.

Moskovskaia Pravda. (Moscow Truth). Moscow: Daily of the Moscow City Party Organization.

Partiinaia Zhizn'. (Party Life). Moscow: Semimonthly journal of the CPSU Central Committee.

Planovoye Khoziaistvo. (Planned Economy). Moscow: Monthly journal of the USSR State Planning Committee.

Pravda. Moscow: Official daily of the CPSU Central Committee.

Problemy Mira i Sotsializma. (Problems of Peace and Socialism). Prague: Russian-language monthly of the "Communist and Workers' Parties."

Riabov, V. S., editor. *Dvina: The Military Maneuvers Carried Out on the Territory of Belorussia in March 1970.* Moscow: Voenizdat, 1970.

Savkin, V. E. *Osnovnyye Printsipy Operativnogo Iskusstva i Taktiki.* (Fundamental Principles of the Military Art and Tactics). Moscow: Voenizdat, 1972.

Sidorenko, A. A. *Nastupleniye.* (The Offensive). Moscow: Voenizdat, 1970.

Sokolovsky, V. D. *Voennaia Strategiia.* (Military Strategy). 3rd edition. Moscow: Voenizdat, 1968.

Solnyshkov, Iu. S. *Ekonomicheskiye Faktory i Vooruzheniye.* (Economic Factors and Armaments). Moscow: Voenizdat, 1973.

Sotsialisticheskaia Industriia. (Socialist Industry). Moscow: Daily of the CPSU Central Committee.

Sovetskaia Belorussiia. (Soviet Belorussia). Minsk: Daily of the Belorussian Communist Party and Government.

Sovetskaia Kirgiziia. (Soviet Kirgizia). Frunze: Daily of the Kirgiz and Frunze Communist Party and the Kirgiz Government.

Sovetskaia Litva. (Soviet Lithuania). Vilnius: Daily of the Lithuanian Communist Party and Government.

Sovetskaia Rossiia. (Soviet Russia). Moscow: Daily of the Russian Republic Bureau of the CPSU Central Committee.

Sovetskii Patriot. (Soviet Patriot). Moscow: Semiweekly of the Volunteer Society for Cooperation with the Armed Forces (DOSAAF).

Soviet Military Review. Moscow: English-language monthly of the Ministry of Defense.

SShA: Ekonomika, Politika, Ideologiia. (USA: Economics, Politics, Ideology). Moscow: Monthly journal of the USA Institute of the USSR Academy of Sciences.

Trud. (Labor). Moscow: Daily of the Central Council of Trade Unions.

Vestnik Protivovozdushnoi Oborony. (Herald of Anti-Air Defense). Moscow: Monthly journal of the PVO (Anti-Air Defense Forces).

Voenno-Istoricheskii Zhurnal. (Military-Historical Journal). Moscow: Monthly historical journal of the Ministry of Defense.

Voennyye Znaniia. (Military Knowledge). Moscow: Monthly journal of the Volunteer Society for Cooperation with the Armed Forces (DOSAAF).

Voennyi Vestnik. (Military Digest). Moscow: Monthly journal of the Ministry of Defense.

Voznenko, V. V. *Nauchno-Tekhnicheskii Progress i Revoliutsiia v Voennom Dele.* (Scientific-Technical Progress and the Revolution in Military Affairs). Moscow: Voenizdat, 1973.

World Marxist Review. Toronto: English-language monthly of the "Communist and Workers' Parties"; North American edition of *Problemy Mira i Sotsializma.*

Yefremov, A. Ye. *Yevropa i Iadernoye Oruzhiye.* (Europe and Nuclear Weapons). Moscow: Voenizdat, 1972.

Yepishev, A. A. *Mogucheye Oruzhiye Partii.* (Mighty Weapon of the Party). Moscow: Voenizdat, 1973.

Zagladin, V. V., editor. *Mezhdunarodnoye Kommunisticheskoye Dvizheniye: Ocherk Strategii i Taktiki.* (The International Communist Movement: Sketch of Strategy and Tactics). Moscow: Politizdat, 1972.

Za Rubezhom. (Life Abroad). Moscow: Weekly foreign affairs journal of the Soviet Journalists' Union.

Zhurkin, V. V., and Primakov, Ye. M., editors. *Mezhdunarodnyye Konflikty.* (International Conflicts). Moscow: Mezhdunarodnyye Otnosheniia, 1972.

Index